JLA

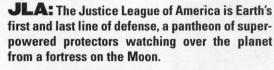

JLA: The Justice League of America is Earth's first and last line of defense, a pantheon of super-powered protectors watching over the planet from a fortress on the Moon.

Superman: The last son of the doomed planet Krypton, Kal-El uses his incredible powers of flight, super-strength, and invulnerability to fight for truth and justice on his adopted home, Earth. When not protecting the planet, he is *Daily Planet* reporter Clark Kent, married to fellow journalist Lois Lane.

Batman: Dedicated to ridding the world of crime since the brutal murder of his parents, billionaire Bruce Wayne dons the cape and cowl of the Dark Knight to battle evil from the shadows of Gotham City.

Wonder Woman: Born an Amazonian princess, Diana was chosen to serve as her people's ambassador of peace in the World of Man. Armed with the Lasso of Truth and indestructible bracelets, she directs her gods-given abilities of strength and speed toward the betterment of mankind.

The Flash: A member of the original Teen Titans when he was known as Kid Flash, Wally West now takes the place of his friend and partner, Barry Allen, who fell in battle as the previous Flash.

Green Lantern: Pilot Hal Jordan was chosen to represent an intergalactic police force created by the oldest beings in existence — the Guardians of the Universe. Protecting Earth and all of Space Sector 2814 from every extra-terrestrial threat imaginable, Hal Jordan shines his light proudly as the Green Lantern.

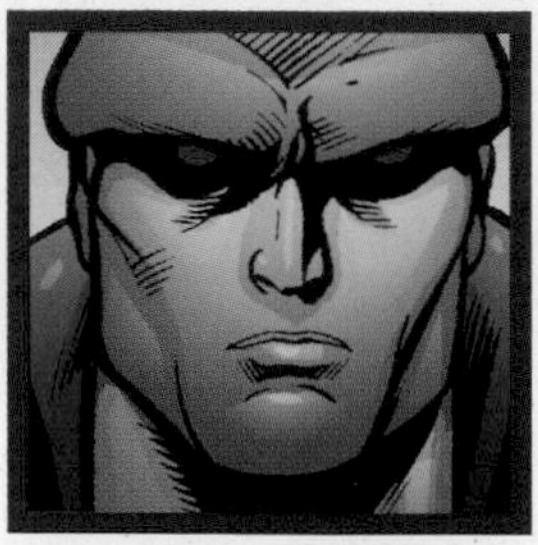

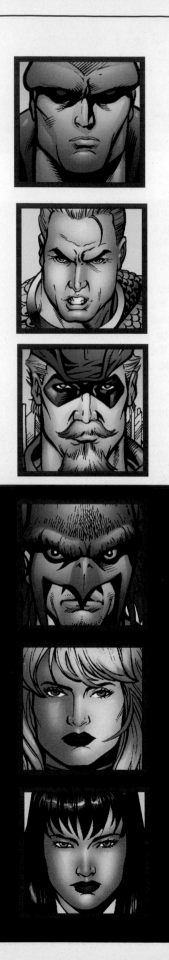

Martian Manhunter: J'onn J'onzz has been a member of the JLA for every one of the team's many incarnations. His strength rivals that of Earth's mightiest heroes, and his shape-shifting abilities allow him to pass anonymously among our planet's populace. His awesome mental powers serve to link the entire League in thought and action.

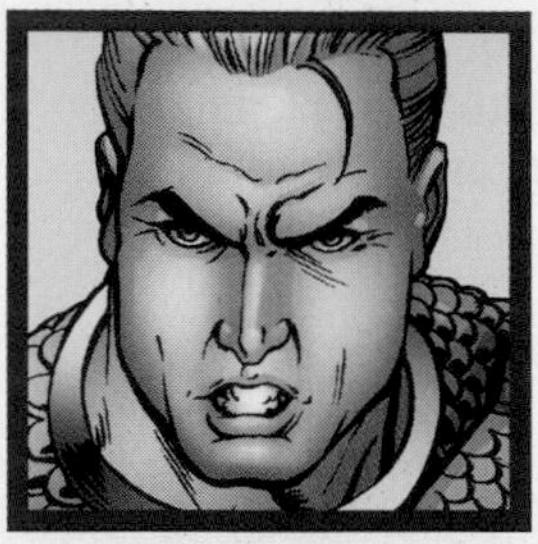

Aquaman: A founding member of the Justice League, Arthur Curry is the royal ruler of a kingdom that covers more than two-thirds of the Earth's surface. His abilities to withstand the awesome pressure of the deep and to communicate with all of the ocean's inhabitants help to make him the undersea world's greatest protector.

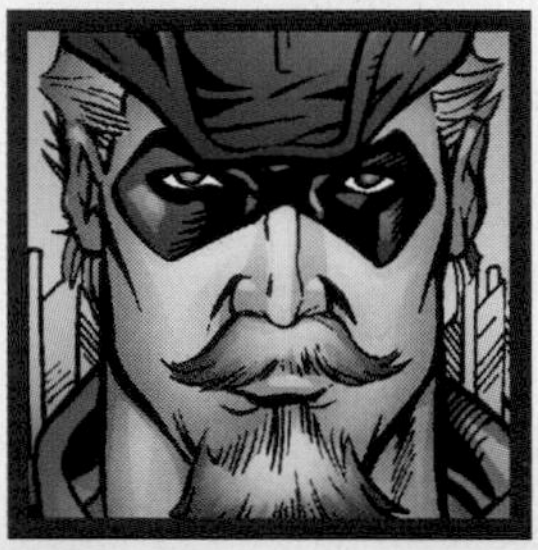

Green Arrow: While stranded on a desert island, millionaire Oliver Queen taught himself amazing archery skills. After his rescue, he used those abilities to fight for the weak and defenseless. Green Arrow has not always seen eye-to-eye with the group's mission. Queen sacrificed his life to save Metropolis, but cosmic forces brought him back from the dead. His body and soul have been reunited, forcing him to re-adjust to a world that has moved on without him.

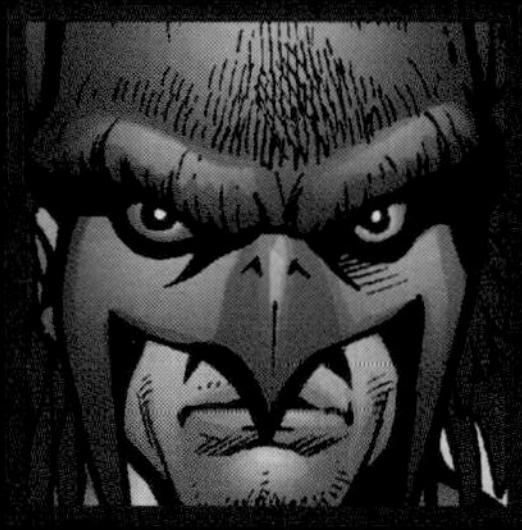

Hawkman: Thousands of years ago, in ancient Egypt, Prince Khufu discovered an alien spacecraft from the planet Thanagar. The ship was powered by a mysterious antigravity element, which the aliens called Nth metal. For centuries, Khufu was reincarnated, life after life. Today, he is Carter Hall, archaeologist, adventurer and hero.

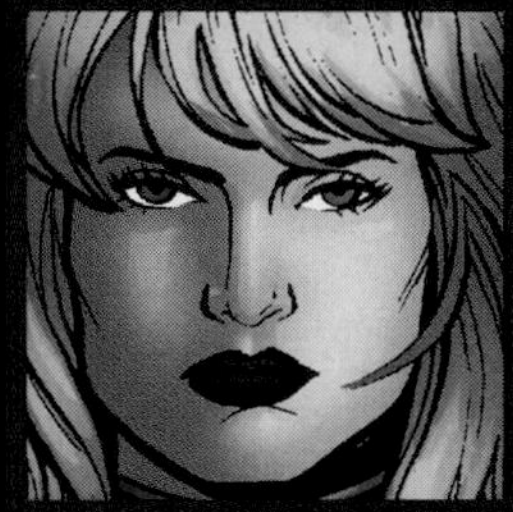

Dinah Lance grew up in the shadow of the legendary Justice Society of America, inheriting the role of Black Canary from her well-intentioned but domineering mother. Armed with a super-powered sonic cry and a mastery of the martial arts, Dinah helped found the JSA's successor, the Justice League of America. When her tempestuous relationship with Oliver Queen — Green Arrow — reached an end, Dinah left the Emerald Archer to blaze her own path.

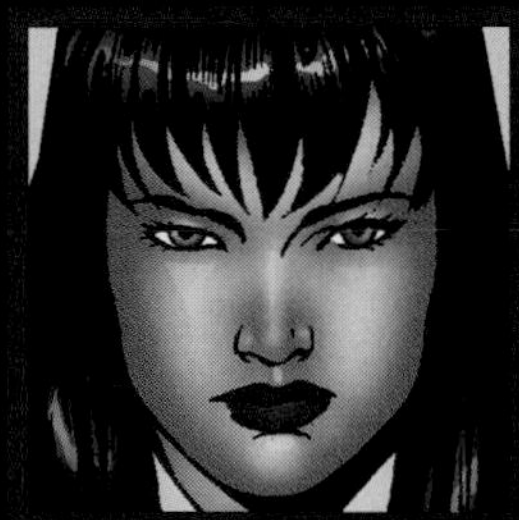

The daughter of the legendary magician Zatara and a popular stage performer in her own right, Zatanna employs powerful spells spoken in reverse to accomplish real magic, though her audiences think it's harmless stage-craft. Zatanna is half *Homo magi*, an inheritance passed down by her mother, who came from a hidden race of beings in another reality. A former member of the JLA, she remains available when needed.

JLA: CRISIS OF CONSCIENCE. Published by DC Comics. Cover, introduction and compilation copyright © 2006 DC Comics. All Rights Reserved. Originally published in single magazine form as JLA 115-119. Copyright © 2005 DC Comics. All Rights Reserved. All characters, their distinctive likenesses and related elements featured in this publication are trademarks of DC Comics. The stories, characters and incidents featured in this publication are entirely fictional. DC Comics does not read or accept unsolicited submissions of ideas, stories or artwork. DC Comics, 1700 Broadway, New York, NY 10019. A Warner Bros. Entertainment Company. Printed in Canada. First Printing. ISBN: 1-4012-0963-7. ISBN 13: 978-1-4012-0963-6. Cover illustration by Rags Morales. Cover color by Tanya & Richard Horie.

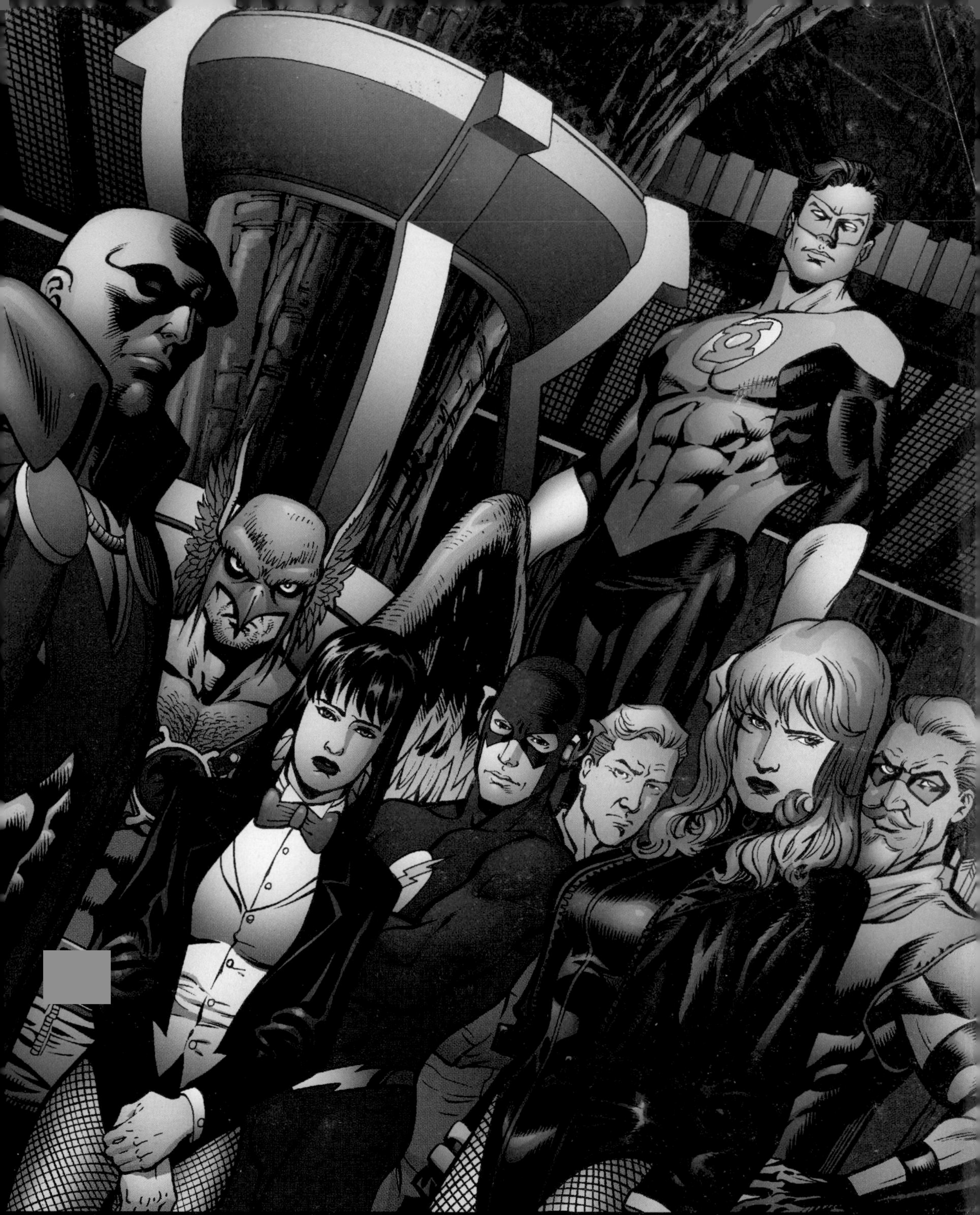

JLA CRISIS OF CONSCIENCE

Geoff Johns & Allan Heinberg Writers Chris Batista Penciller Mark Farmer Inker David Baron Colorist Ken Lopez Rob Leigh Letterers Rags Morales & Mark Farmer Original series covers Superman created by Jerry Siegel and Joe Shuster Batman created by Bob Kane

The Secret Society of Super-Villains:
Under the leadership of The Wizard, an alliance of super-villains was formed, working in secret to bring down Earth's costumed champions. Their goal is to leave humanity unprotected, and perfect prey for their global ambitions.

The Wizard:
William Asmodeus Zard is a career criminal, first serving prison time in the 1930s. In between incarcerations, he journeyed to Tibet and studied the mystic arts, returning to America after World War II as the Wizard. Since then, he has used his arcane powers to attempt world domination, only to be thwarted by the Justice Society of America and the Justice League.

Chronos:
Petty thief David Clinton spent his multiple jail terms studying – and ultimately mastering – time itself. At first he used time-themed weapons to commit his crimes, but then he sold his soul to the demon Neron in exchange for inherent chronal powers. Since gaining his mystically based abilities, he has battled the Atom and the Justice League with renewed vigor.

Star Sapphire:
There have been several women claiming to be Star Sapphire. Perhaps the most mysterious one is a French native who has taken possession of the uniform once worn by the alien Queen of Zamaron. It remains to be determined how she obtained it and exactly what her powers are.

Felix Faust:
The magician Felix Faust counts his age in terms of millennia, inhabiting one body after another. In the 21st century, he inhabits the body of Dekan Drache and this is his most powerful incarnation yet, thanks to the advanced knowledge and experience he has accumulated. A perennial thorn in the Justice League's side, he is also one of their deadliest opponents.

Floronic Man:
Originally a criminal from another dimension, the man known as Woodrue was banished to Earth, only to thrive in his new home. As "Jason Woodrue" he became a botany professor, improving his knowledge and control of the indigenous plant life. One of his experiments transformed him from fauna to flora, and in this new amoral incarnation, he remains a threat to all manner of life on Earth.

Matter Master:
Mark Mandrill discovered the rare chemical Menthachem, which grants him the ability to control the very properties of matter. Rather than help others with this astonishing scientific breakthrough, he has chosen to exploit the chemical and seek personal gain. Yet such attempts have only led to his defeat at the hands of Hawkman and Sargon the Sorcerer.

The cloistered world of super-heroes was shattered when Sue Dibny, wife of the Elongated Man, was killed in her home. The investigation into the grisly crime baffled the world's greatest detectives, from Batman to Mr. Miracle.

Evidence suggested that Dr. Light might have been responsible, and this was especially alarming news to a select group of Justice Leaguers. It meant that a horrible secret, held for years, was finally out in the open. It was revealed that Light had attacked Sue before. He had infiltrated the JLA's orbiting satellite headquarters, where he brutally assaulted and raped Sue. When the JLA subdued him, the League was divided over his punishment. Finally they decieded that Zatanna would use her mystic powers to alter his mind, removing knowledge of their identities and softening his personality. Batman arrived moments before Zatanna performed her spell, and when he objected, they erased the knowledge from his mind.

Despite their precautions, it seemed as if Dr. Light had struck again, with devastating consequences. As the Leaguers tracked him, they had to first get past Deathstroke the Terminator. During the melee, the magical bonds on Light's mind shattered and he remembered what had been done to him. More vicious than ever, he swore vengeance against the costumed champions.

And the word spread. Angered by the notion that the heroes had tampered with their minds, their very personalities, the villains determined to strike back. Armed with this powerful impetus, Lex Luthor and others formed a Society focused upon a single goal: **revenge**.

As the murder investigation continued, it was learned that it was Jean Loring, the Atom's estranged ex-wife, who had accidentally killed Sue. Using a spare Atom outfit, complete with size and weight controls, Jean visited her old friend Sue, microscopically entering her brain. The goal was to injure her in her own home, sending a shock wave throughout the super-hero community and reuniting loved ones, including Jean and Ray Palmer. Unused to the powers and the biology, Jean had caused Sue's brain to hemorrhage.

Dr. Mid-Nite uncovered the evidence of Jean's actions, and informed J'onn J'onzz who telepathically informed the rest of the JLA. Jean was taken into custody and locked away at Arkham Asylum, Gotham City's home for the criminally insane. Palmer, mad with grief, used his abilities to shrink until he had disappeared entirely, removing himself from all contact with his comrades.

However, it remains for the JLA to confront the consequences of their actions — consequences that threaten to ripple out of control...

JLA #115
by Rags Morales & Mark Farmer

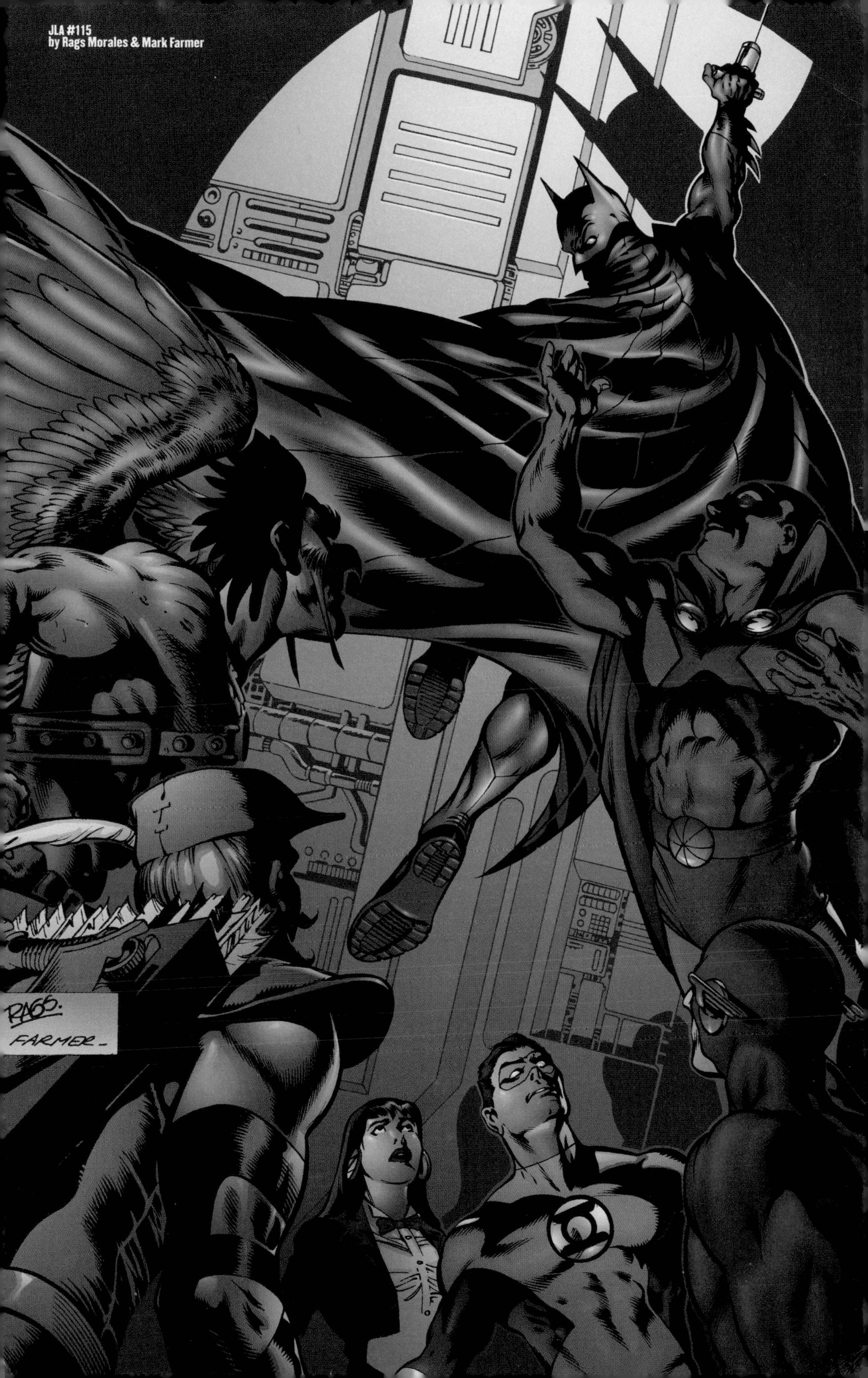
RAGS.
FARMER-

JLA

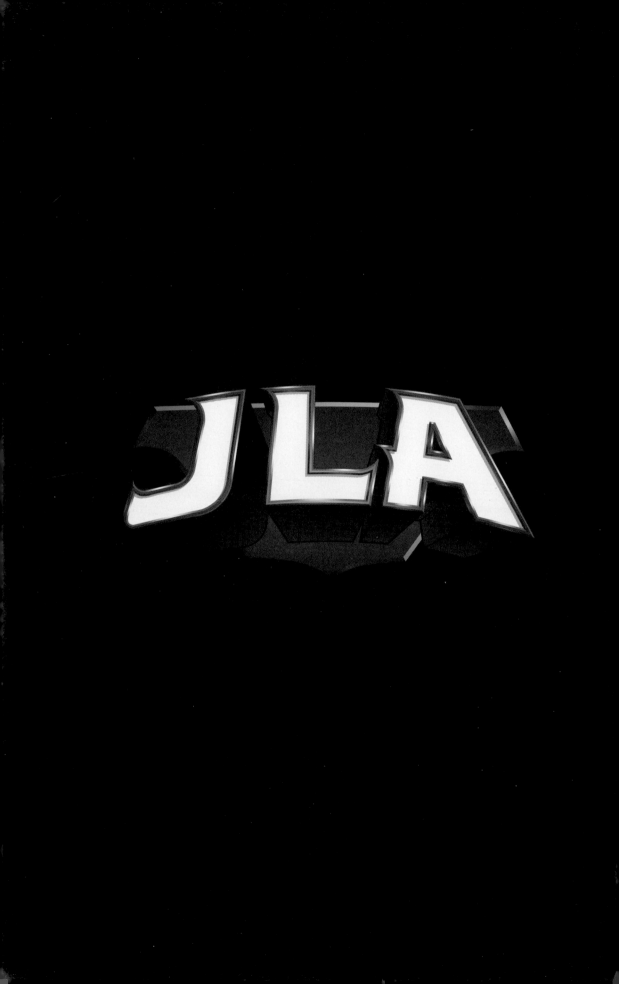

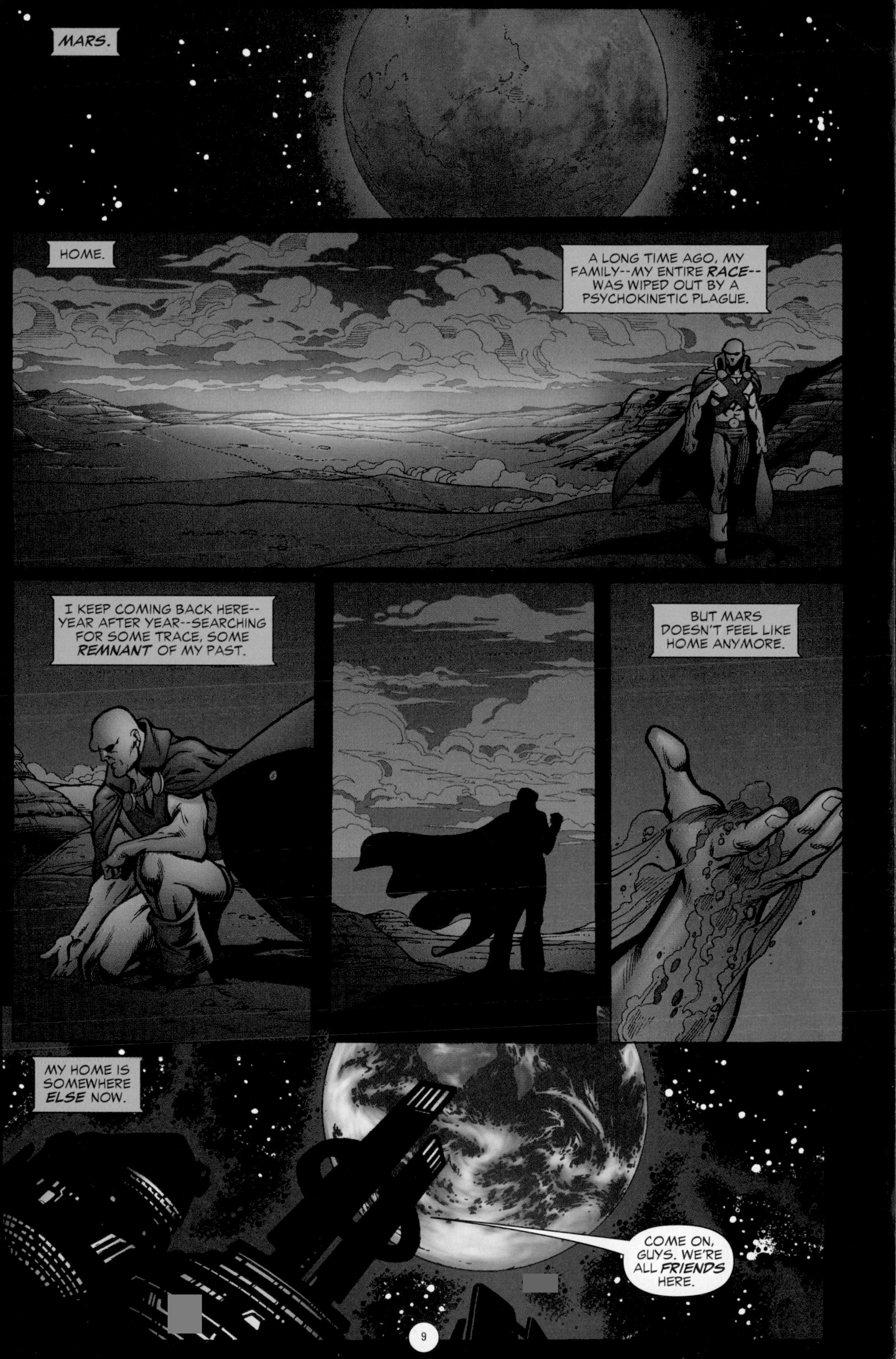
MARS.
HOME.
A LONG TIME AGO, MY FAMILY--MY ENTIRE RACE--WAS WIPED OUT BY A PSYCHOKINETIC PLAGUE.
I KEEP COMING BACK HERE--YEAR AFTER YEAR--SEARCHING FOR SOME TRACE, SOME REMNANT OF MY PAST.
BUT MARS DOESN'T FEEL LIKE HOME ANYMORE.
MY HOME IS SOMEWHERE ELSE NOW.
COME ON, GUYS. WE'RE ALL FRIENDS HERE.

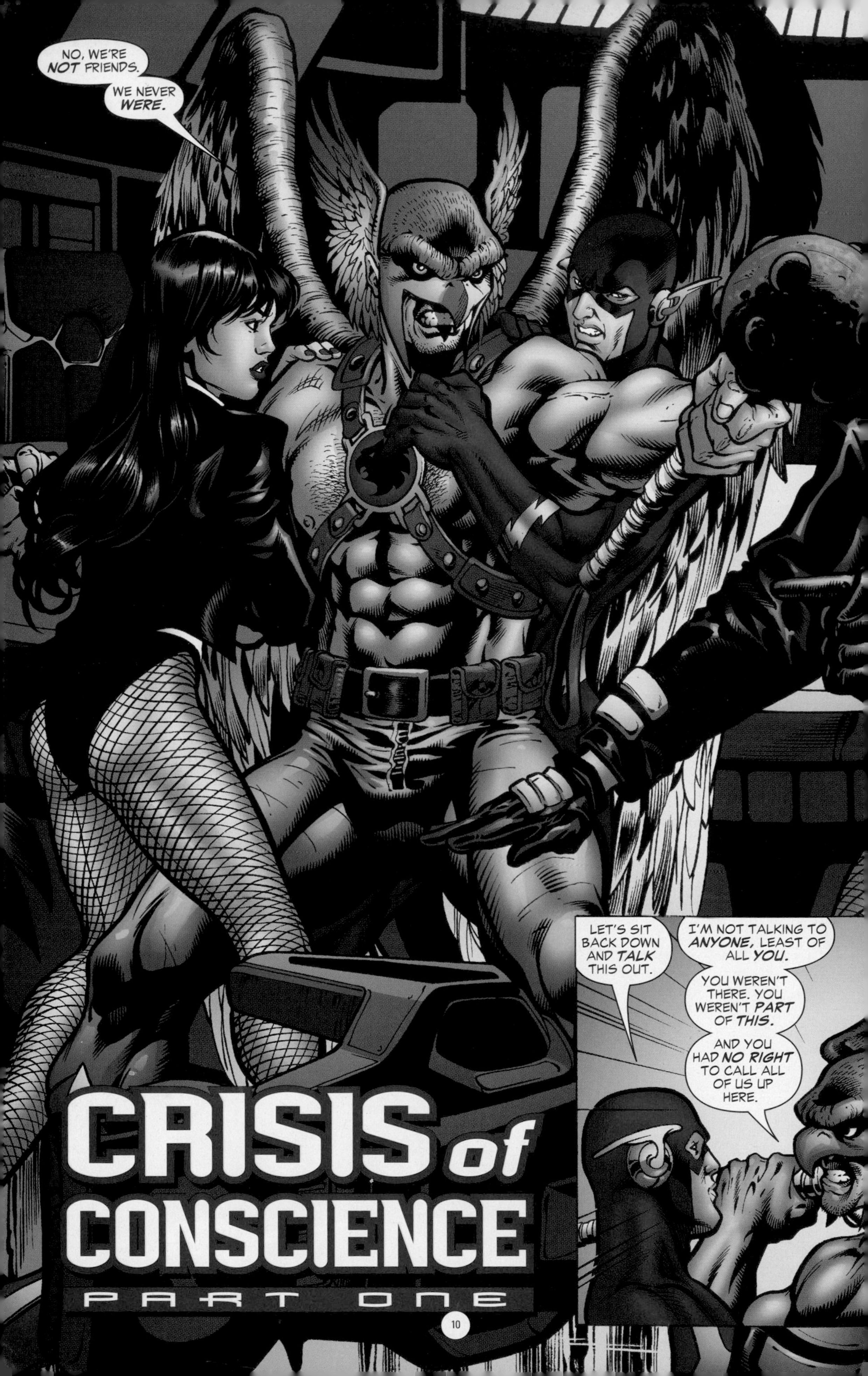

NO, WE'RE NOT FRIENDS.
WE NEVER WERE.
CRISIS of CONSCIENCE
PART ONE
LET'S SIT BACK DOWN AND TALK THIS OUT.
I'M NOT TALKING TO ANYONE, LEAST OF ALL YOU.
YOU WEREN'T THERE. YOU WEREN'T PART OF THIS.
AND YOU HAD NO RIGHT TO CALL ALL OF US UP HERE.

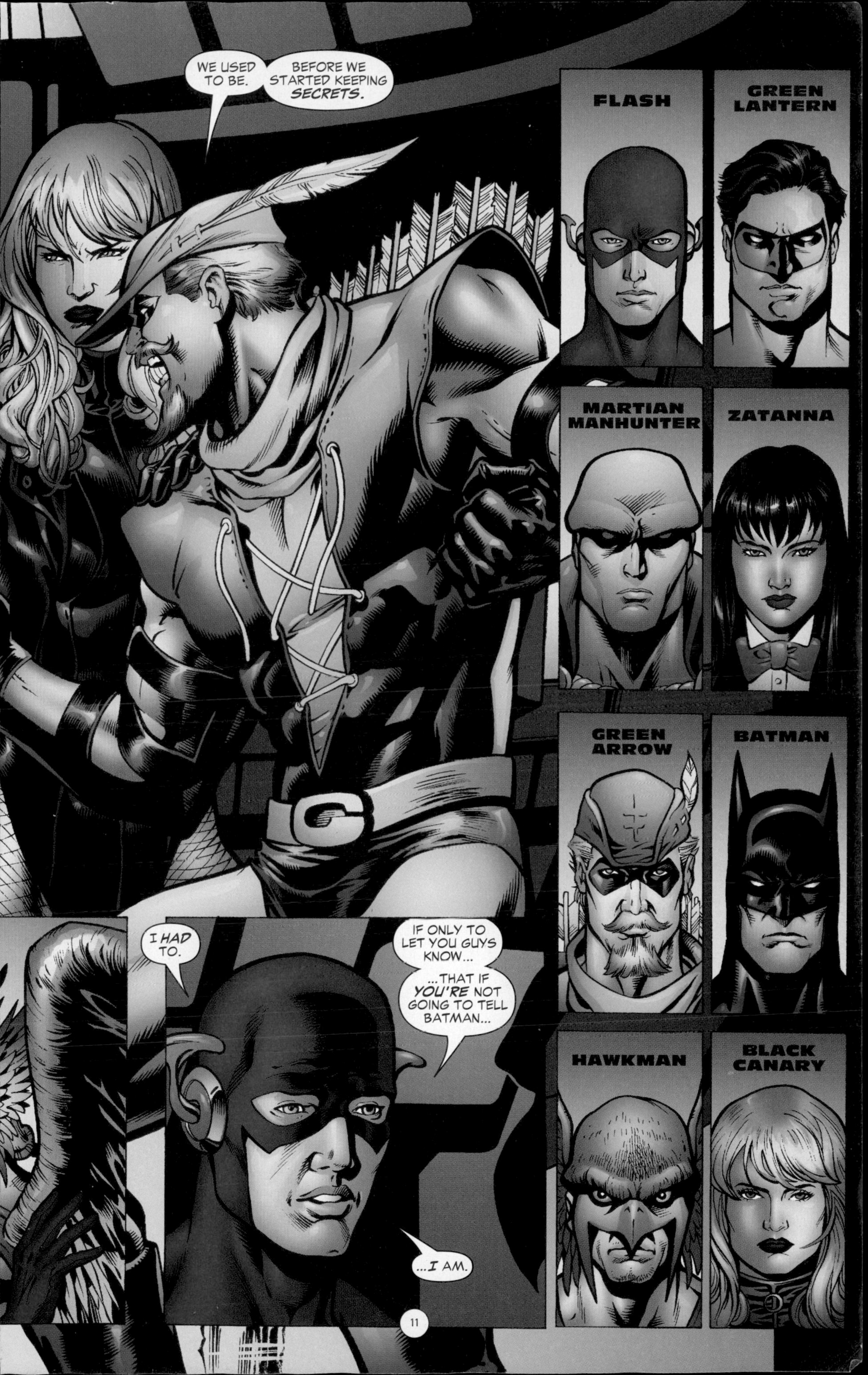

WE USED TO BE.
BEFORE WE STARTED KEEPING *SECRETS*.
FLASH
GREEN LANTERN
MARTIAN MANHUNTER
ZATANNA
GREEN ARROW
BATMAN
HAWKMAN
BLACK CANARY
I *HAD* TO.
IF ONLY TO LET YOU GUYS KNOW...
...THAT IF *YOU'RE* NOT GOING TO TELL BATMAN...
...*I* AM.

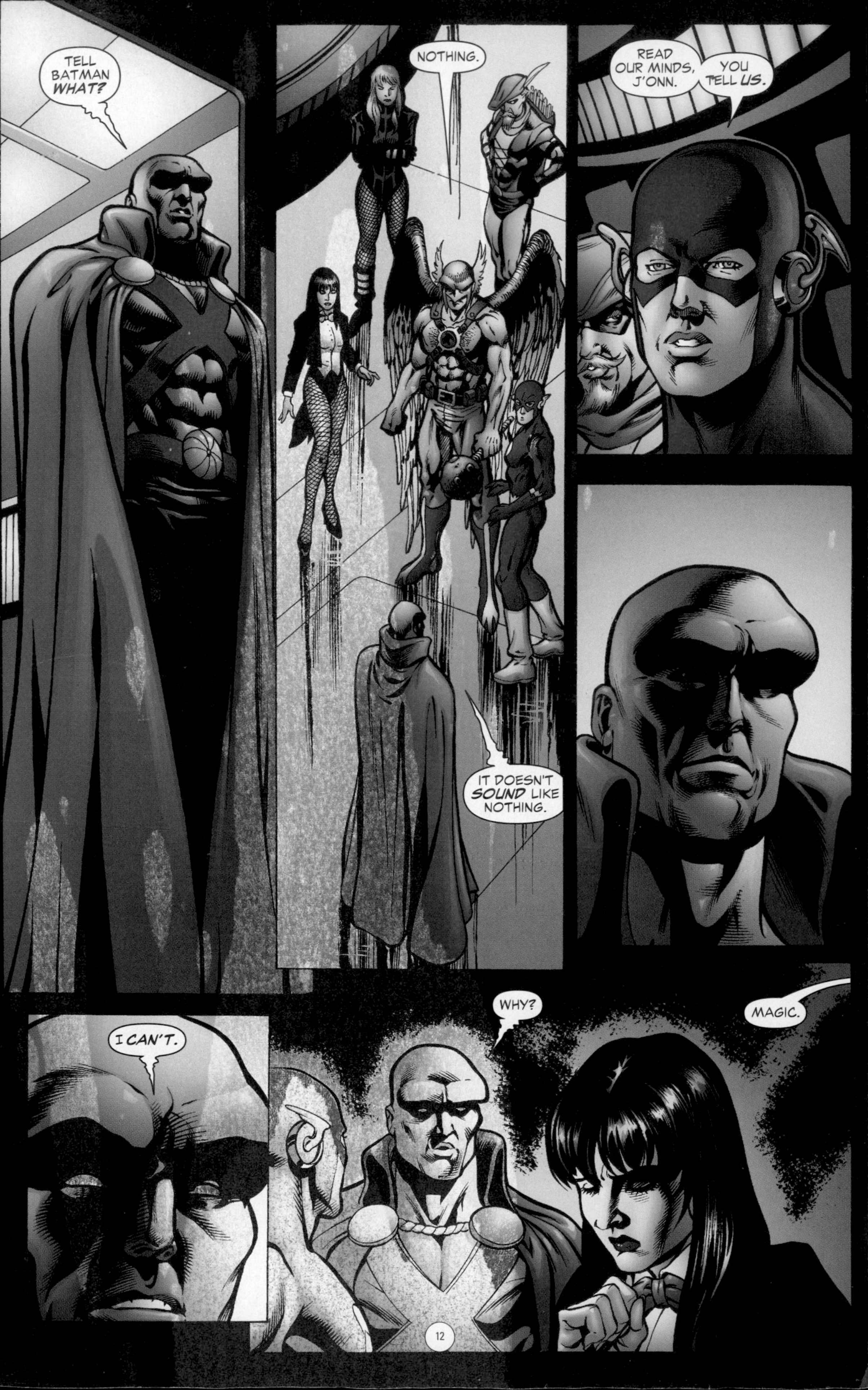
TELL BATMAN WHAT?
NOTHING.
IT DOESN'T SOUND LIKE NOTHING.
READ OUR MINDS, J'ONN.
YOU TELL US.
I CAN'T.
WHY?
MAGIC.

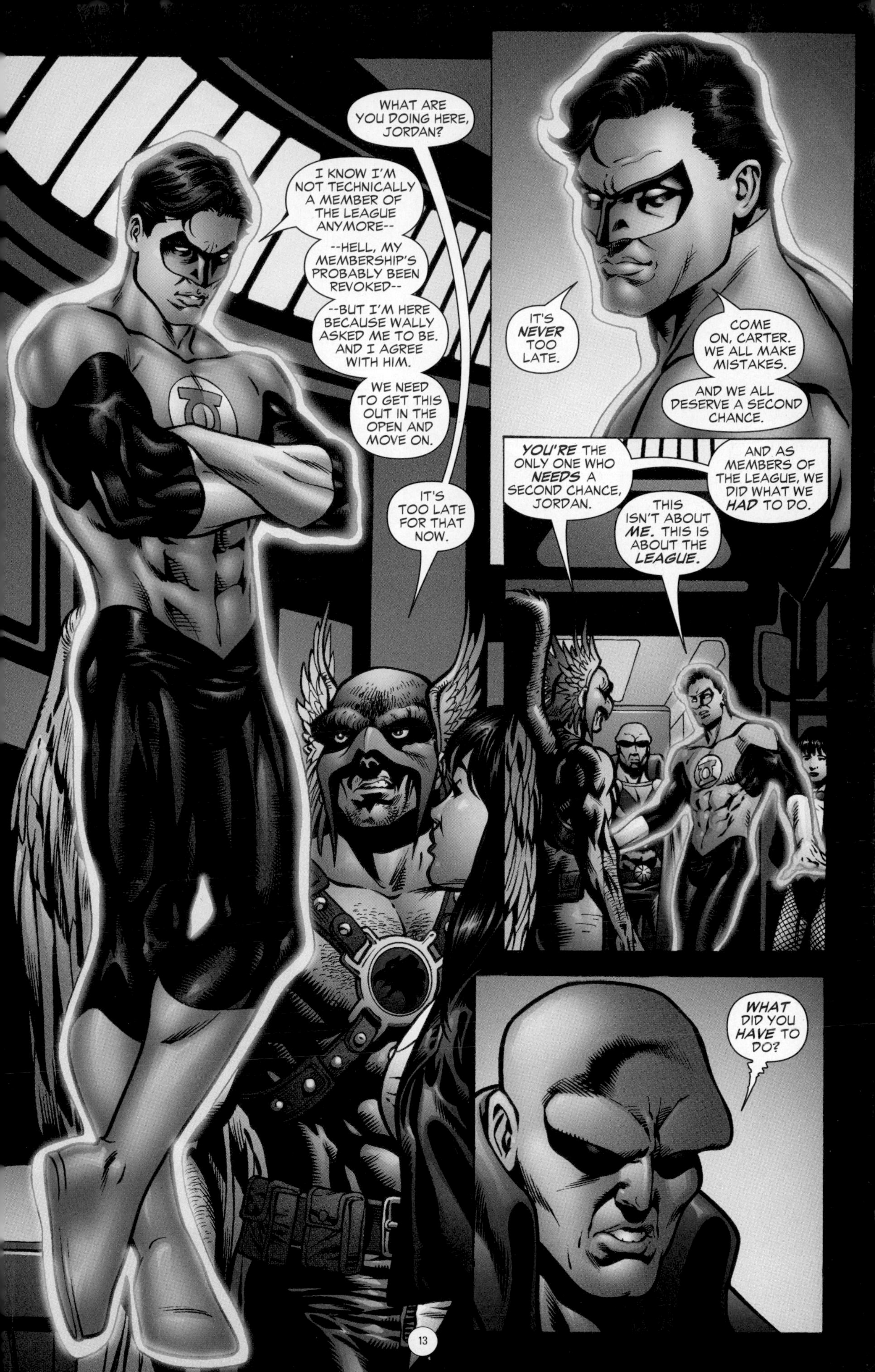
WHAT ARE YOU DOING HERE, JORDAN?
I KNOW I'M NOT TECHNICALLY A MEMBER OF THE LEAGUE ANYMORE--
--HELL, MY MEMBERSHIP'S PROBABLY BEEN REVOKED--
--BUT I'M HERE BECAUSE WALLY ASKED ME TO BE. AND I AGREE WITH HIM.
WE NEED TO GET THIS OUT IN THE OPEN AND MOVE ON.
IT'S TOO LATE FOR THAT NOW.
IT'S NEVER TOO LATE.
COME ON, CARTER. WE ALL MAKE MISTAKES.
AND WE ALL DESERVE A SECOND CHANCE.
YOU'RE THE ONLY ONE WHO NEEDS A SECOND CHANCE, JORDAN.
AND AS MEMBERS OF THE LEAGUE, WE DID WHAT WE HAD TO DO.
THIS ISN'T ABOUT ME. THIS IS ABOUT THE LEAGUE.
WHAT DID YOU HAVE TO DO?

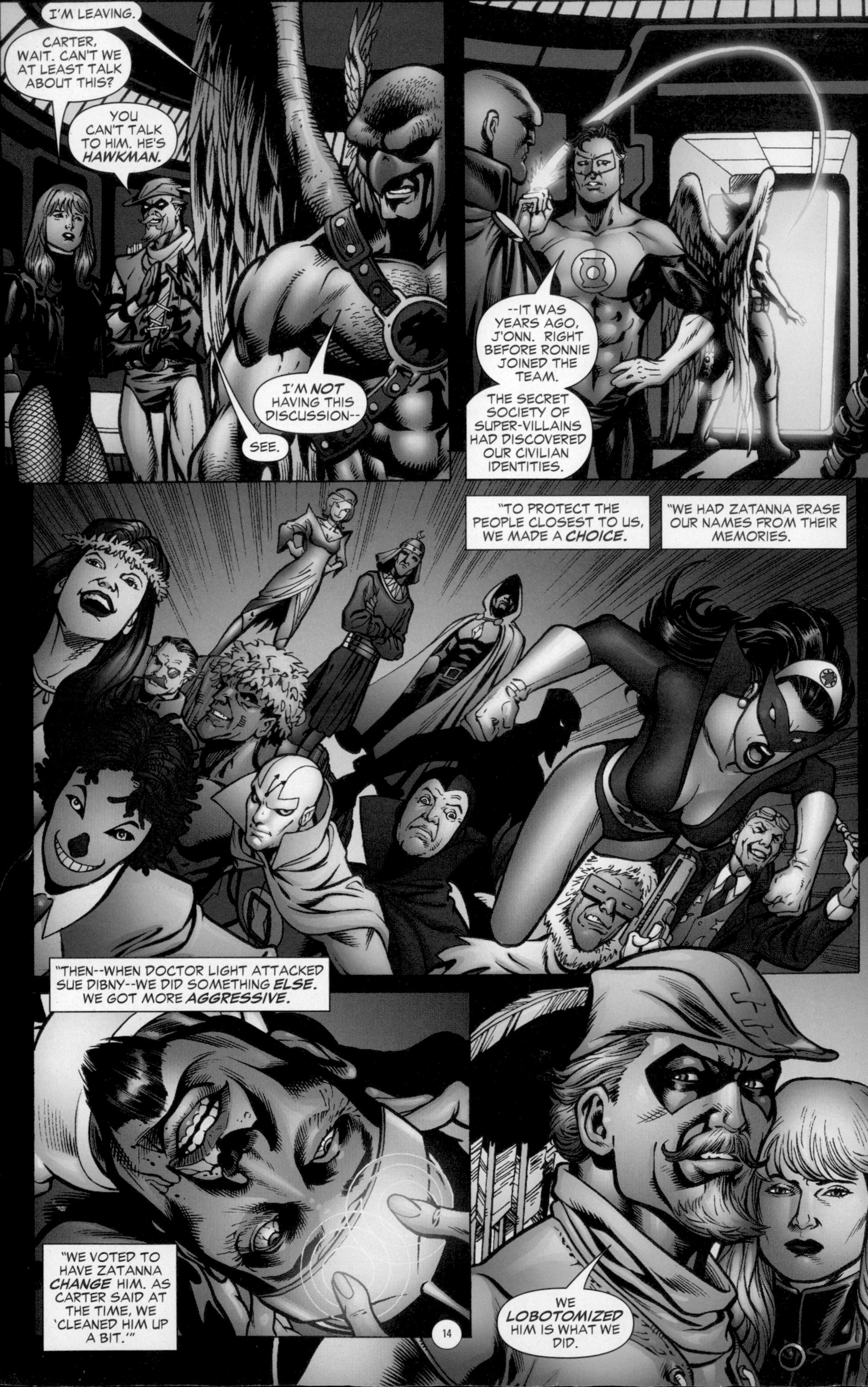

I'M LEAVING.
CARTER, WAIT. CAN'T WE AT LEAST TALK ABOUT THIS?
YOU CAN'T TALK TO HIM. HE'S *HAWKMAN.*
I'M *NOT* HAVING THIS DISCUSSION--
SEE.
--IT WAS YEARS AGO, J'ONN. RIGHT BEFORE RONNIE JOINED THE TEAM.
THE SECRET SOCIETY OF SUPER-VILLAINS HAD DISCOVERED OUR CIVILIAN IDENTITIES.
"TO PROTECT THE PEOPLE CLOSEST TO US, WE MADE A *CHOICE.*
"WE HAD ZATANNA ERASE OUR NAMES FROM THEIR MEMORIES.
"THEN--WHEN DOCTOR LIGHT ATTACKED SUE DIBNY--WE DID SOMETHING *ELSE.* WE GOT MORE *AGGRESSIVE.*
"WE VOTED TO HAVE ZATANNA *CHANGE* HIM. AS CARTER SAID AT THE TIME, WE 'CLEANED HIM UP A BIT.'"
WE *LOBOTOMIZED* HIM IS WHAT WE DID.

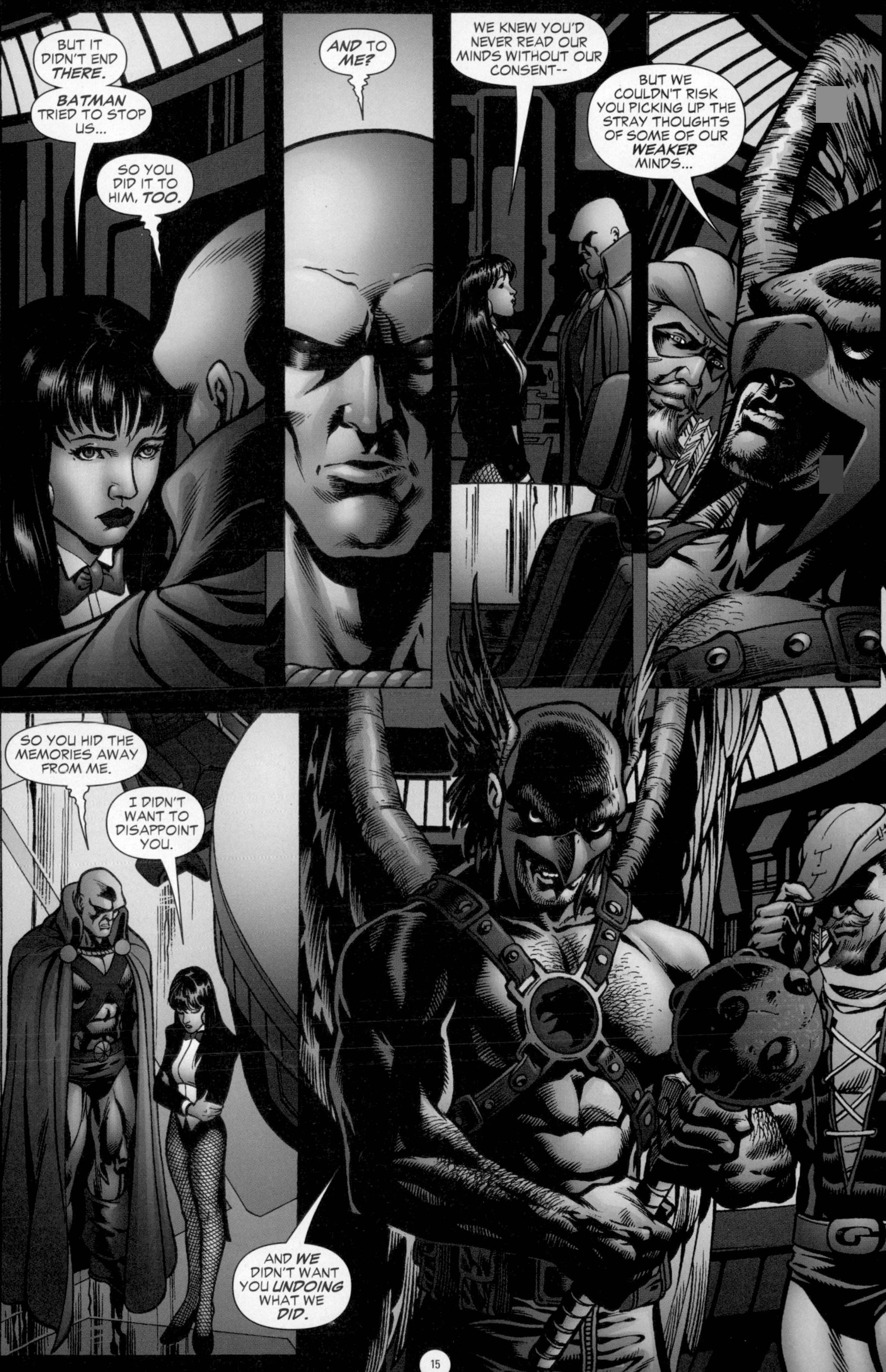
BUT IT DIDN'T END THERE.
BATMAN TRIED TO STOP US...
SO YOU DID IT TO HIM, TOO.
AND TO ME?
WE KNEW YOU'D NEVER READ OUR MINDS WITHOUT OUR CONSENT--
BUT WE COULDN'T RISK YOU PICKING UP THE STRAY THOUGHTS OF SOME OF OUR WEAKER MINDS...
SO YOU HID THE MEMORIES AWAY FROM ME.
I DIDN'T WANT TO DISAPPOINT YOU.
AND WE DIDN'T WANT YOU UNDOING WHAT WE DID.

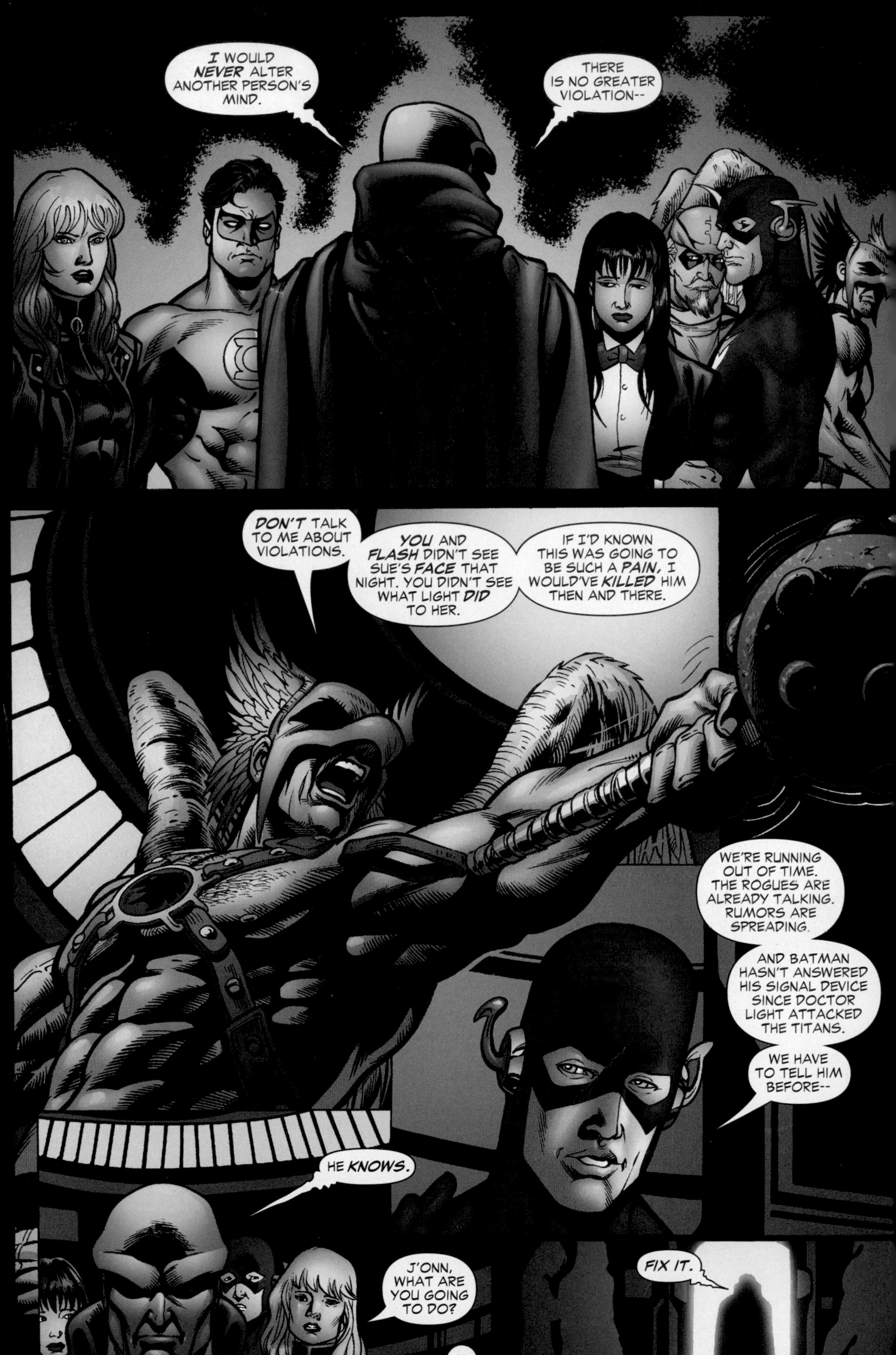
I WOULD NEVER ALTER ANOTHER PERSON'S MIND.
THERE IS NO GREATER VIOLATION--
DON'T TALK TO ME ABOUT VIOLATIONS.
YOU AND FLASH DIDN'T SEE SUE'S FACE THAT NIGHT. YOU DIDN'T SEE WHAT LIGHT DID TO HER.
IF I'D KNOWN THIS WAS GOING TO BE SUCH A PAIN, I WOULD'VE KILLED HIM THEN AND THERE.
WE'RE RUNNING OUT OF TIME. THE ROGUES ARE ALREADY TALKING. RUMORS ARE SPREADING.
AND BATMAN HASN'T ANSWERED HIS SIGNAL DEVICE SINCE DOCTOR LIGHT ATTACKED THE TITANS.
WE HAVE TO TELL HIM BEFORE--
HE KNOWS.
J'ONN, WHAT ARE YOU GOING TO DO?
FIX IT.

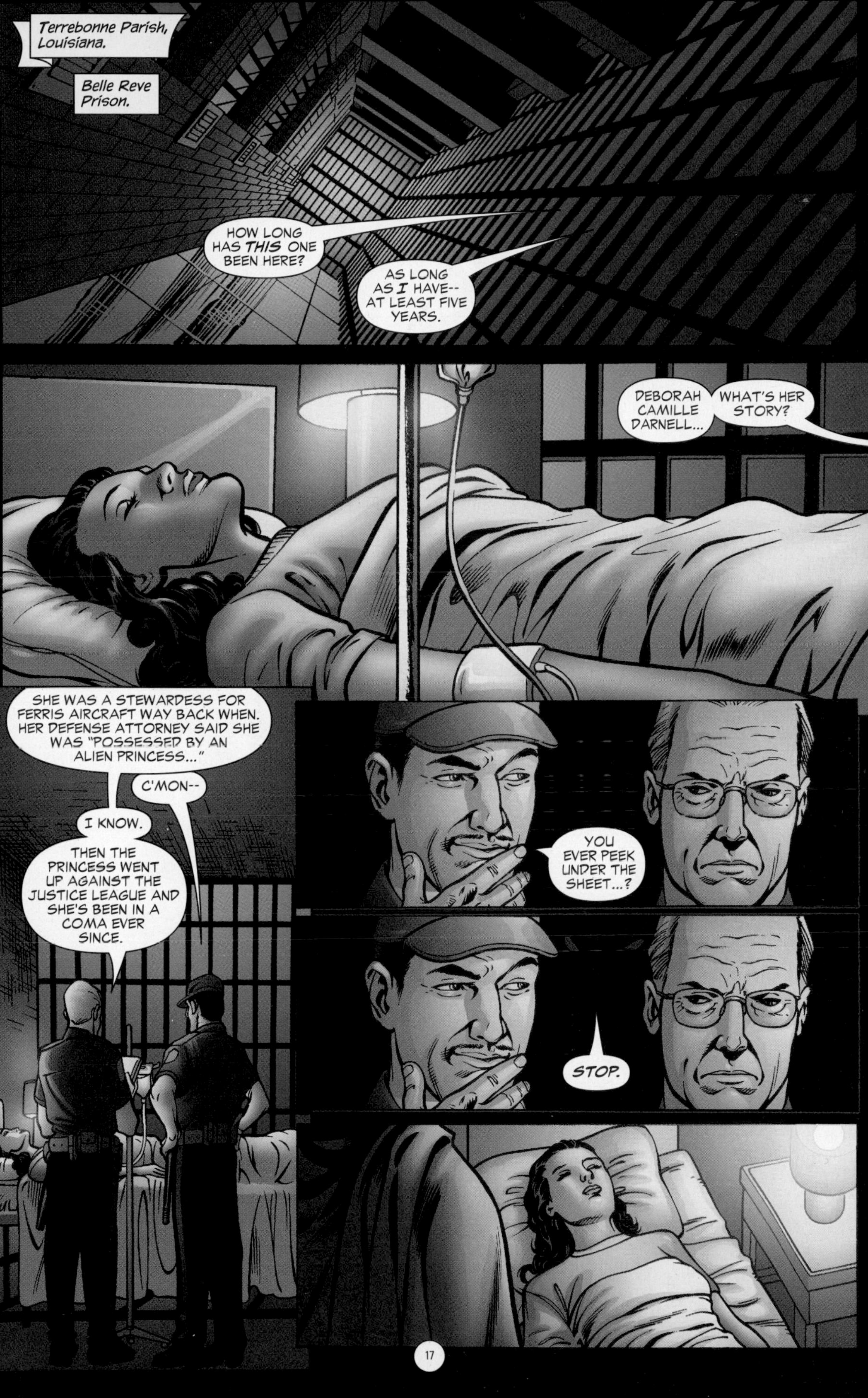
Terrebonne Parish, Louisiana.
Belle Reve Prison.
HOW LONG HAS THIS ONE BEEN HERE?
AS LONG AS I HAVE-- AT LEAST FIVE YEARS.
DEBORAH CAMILLE DARNELL...
WHAT'S HER STORY?
SHE WAS A STEWARDESS FOR FERRIS AIRCRAFT WAY BACK WHEN. HER DEFENSE ATTORNEY SAID SHE WAS "POSSESSED BY AN ALIEN PRINCESS..."
C'MON--
I KNOW.
THEN THE PRINCESS WENT UP AGAINST THE JUSTICE LEAGUE AND SHE'S BEEN IN A COMA EVER SINCE.
YOU EVER PEEK UNDER THE SHEET...?
STOP.

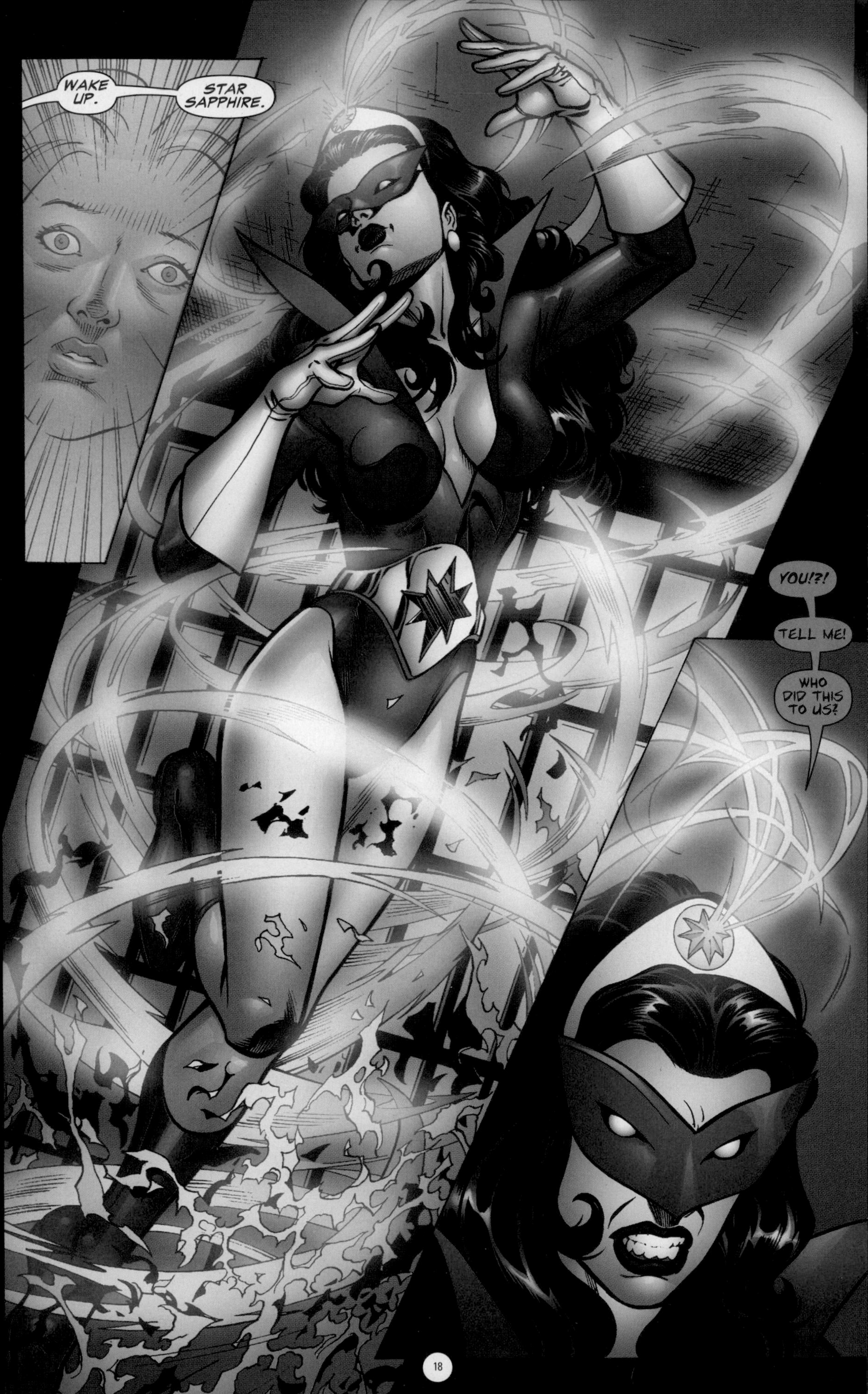
WAKE UP.
STAR SAPPHIRE.
YOU!?!
TELL ME!
WHO DID THIS TO US?

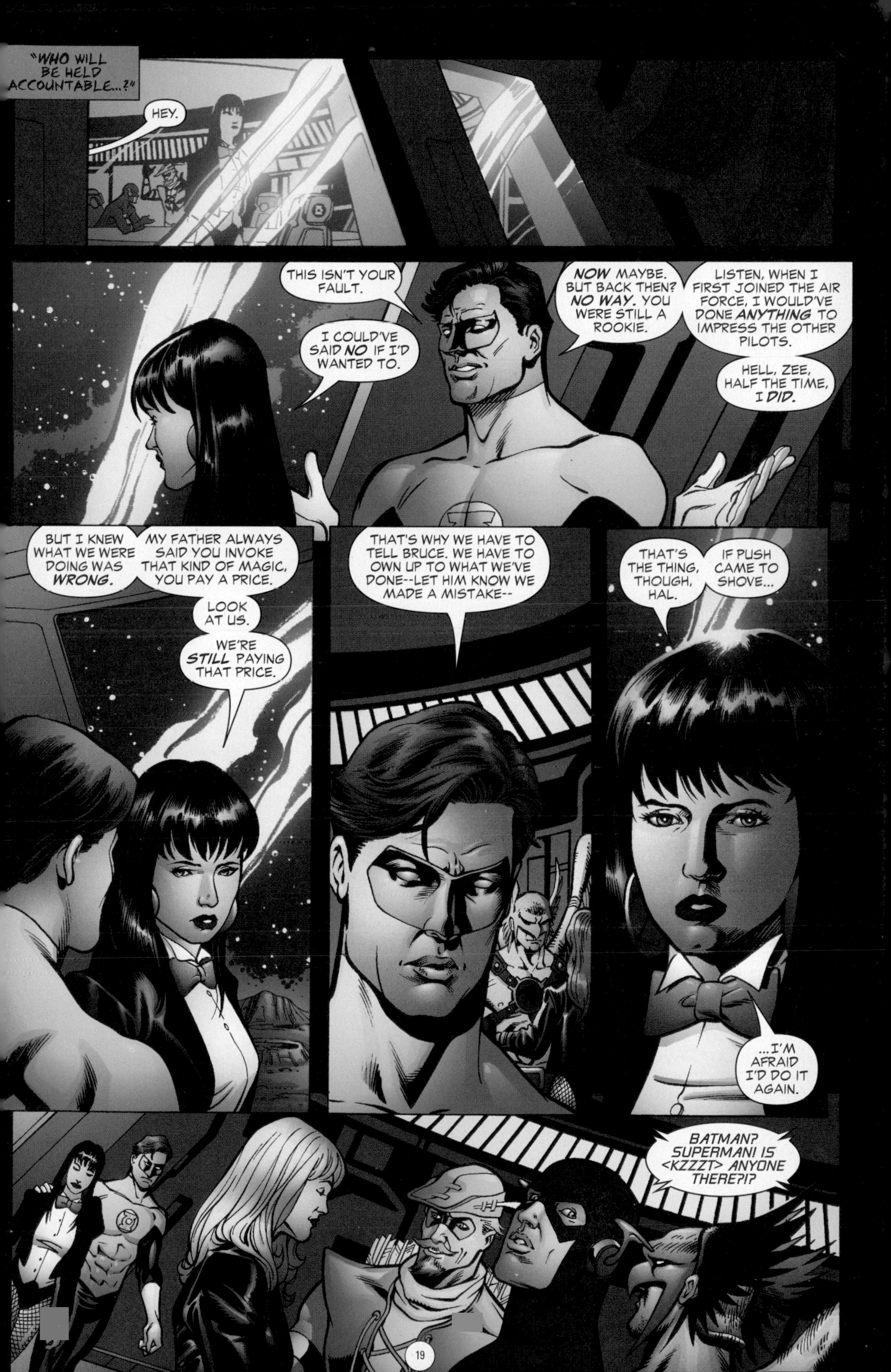
"WHO WILL BE HELD ACCOUNTABLE...?"
HEY.
THIS ISN'T YOUR FAULT.
I COULD'VE SAID NO IF I'D WANTED TO.
NOW MAYBE. BUT BACK THEN? NO WAY. YOU WERE STILL A ROOKIE.
LISTEN, WHEN I FIRST JOINED THE AIR FORCE, I WOULD'VE DONE ANYTHING TO IMPRESS THE OTHER PILOTS.
HELL, ZEE, HALF THE TIME, I DID.
BUT I KNEW WHAT WE WERE DOING WAS WRONG.
MY FATHER ALWAYS SAID YOU INVOKE THAT KIND OF MAGIC, YOU PAY A PRICE.
LOOK AT US.
WE'RE STILL PAYING THAT PRICE.
THAT'S WHY WE HAVE TO TELL BRUCE. WE HAVE TO OWN UP TO WHAT WE'VE DONE--LET HIM KNOW WE MADE A MISTAKE--
THAT'S THE THING, THOUGH, HAL.
IF PUSH CAME TO SHOVE...
...I'M AFRAID I'D DO IT AGAIN.
BATMAN? SUPERMAN! IS <KZZZT> ANYONE THERE?!?

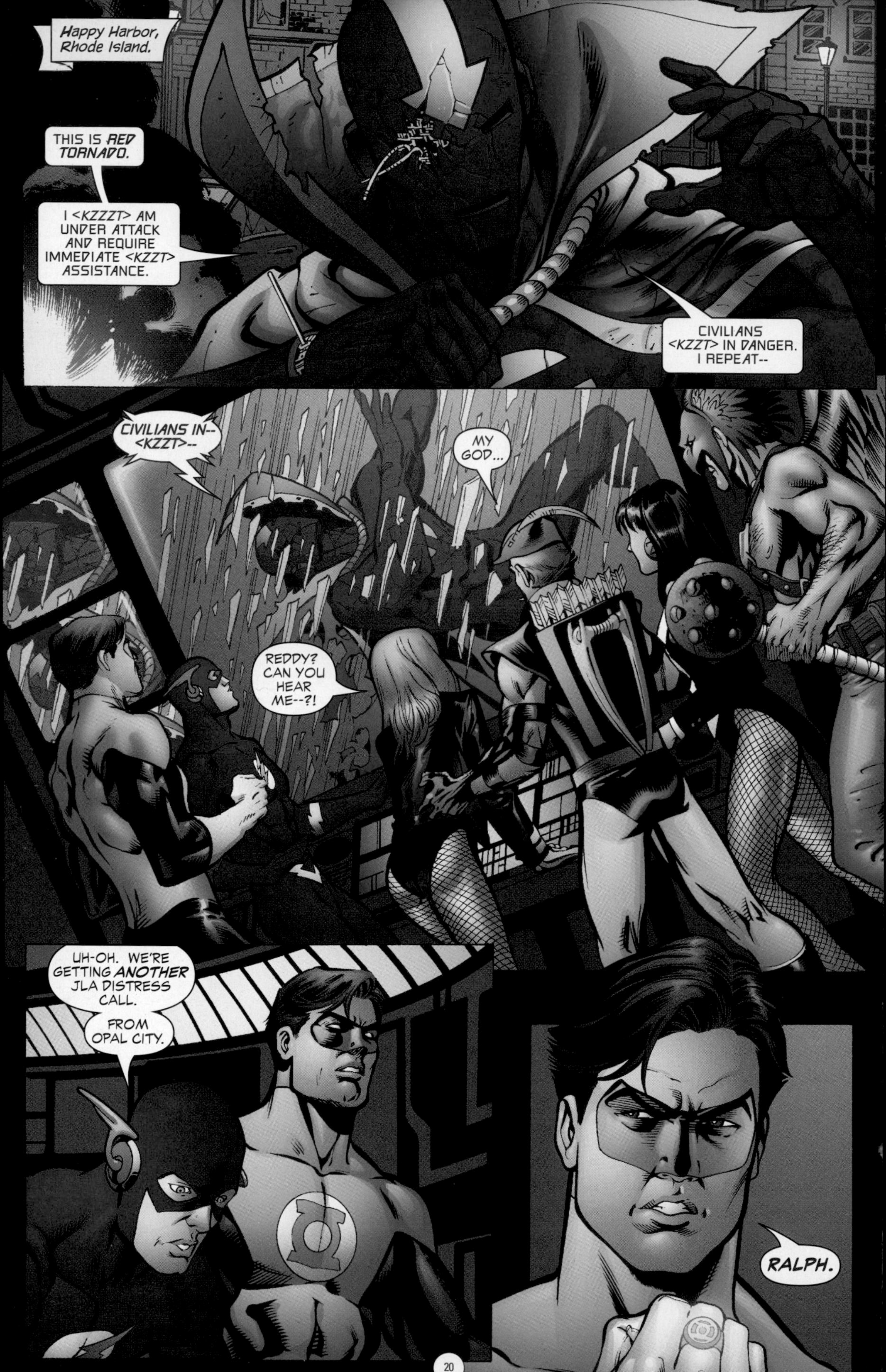
Happy Harbor, Rhode Island.
THIS IS RED TORNADO.
I <KZZZT> AM UNDER ATTACK AND REQUIRE IMMEDIATE <KZZT> ASSISTANCE.
CIVILIANS <KZZT> IN DANGER. I REPEAT--
CIVILIANS IN-- <KZZT>--
MY GOD...
REDDY? CAN YOU HEAR ME--?!
UH-OH. WE'RE GETTING ANOTHER JLA DISTRESS CALL.
FROM OPAL CITY.
RALPH.

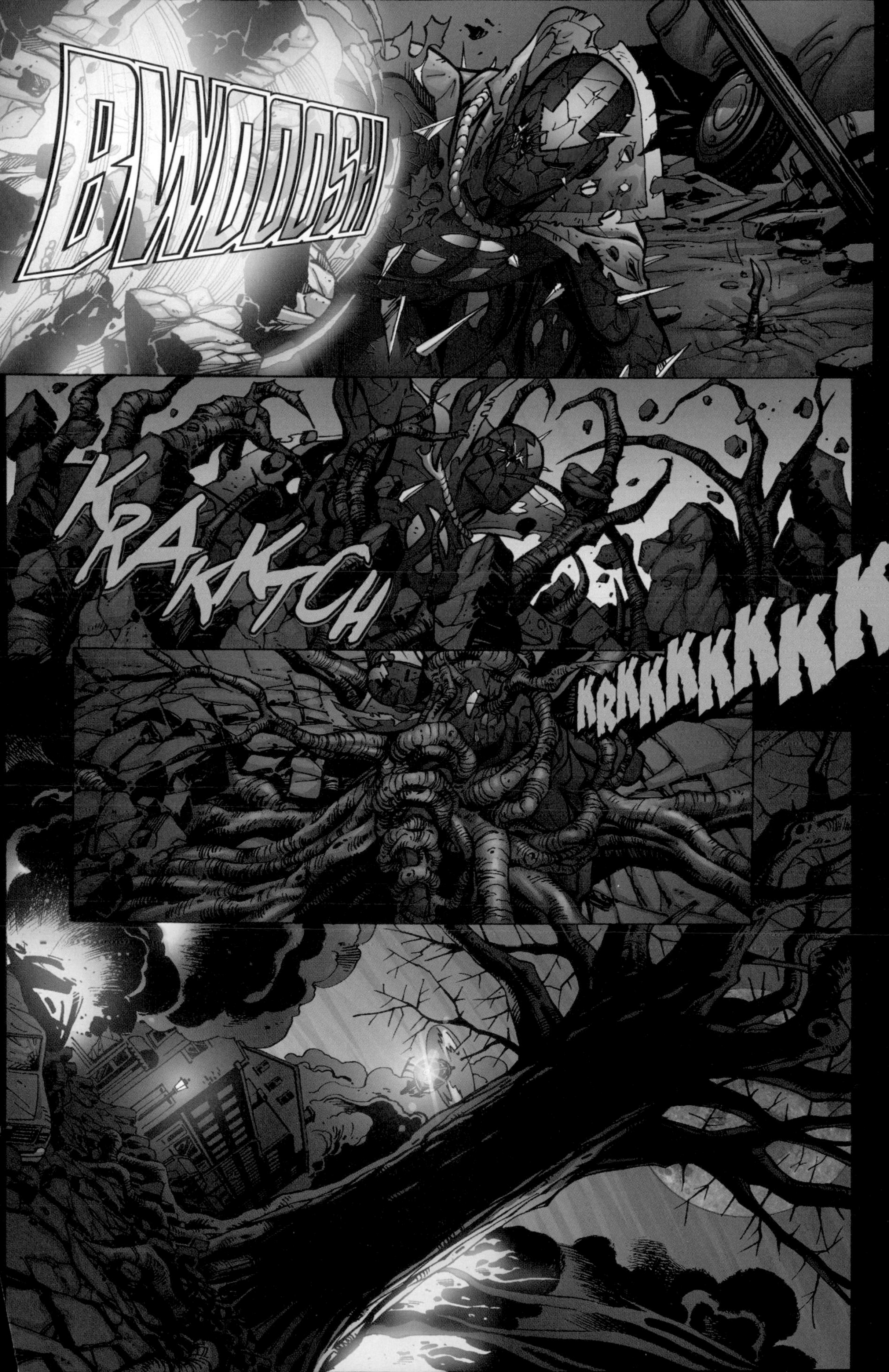
BWOOOOSH
KRAKKTCH
KRKKKKKKKK

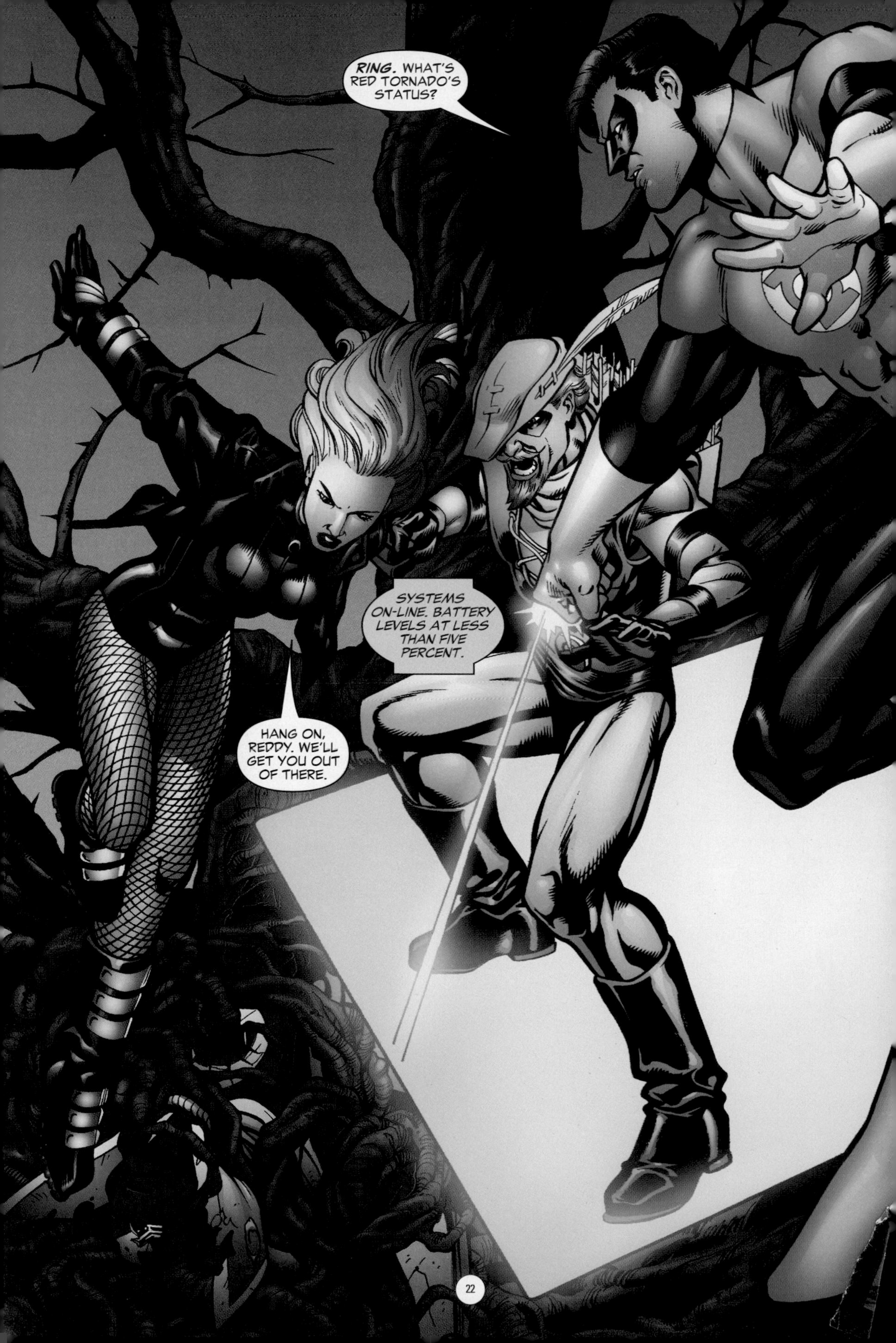
RING. WHAT'S RED TORNADO'S STATUS?
SYSTEMS ON-LINE. BATTERY LEVELS AT LESS THAN FIVE PERCENT.
HANG ON, REDDY. WE'LL GET YOU OUT OF THERE.

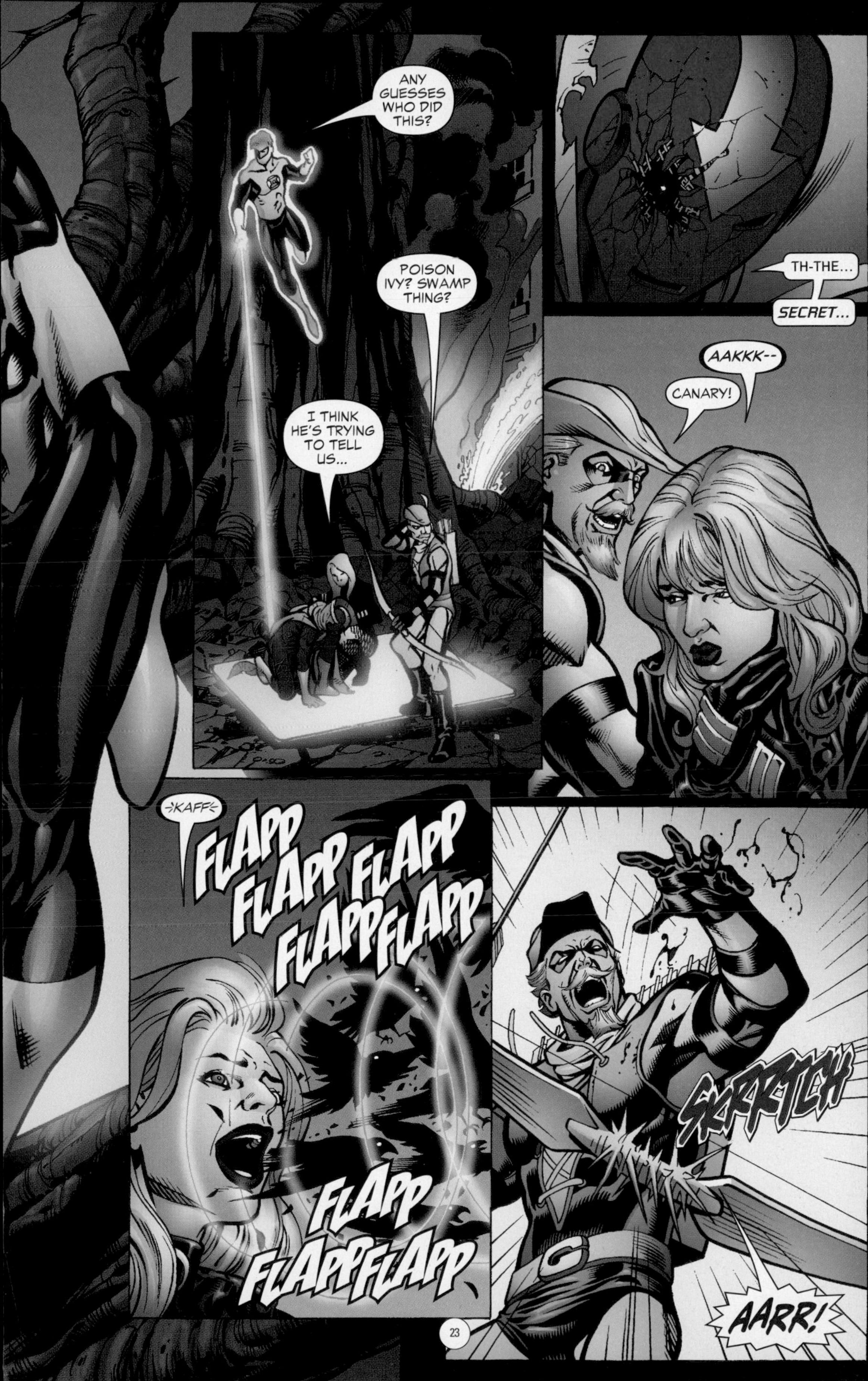
ANY GUESSES WHO DID THIS?
POISON IVY? SWAMP THING?
I THINK HE'S TRYING TO TELL US...
TH-THE...
SECRET...
AAKKK--
CANARY!
KAFF
FLAPP FLAPP FLAPP FLAPP FLAPP
FLAPP FLAPP FLAPP
SKRRTCH
AARR!

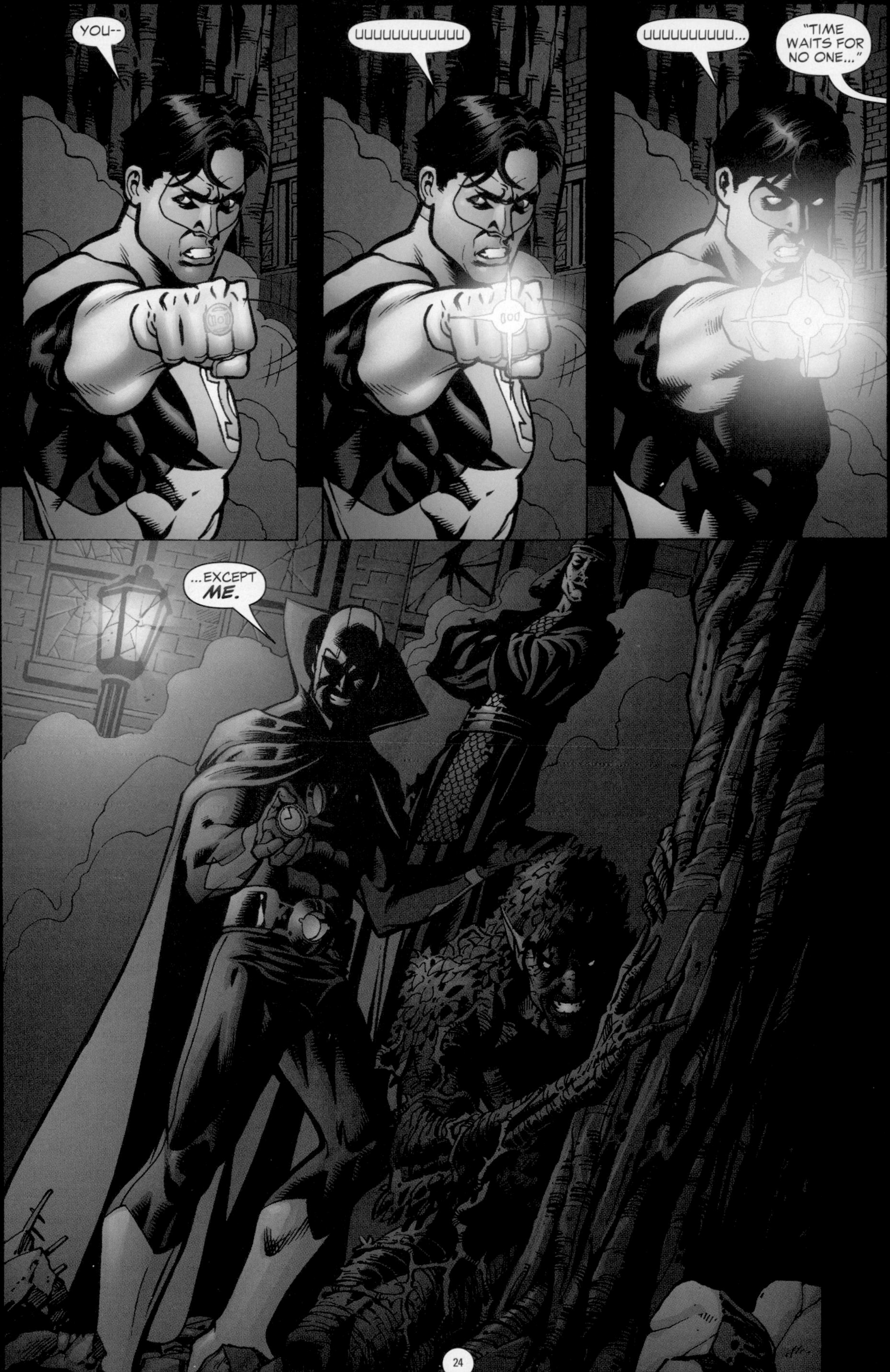
YOU--
UUUUUUUUUUUU
UUUUUUUUUU...
"TIME WAITS FOR NO ONE..."
...EXCEPT ME.

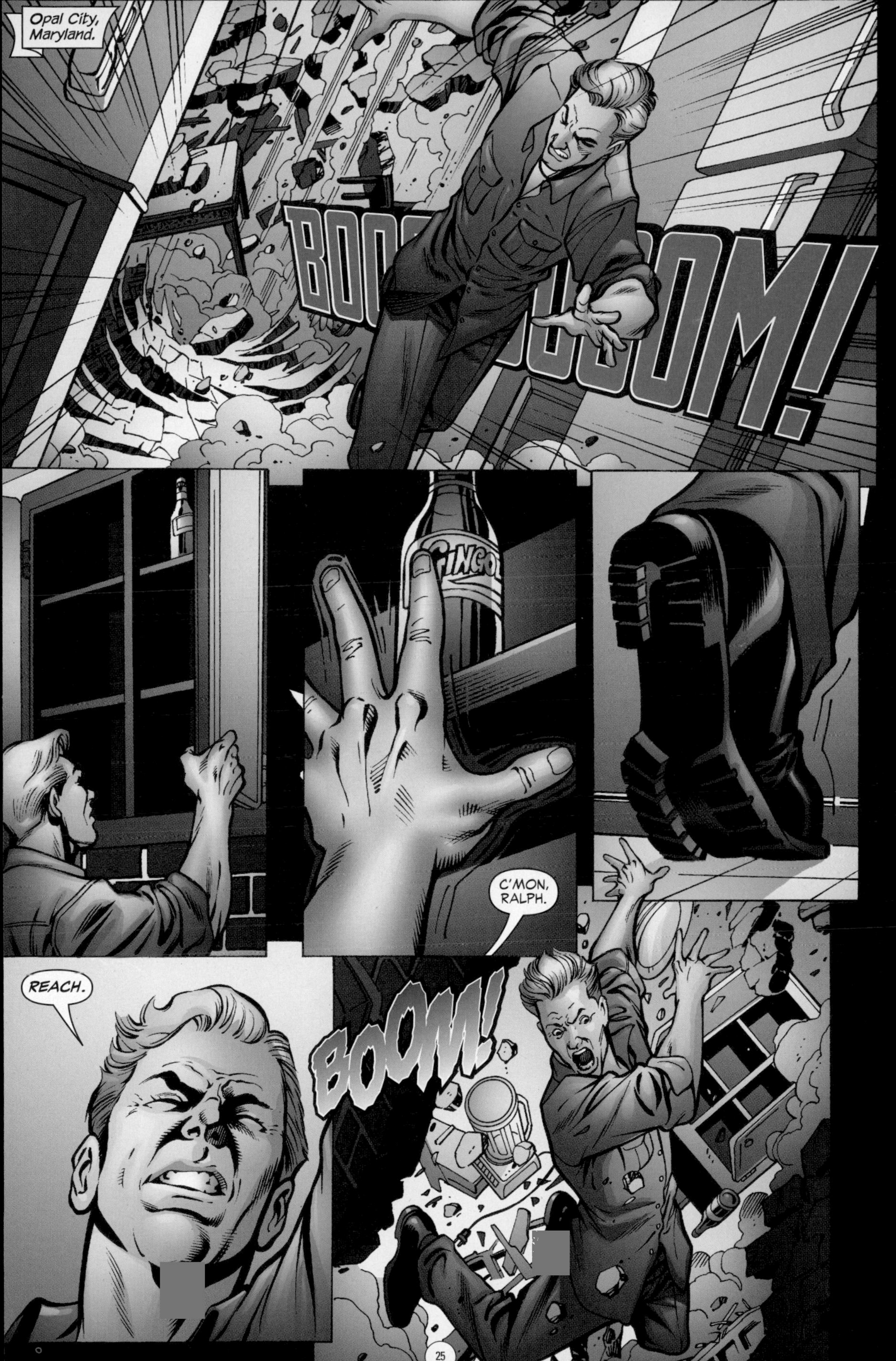

Opal City, Maryland.
C'MON, RALPH.
REACH.
BOOM!

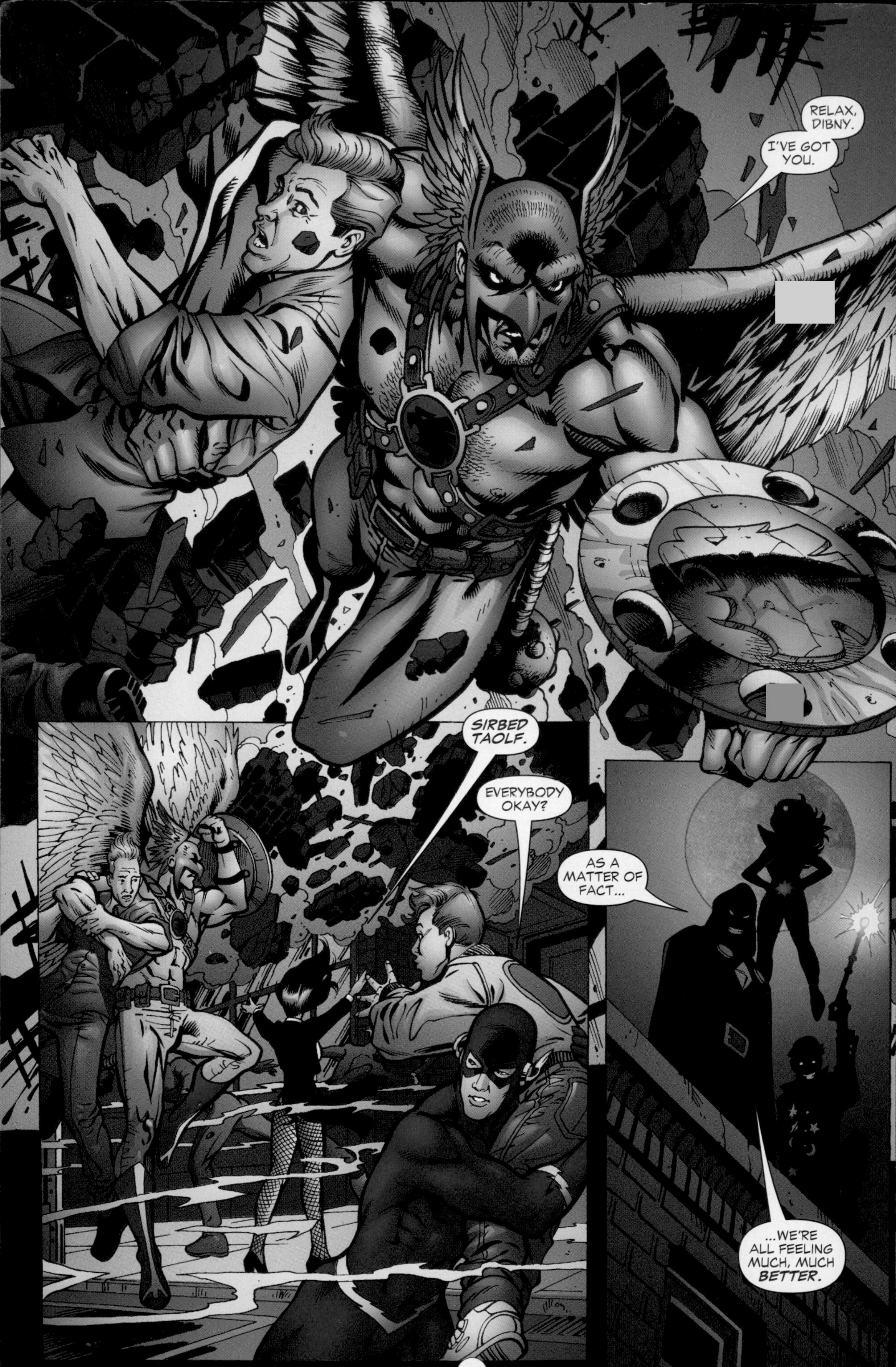
RELAX, DIBNY.
I'VE GOT YOU.
SIRBED TAOLF.
EVERYBODY OKAY?
AS A MATTER OF FACT...
...WE'RE ALL FEELING MUCH, MUCH BETTER.

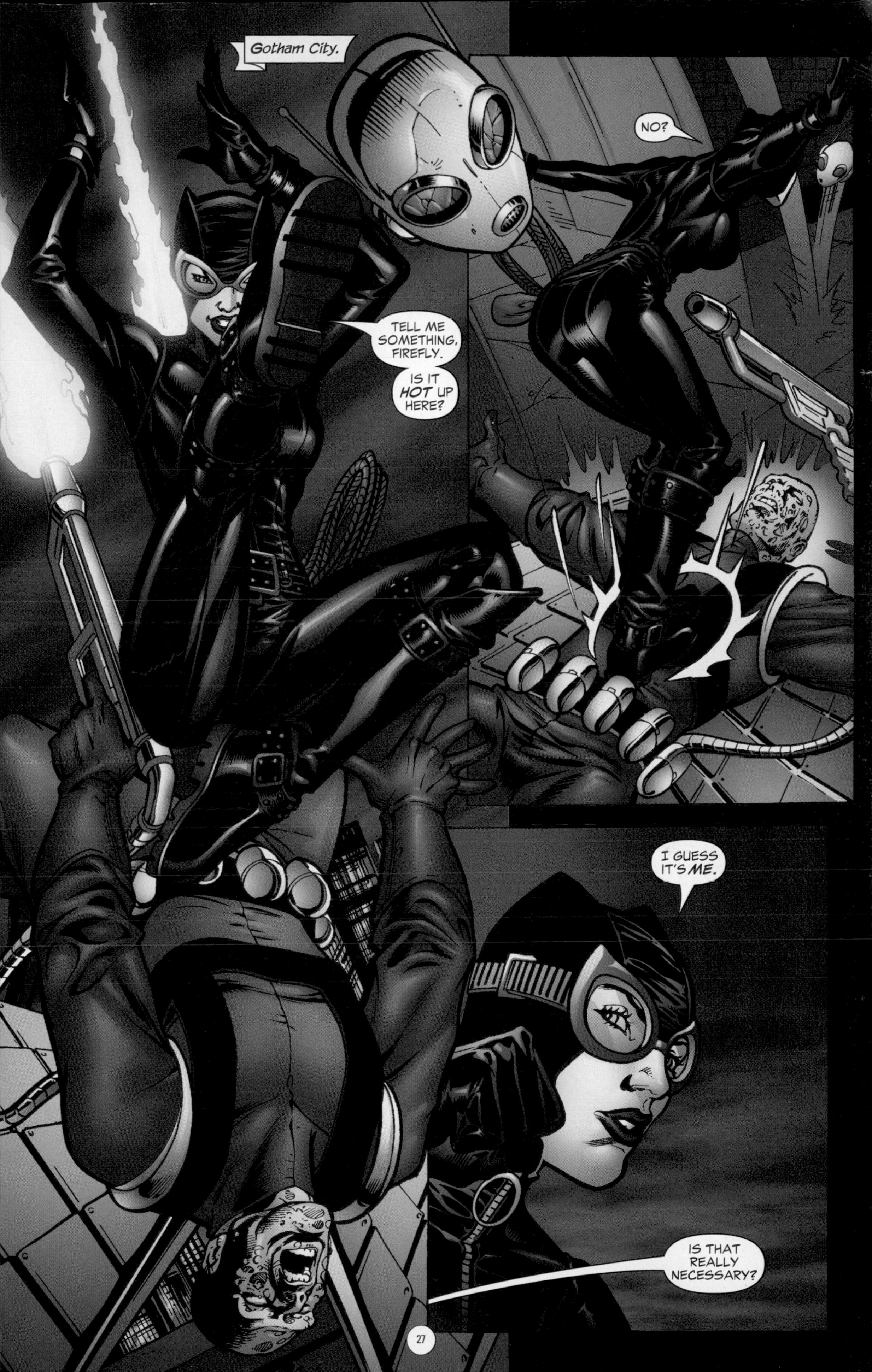
Gotham City.
TELL ME SOMETHING, FIREFLY.
IS IT HOT UP HERE?
NO?
I GUESS IT'S ME.
IS THAT REALLY NECESSARY?

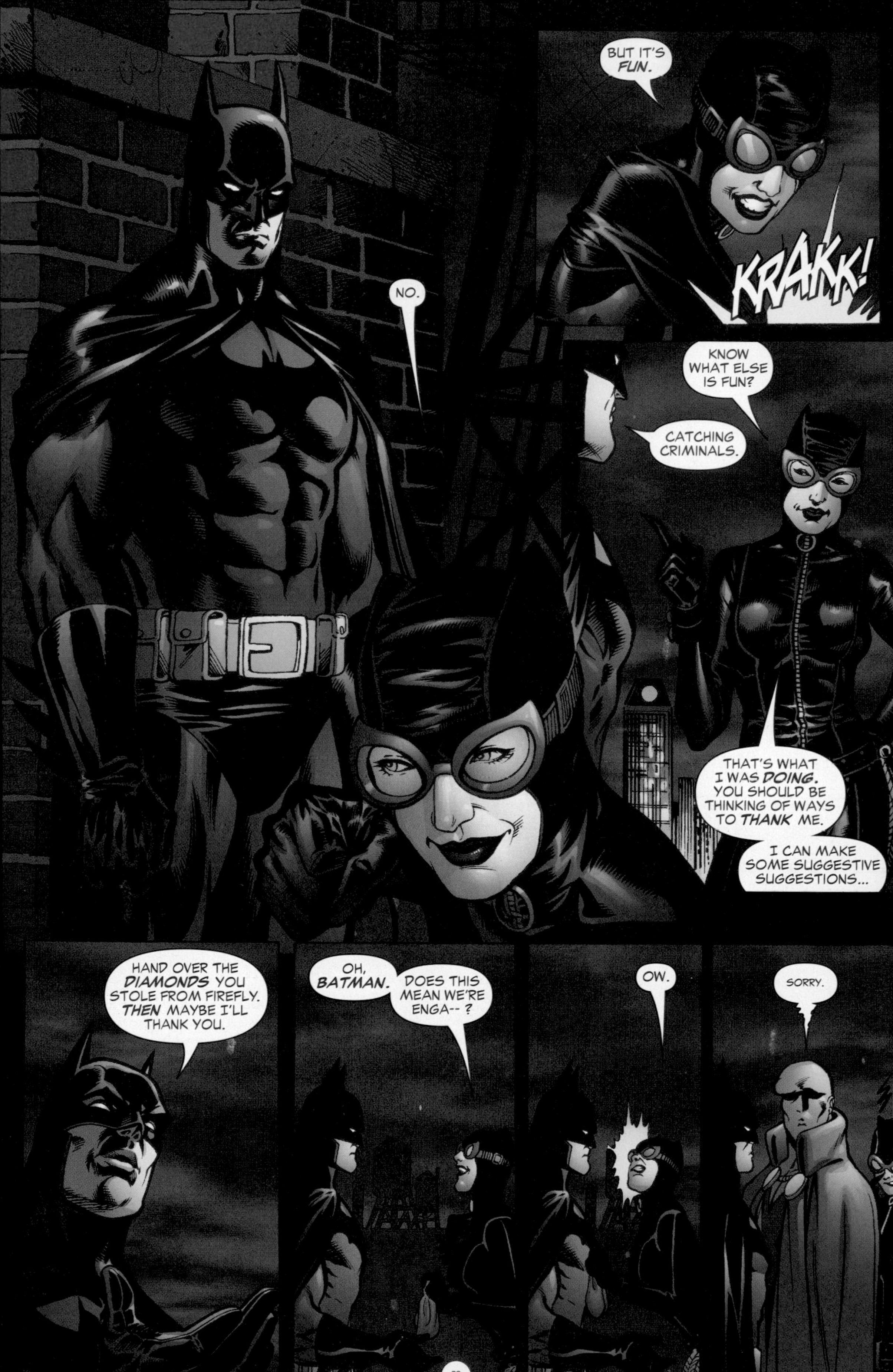
NO.
BUT IT'S FUN.
KRAKK!
KNOW WHAT ELSE IS FUN?
CATCHING CRIMINALS.
THAT'S WHAT I WAS DOING. YOU SHOULD BE THINKING OF WAYS TO THANK ME.
I CAN MAKE SOME SUGGESTIVE SUGGESTIONS...
HAND OVER THE DIAMONDS YOU STOLE FROM FIREFLY. THEN MAYBE I'LL THANK YOU.
OH, BATMAN.
DOES THIS MEAN WE'RE ENGA-- ?
OW.
SORRY.

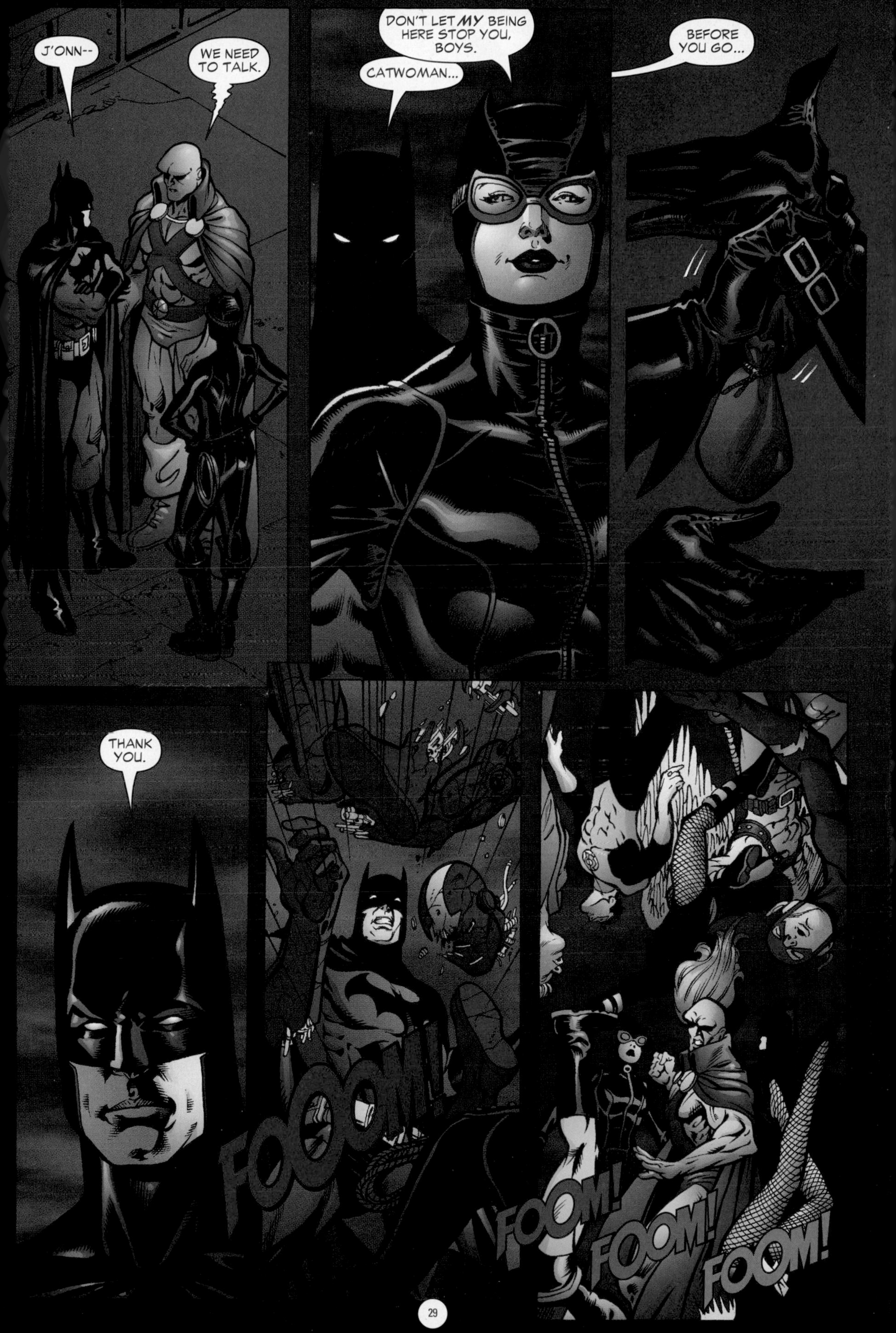
J'ONN--
WE NEED TO TALK.
CATWOMAN...
DON'T LET MY BEING HERE STOP YOU, BOYS.
BEFORE YOU GO...
THANK YOU.
FOOOM!
FOOM!
FOOM!
FOOM!

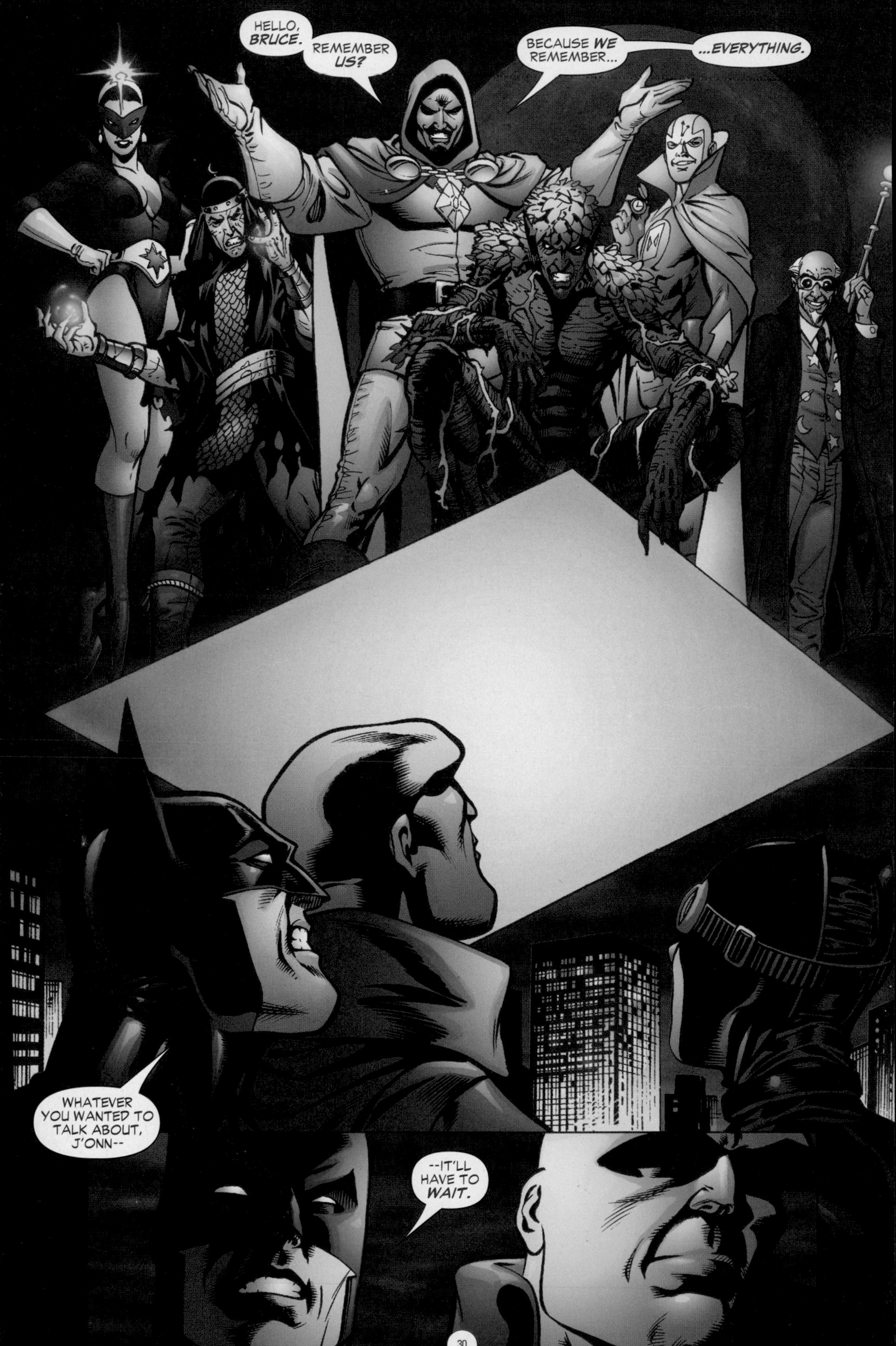
HELLO, BRUCE.
REMEMBER US?
BECAUSE WE REMEMBER...
...EVERYTHING.
WHATEVER YOU WANTED TO TALK ABOUT, J'ONN--
--IT'LL HAVE TO WAIT.

JLA #116
by Rags Morales & Mark Farmer

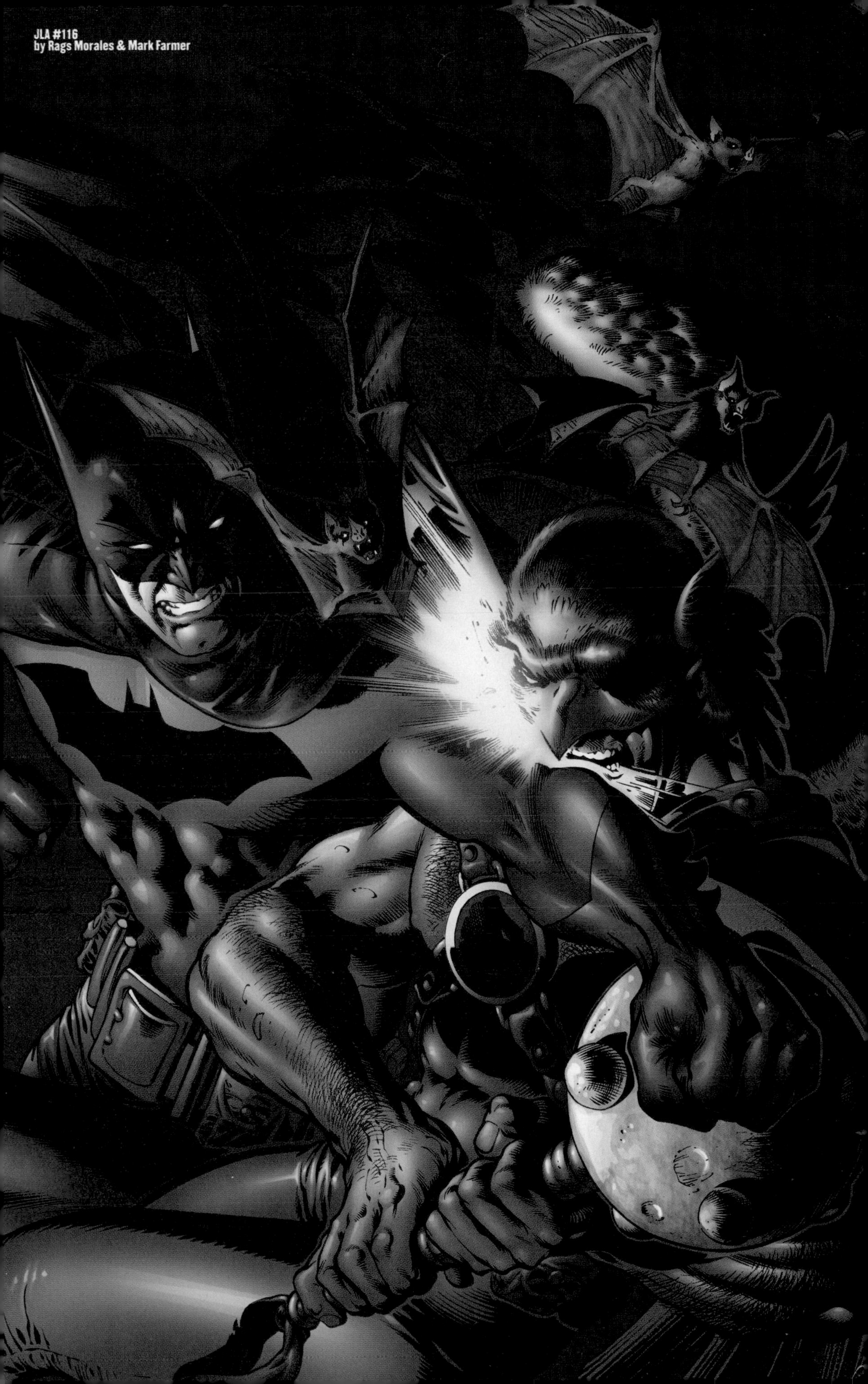

JLA

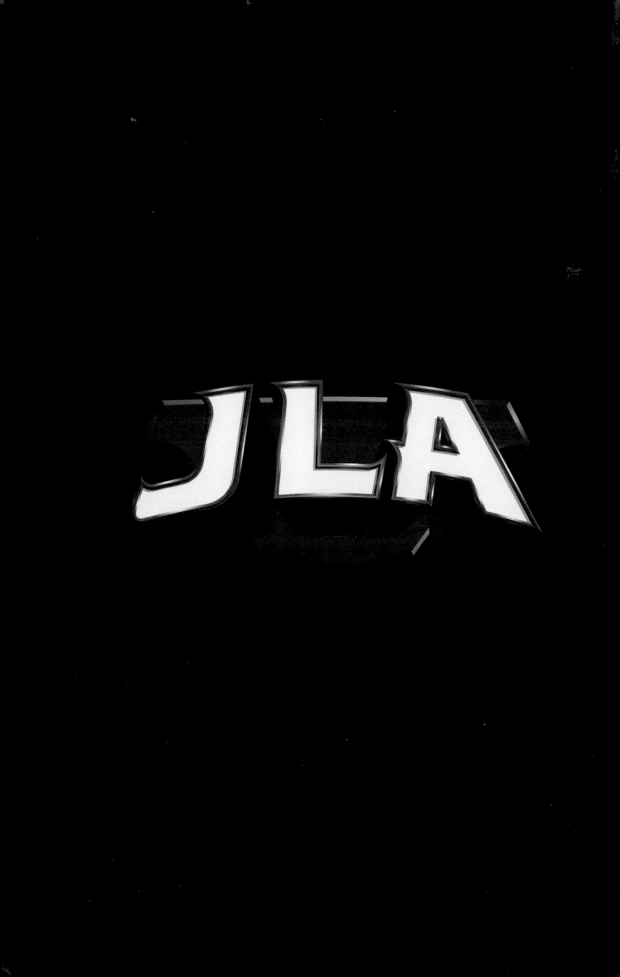

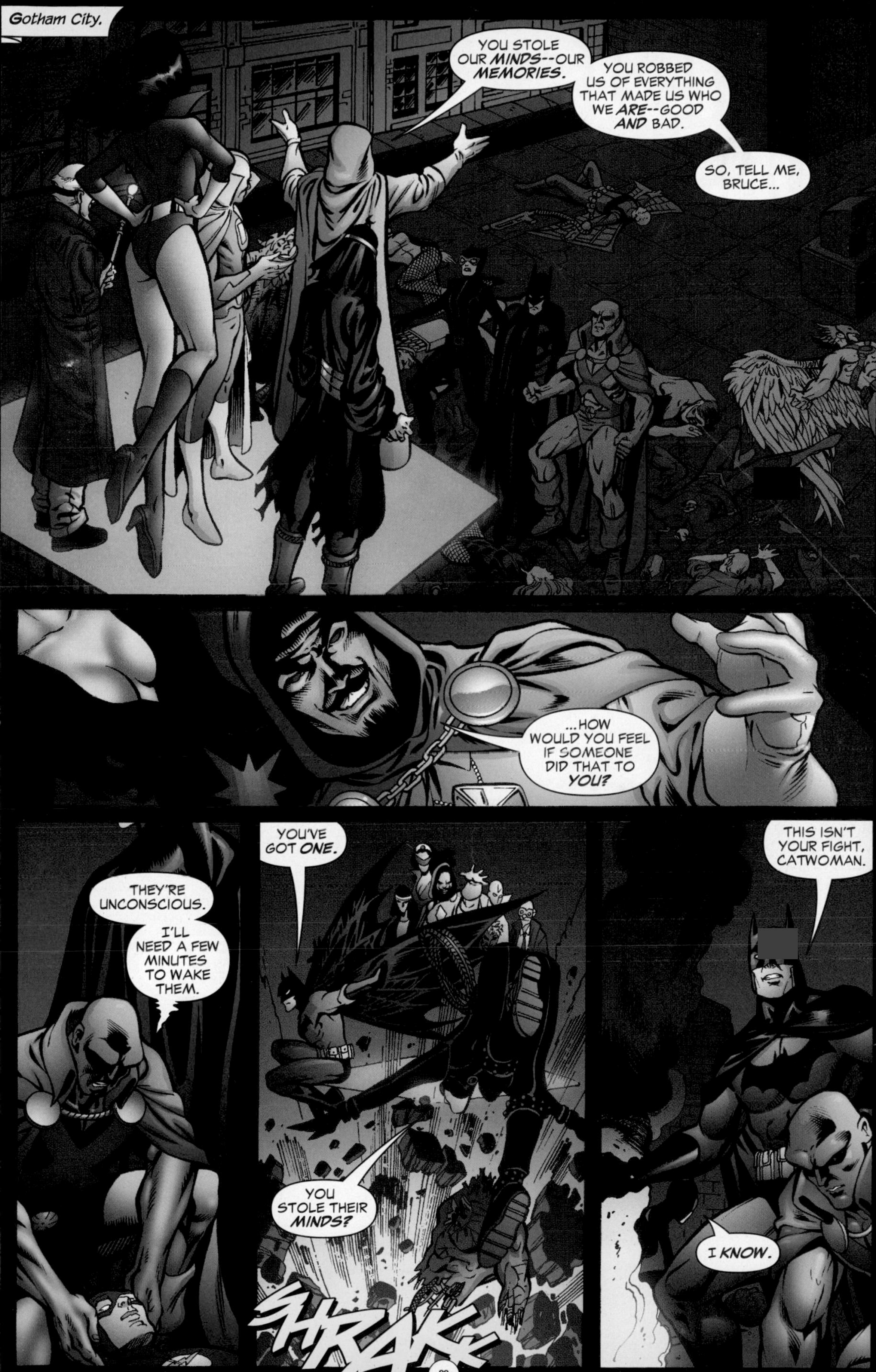
Gotham City.
YOU STOLE OUR *MINDS*--OUR *MEMORIES.*
YOU ROBBED US OF EVERYTHING THAT MADE US WHO WE *ARE*--GOOD *AND* BAD.
SO, TELL ME, BRUCE...
...HOW WOULD YOU FEEL IF SOMEONE DID THAT TO *YOU?*
THEY'RE UNCONSCIOUS.
I'LL NEED A FEW MINUTES TO WAKE THEM.
YOU'VE GOT *ONE.*
YOU STOLE THEIR *MINDS?*
SHRAKK
THIS ISN'T YOUR FIGHT, CATWOMAN.
I *KNOW.*

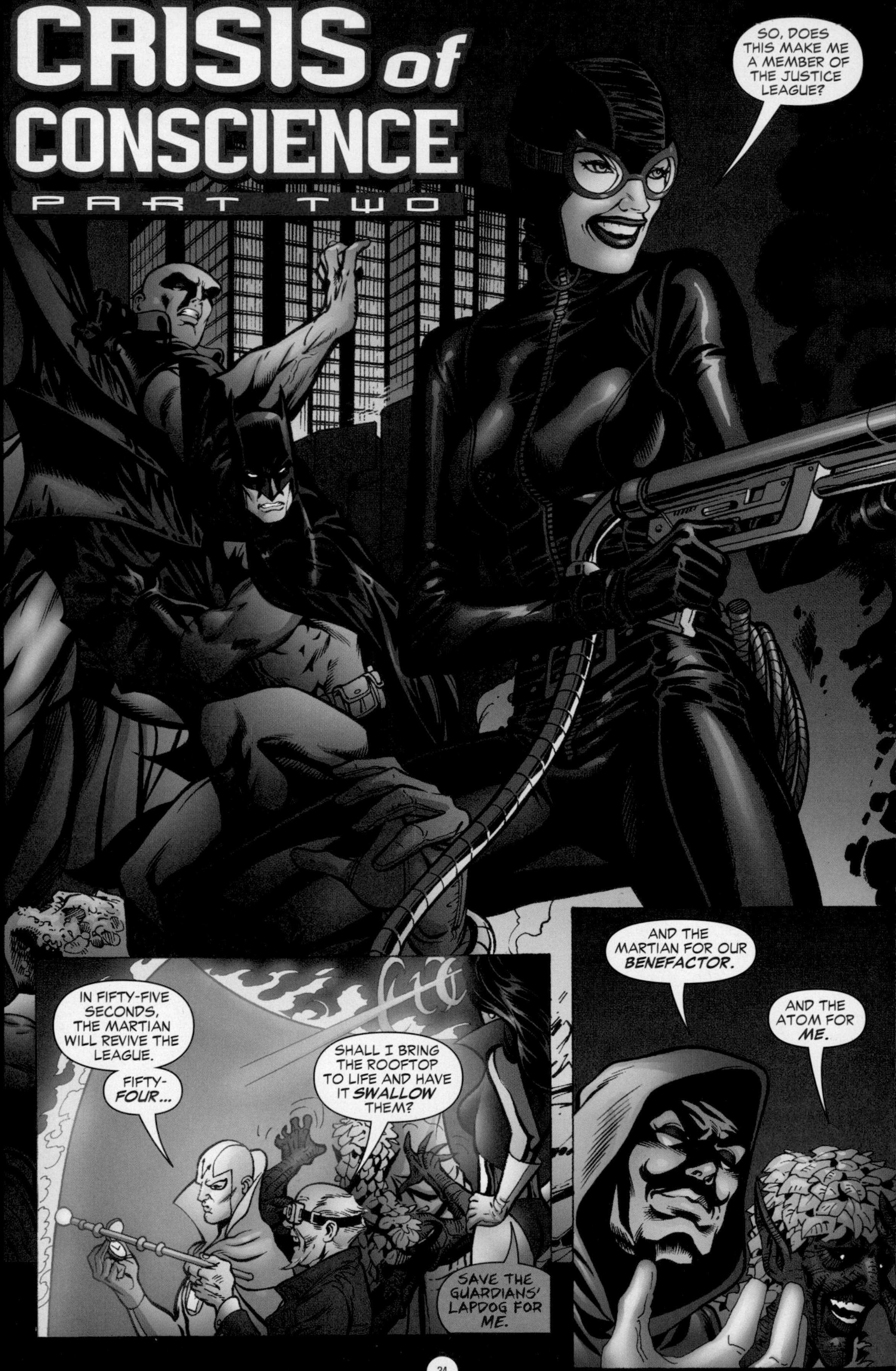
CRISIS of CONSCIENCE
PART TWO
SO, DOES THIS MAKE ME A MEMBER OF THE JUSTICE LEAGUE?
IN FIFTY-FIVE SECONDS, THE MARTIAN WILL REVIVE THE LEAGUE.
FIFTY-FOUR...
SHALL I BRING THE ROOFTOP TO LIFE AND HAVE IT SWALLOW THEM?
SAVE THE GUARDIANS' LAPDOG FOR ME.
AND THE MARTIAN FOR OUR BENEFACTOR.
AND THE ATOM FOR ME.

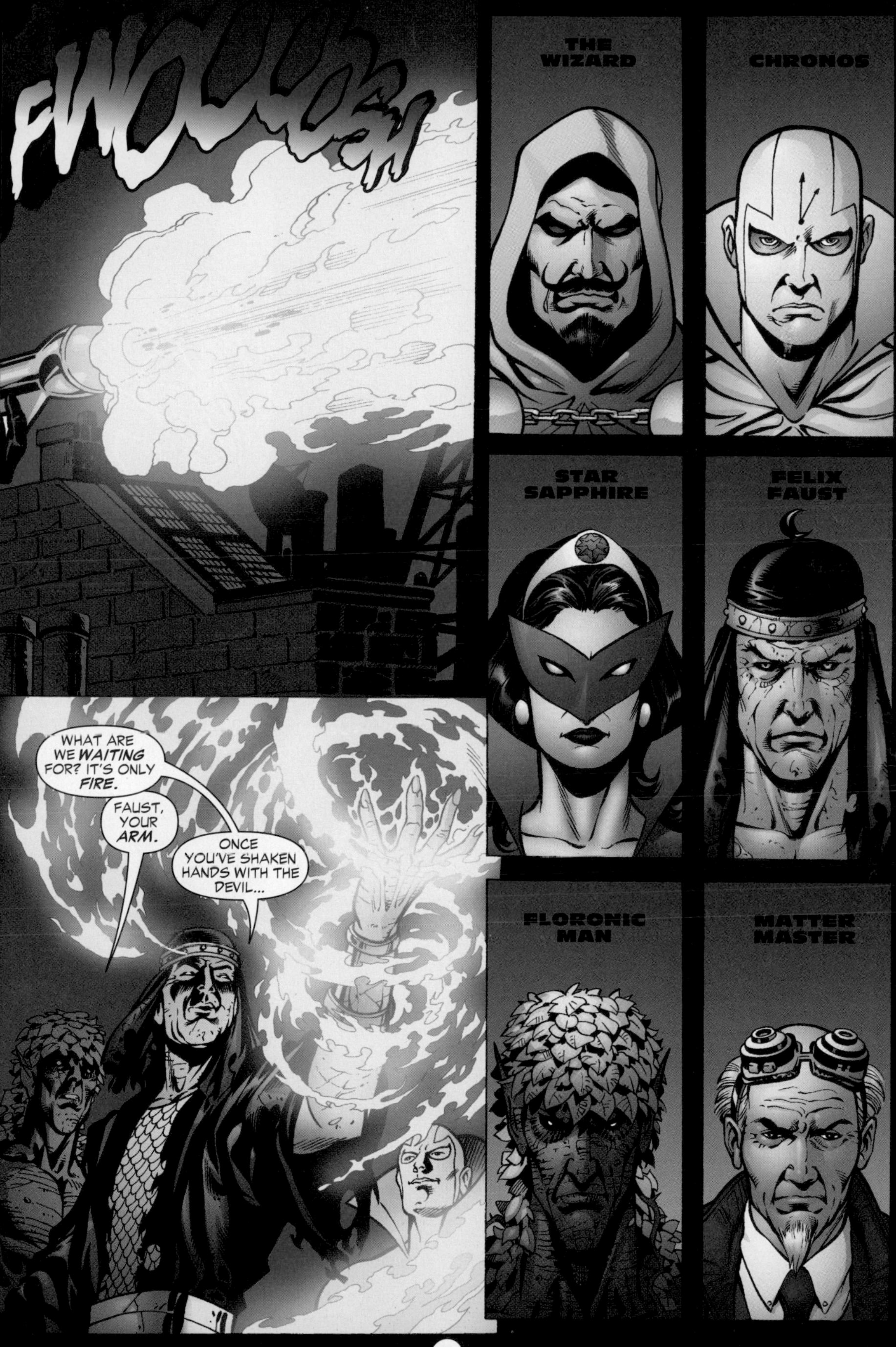

FWOOOSH
THE WIZARD
CHRONOS
STAR SAPPHIRE
FELIX FAUST
WHAT ARE WE WAITING FOR? IT'S ONLY FIRE.
FAUST, YOUR ARM.
ONCE YOU'VE SHAKEN HANDS WITH THE DEVIL...
FLORONIC MAN
MATTER MASTER

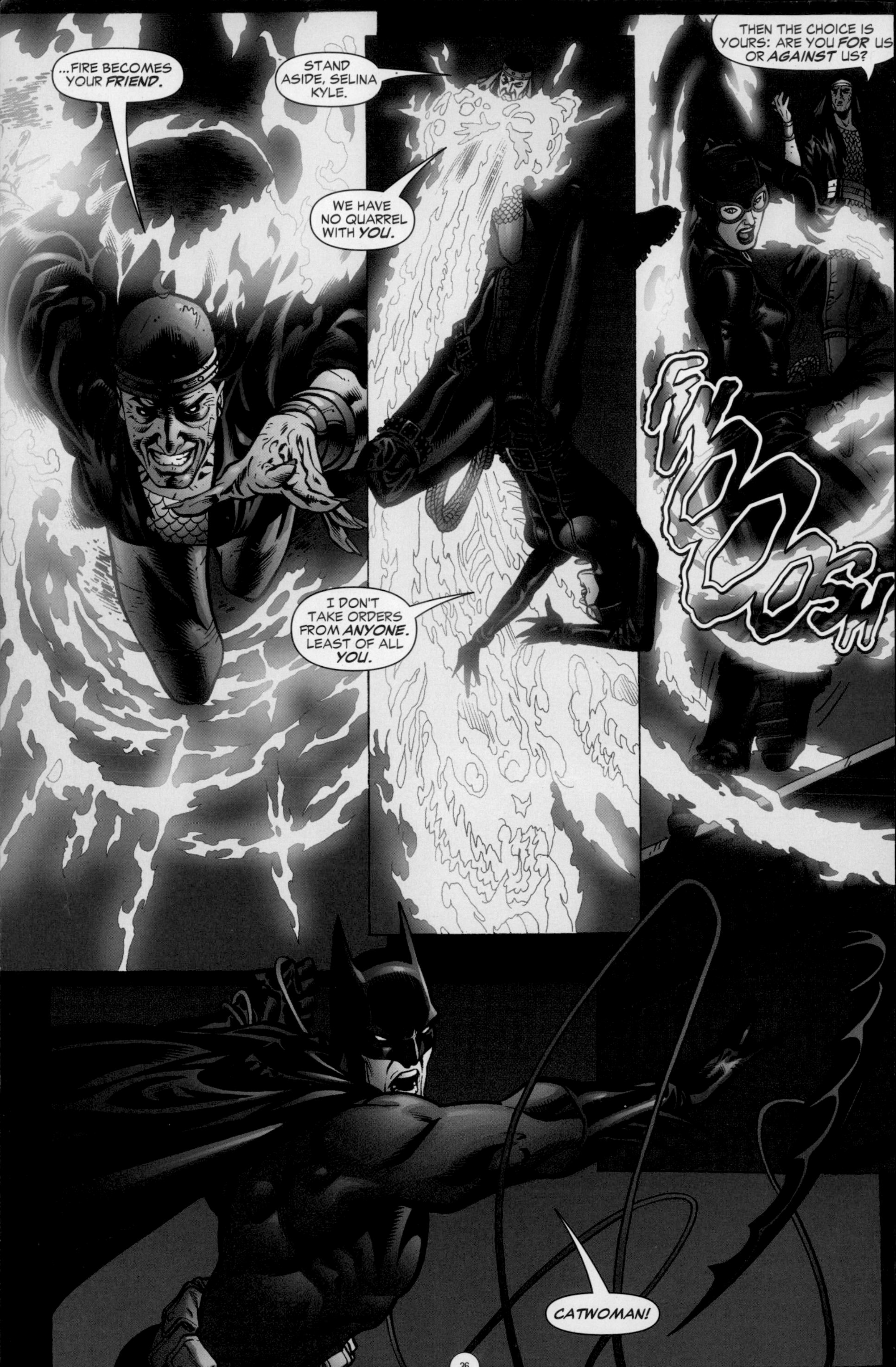
...FIRE BECOMES YOUR FRIEND.
STAND ASIDE, SELINA KYLE.
WE HAVE NO QUARREL WITH YOU.
I DON'T TAKE ORDERS FROM ANYONE. LEAST OF ALL YOU.
THEN THE CHOICE IS YOURS: ARE YOU FOR US OR AGAINST US?
CATWOMAN!

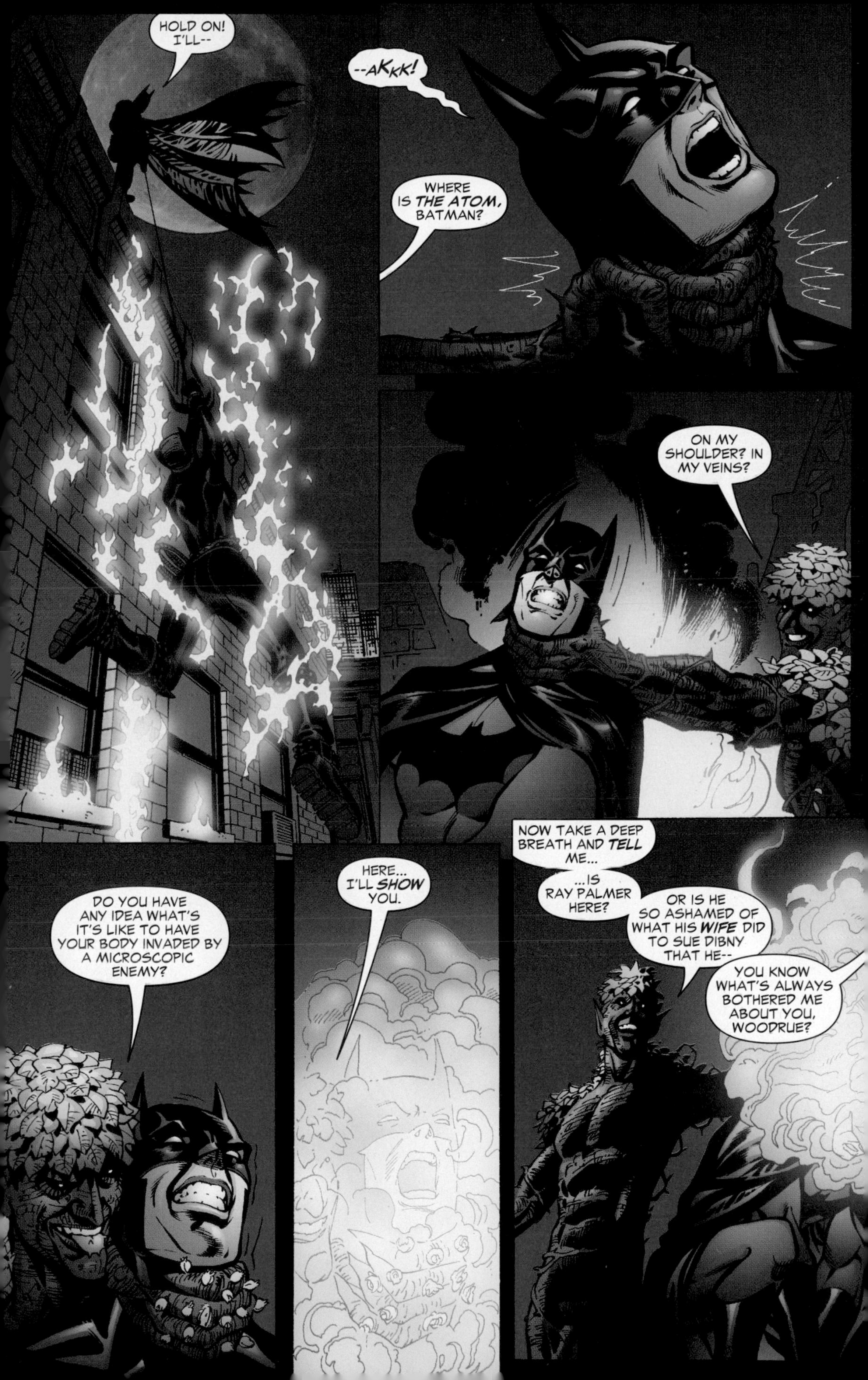
HOLD ON! I'LL--
--AKKK!
WHERE IS THE ATOM, BATMAN?
ON MY SHOULDER? IN MY VEINS?
DO YOU HAVE ANY IDEA WHAT'S IT'S LIKE TO HAVE YOUR BODY INVADED BY A MICROSCOPIC ENEMY?
HERE... I'LL SHOW YOU.
NOW TAKE A DEEP BREATH AND TELL ME...
...IS RAY PALMER HERE?
OR IS HE SO ASHAMED OF WHAT HIS WIFE DID TO SUE DIBNY THAT HE--
YOU KNOW WHAT'S ALWAYS BOTHERED ME ABOUT YOU, WOODRUE?

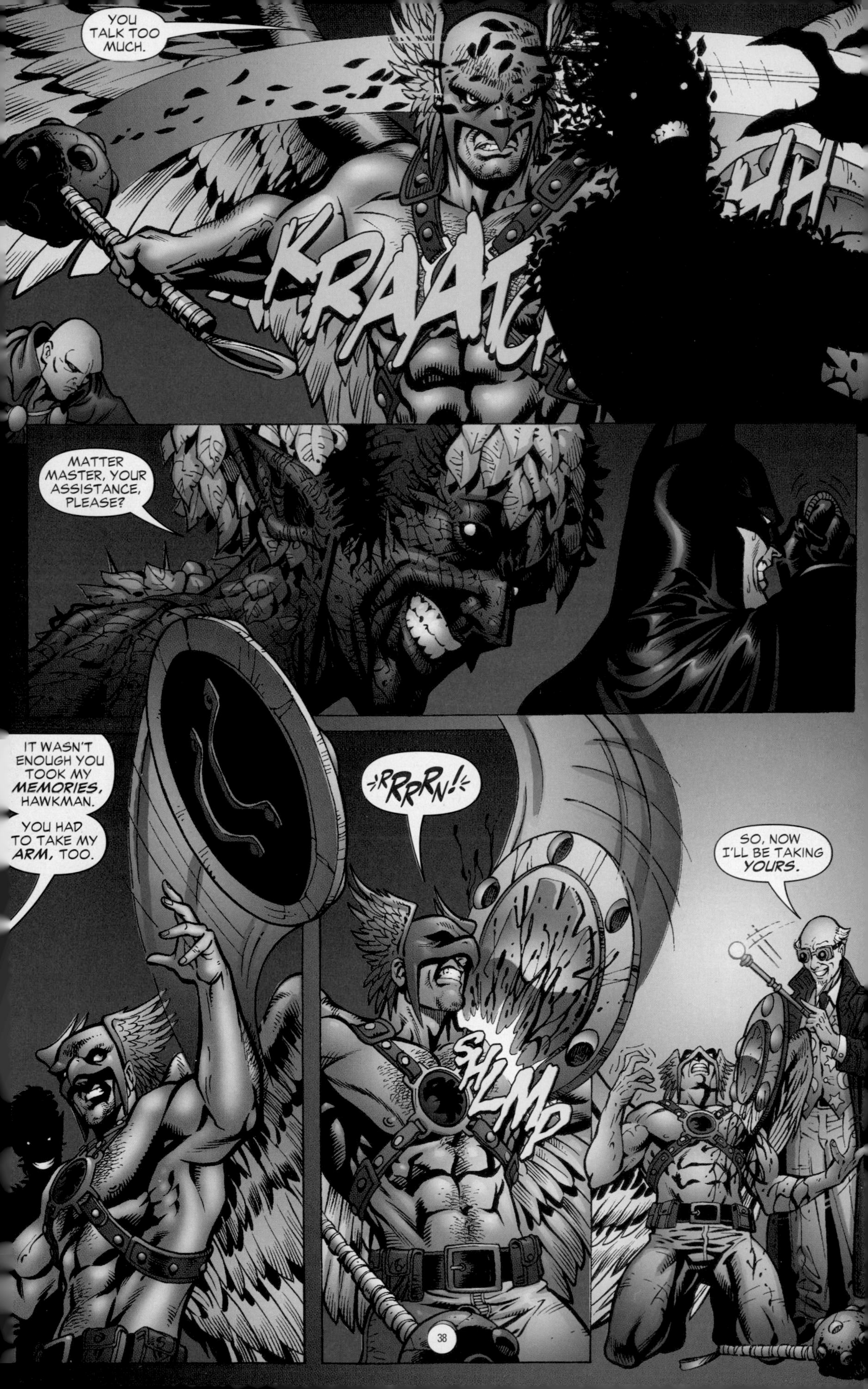
YOU TALK TOO MUCH.
KRAAACK
MATTER MASTER, YOUR ASSISTANCE, PLEASE?
IT WASN'T ENOUGH YOU TOOK MY MEMORIES, HAWKMAN.
YOU HAD TO TAKE MY ARM, TOO.
RRRRN!
SHLMP
SO, NOW I'LL BE TAKING YOURS.

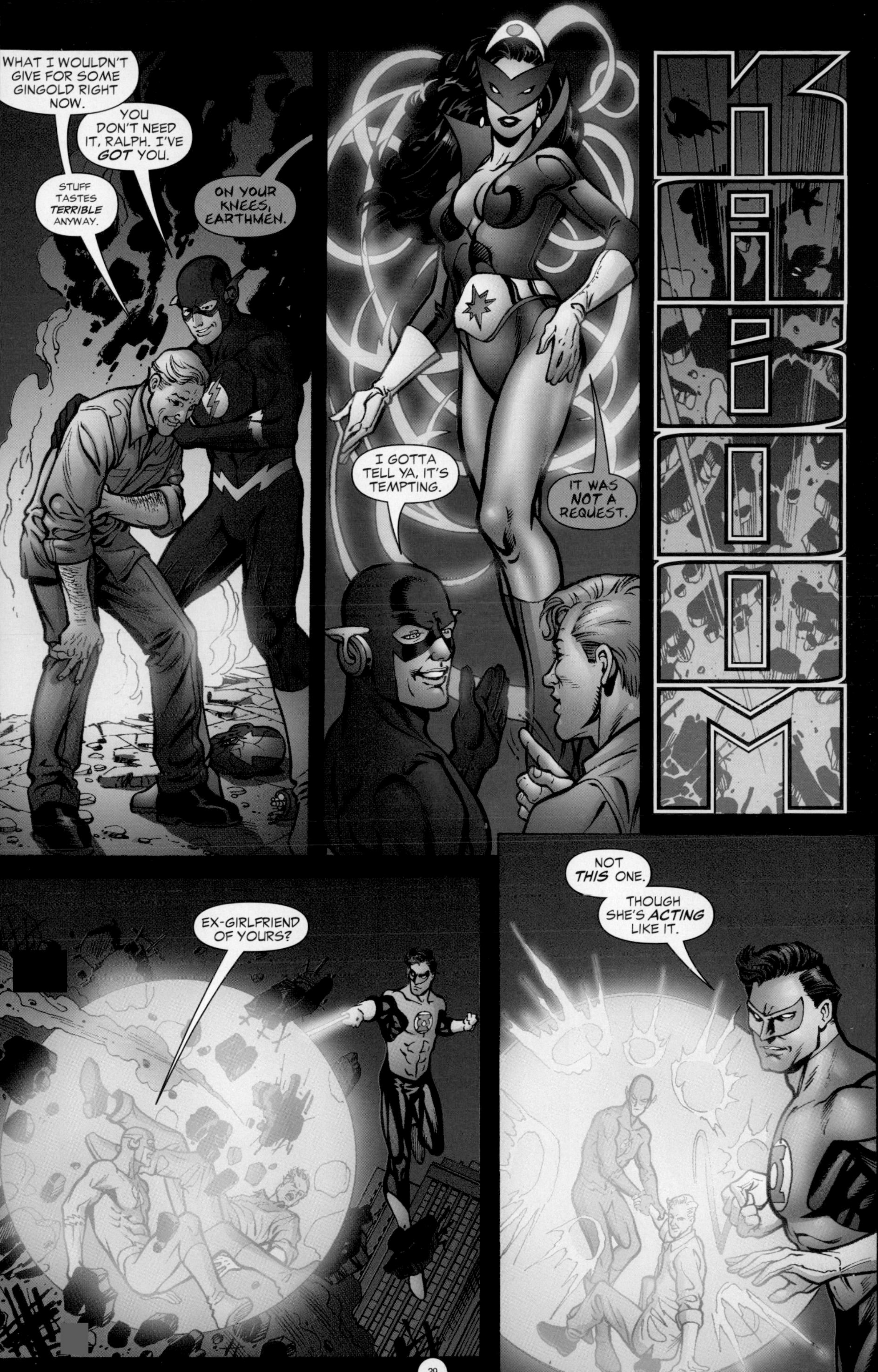
WHAT I WOULDN'T GIVE FOR SOME GINGOLD RIGHT NOW.
YOU DON'T NEED IT, RALPH. I'VE GOT YOU.
STUFF TASTES TERRIBLE ANYWAY.
ON YOUR KNEES, EARTHMEN.
I GOTTA TELL YA, IT'S TEMPTING.
IT WAS NOT A REQUEST.
EX-GIRLFRIEND OF YOURS?
NOT THIS ONE.
THOUGH SHE'S ACTING LIKE IT.

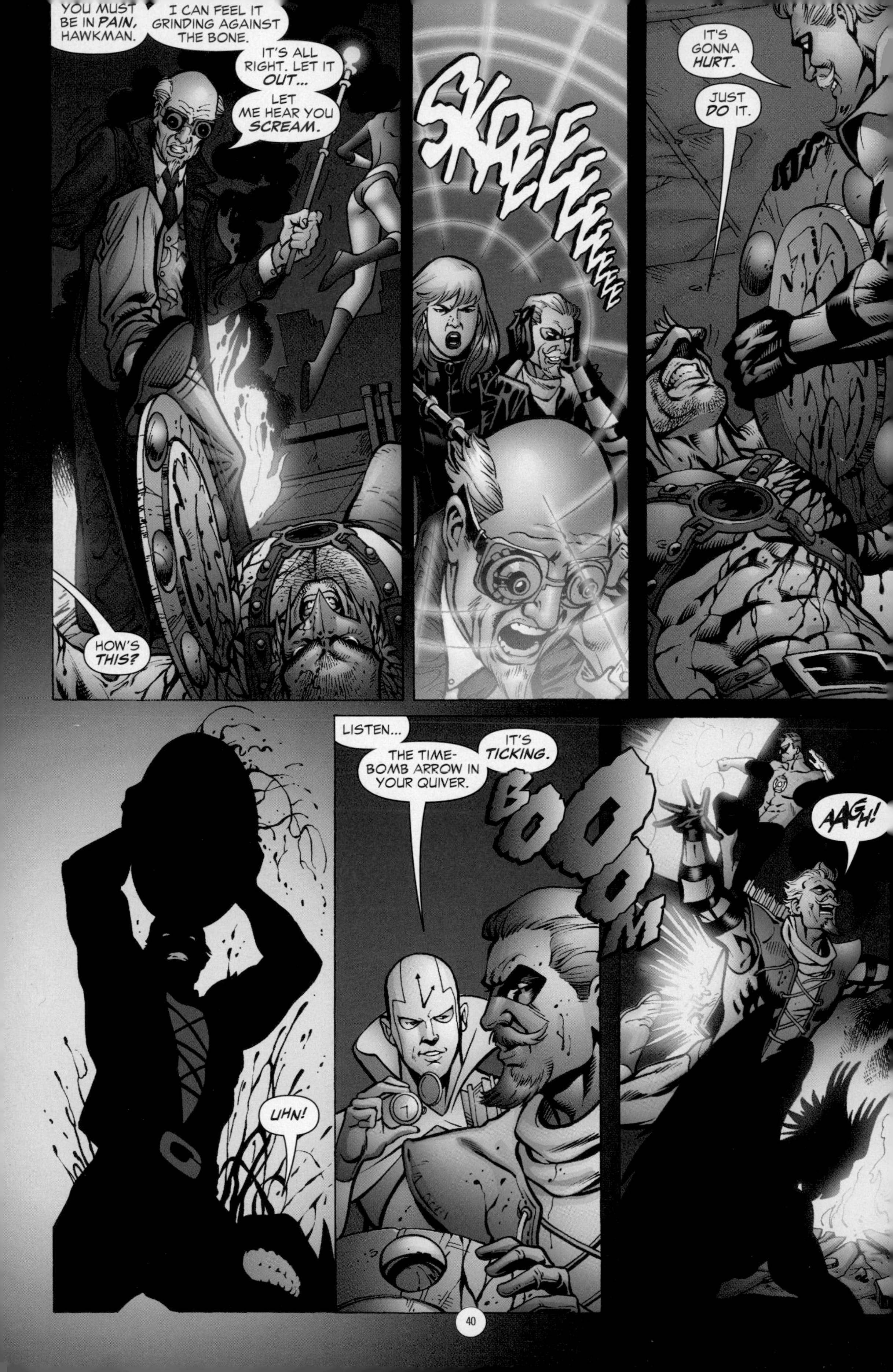
YOU MUST BE IN PAIN, HAWKMAN.
I CAN FEEL IT GRINDING AGAINST THE BONE.
IT'S ALL RIGHT. LET IT OUT...
LET ME HEAR YOU SCREAM.
HOW'S THIS?
SKREEEEEEEEEE
IT'S GONNA HURT.
JUST DO IT.
UHN!
LISTEN...
THE TIME-BOMB ARROW IN YOUR QUIVER.
IT'S TICKING.
BOOOOM
AAGH!

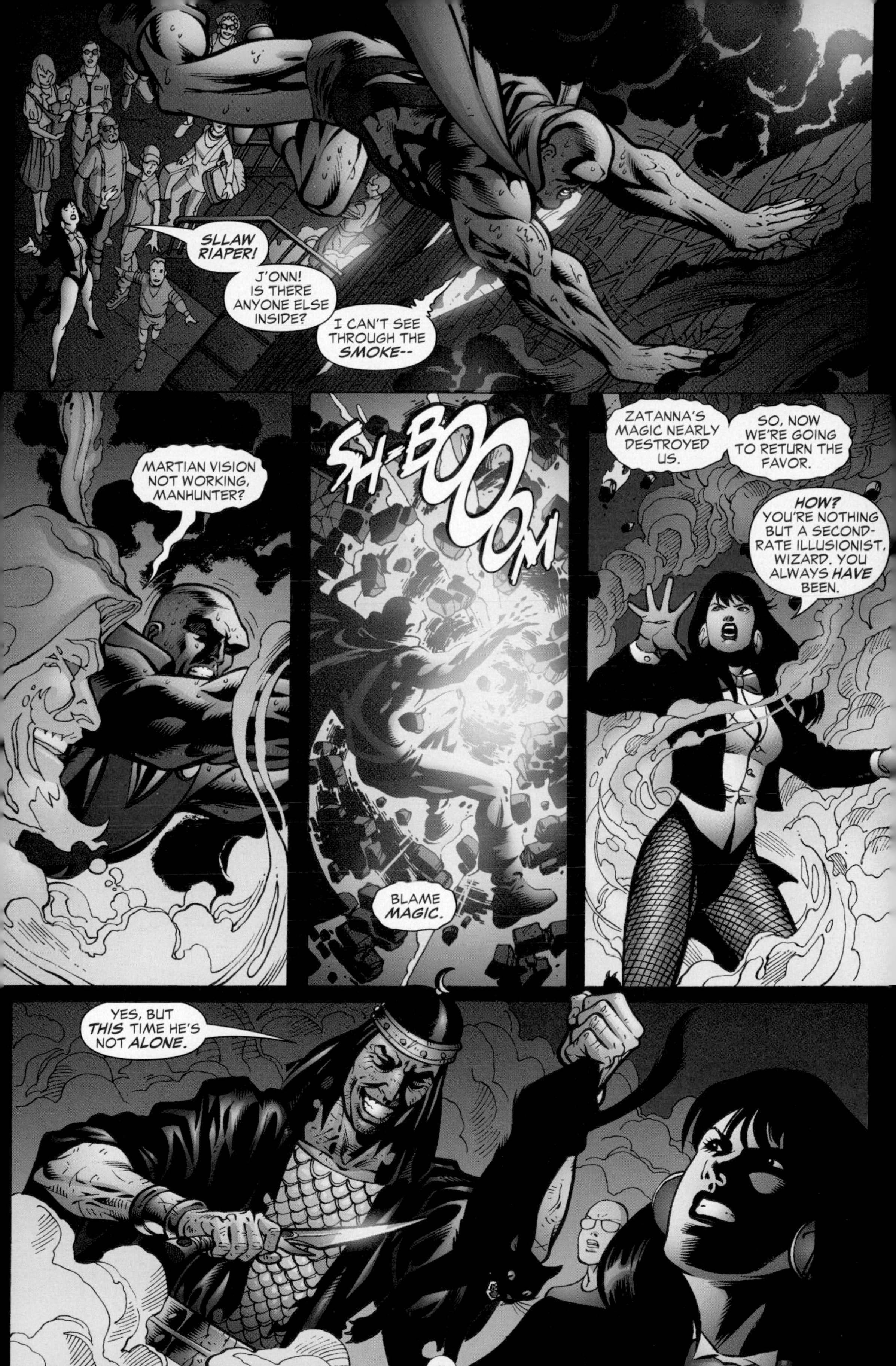
SLLAW RIAPER!
J'ONN! IS THERE ANYONE ELSE INSIDE?
I CAN'T SEE THROUGH THE SMOKE--
MARTIAN VISION NOT WORKING, MANHUNTER?
SH-BOOOOM
BLAME MAGIC.
ZATANNA'S MAGIC NEARLY DESTROYED US.
SO, NOW WE'RE GOING TO RETURN THE FAVOR.
HOW? YOU'RE NOTHING BUT A SECOND-RATE ILLUSIONIST, WIZARD. YOU ALWAYS HAVE BEEN.
YES, BUT THIS TIME HE'S NOT ALONE.

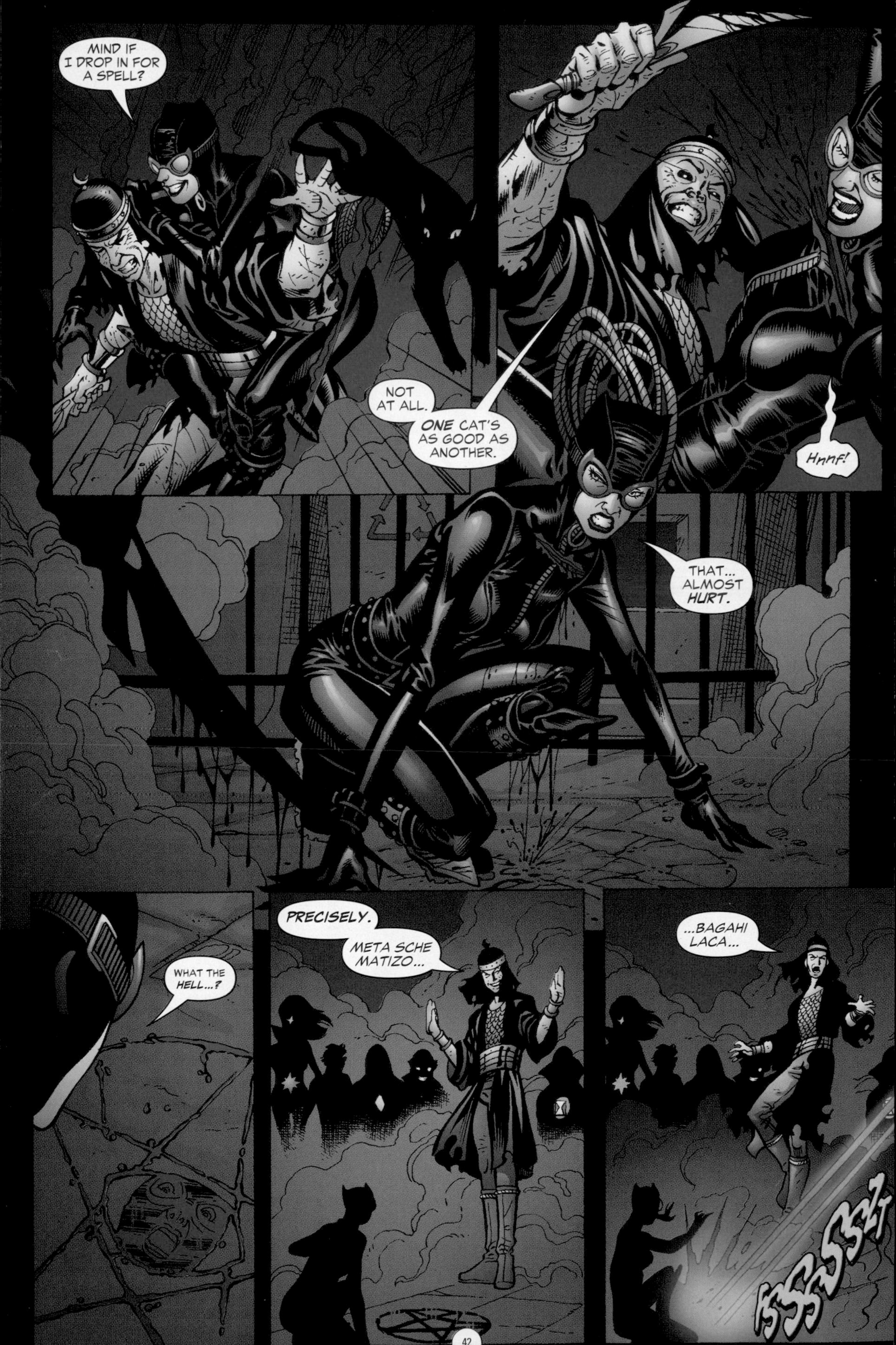
MIND IF I DROP IN FOR A SPELL?
NOT AT ALL.
ONE CAT'S AS GOOD AS ANOTHER.
Hnnf!
THAT... ALMOST HURT.
WHAT THE HELL...?
PRECISELY.
META SCHE MATIZO...
...BAGAHI LACA...
FSSSSSSZZT

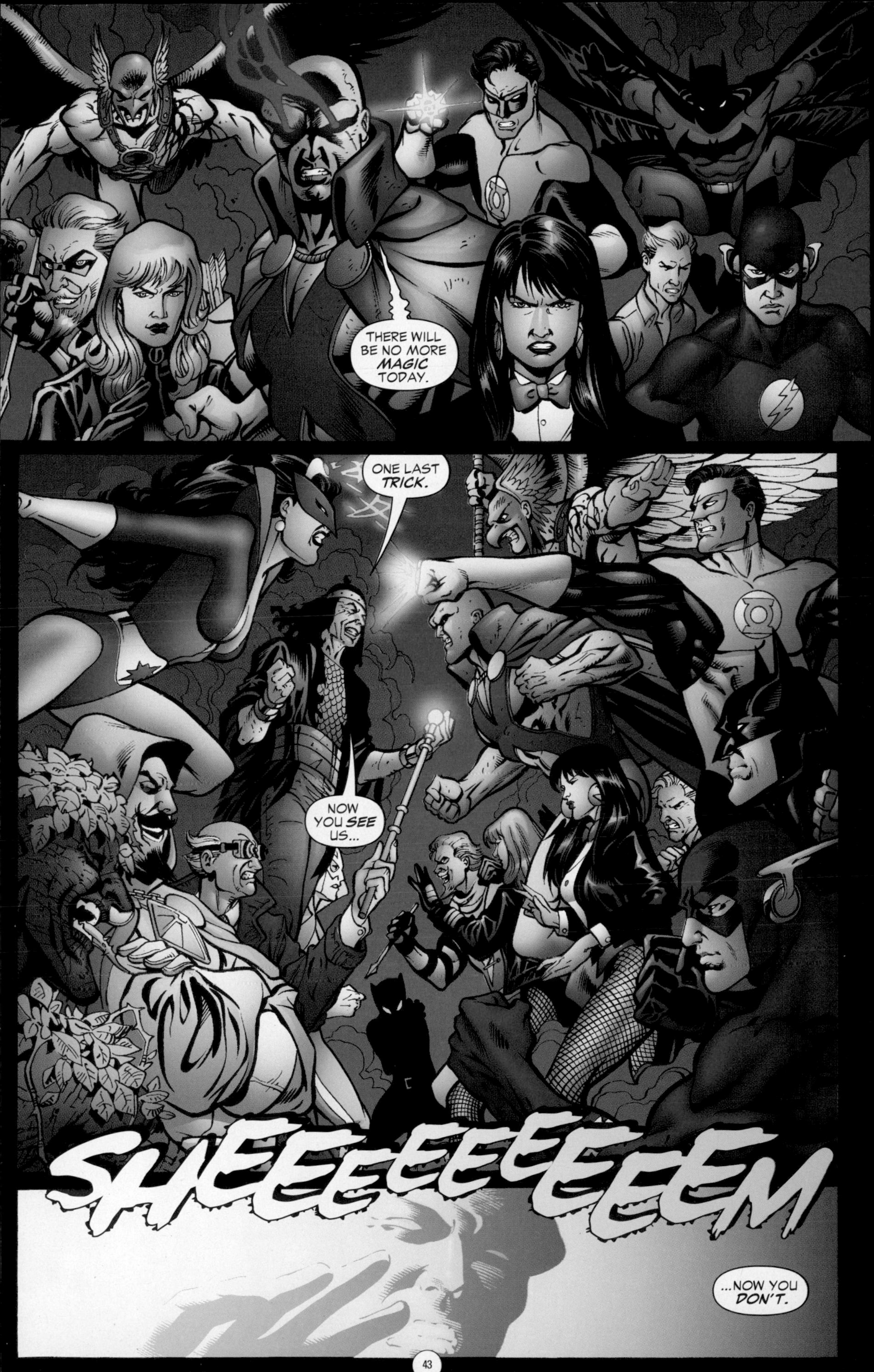
THERE WILL BE NO MORE MAGIC TODAY.
ONE LAST TRICK.
NOW YOU SEE US...
SHEEEEEEEEEEEEM
...NOW YOU DON'T.

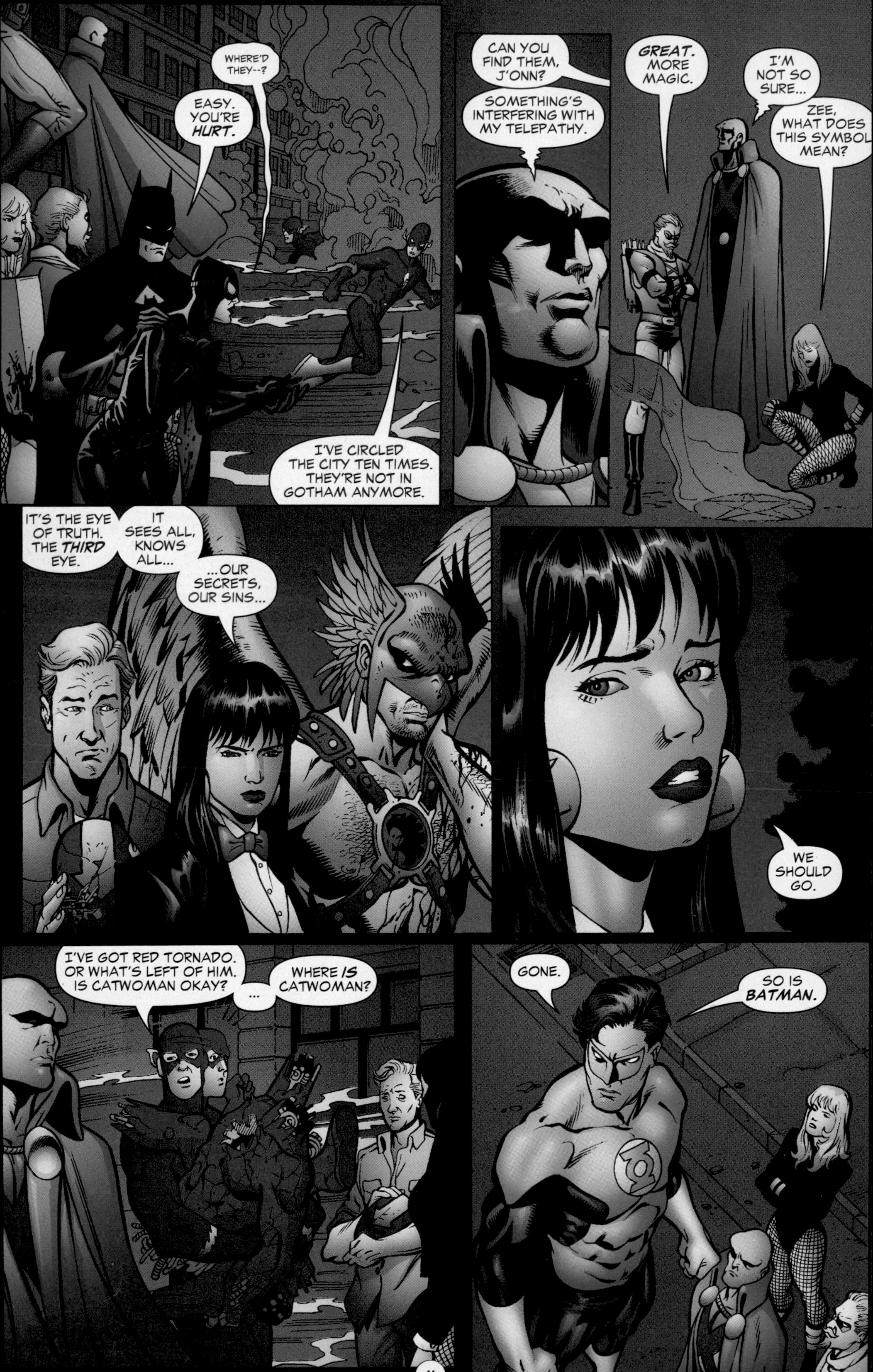
WHERE'D THEY--?
EASY. YOU'RE HURT.
I'VE CIRCLED THE CITY TEN TIMES. THEY'RE NOT IN GOTHAM ANYMORE.
CAN YOU FIND THEM, J'ONN?
SOMETHING'S INTERFERING WITH MY TELEPATHY.
GREAT. MORE MAGIC.
I'M NOT SO SURE...
ZEE, WHAT DOES THIS SYMBOL MEAN?
IT'S THE EYE OF TRUTH. THE THIRD EYE.
IT SEES ALL, KNOWS ALL...
...OUR SECRETS, OUR SINS...
WE SHOULD GO.
I'VE GOT RED TORNADO. OR WHAT'S LEFT OF HIM. IS CATWOMAN OKAY?
...
WHERE IS CATWOMAN?
GONE.
SO IS BATMAN.

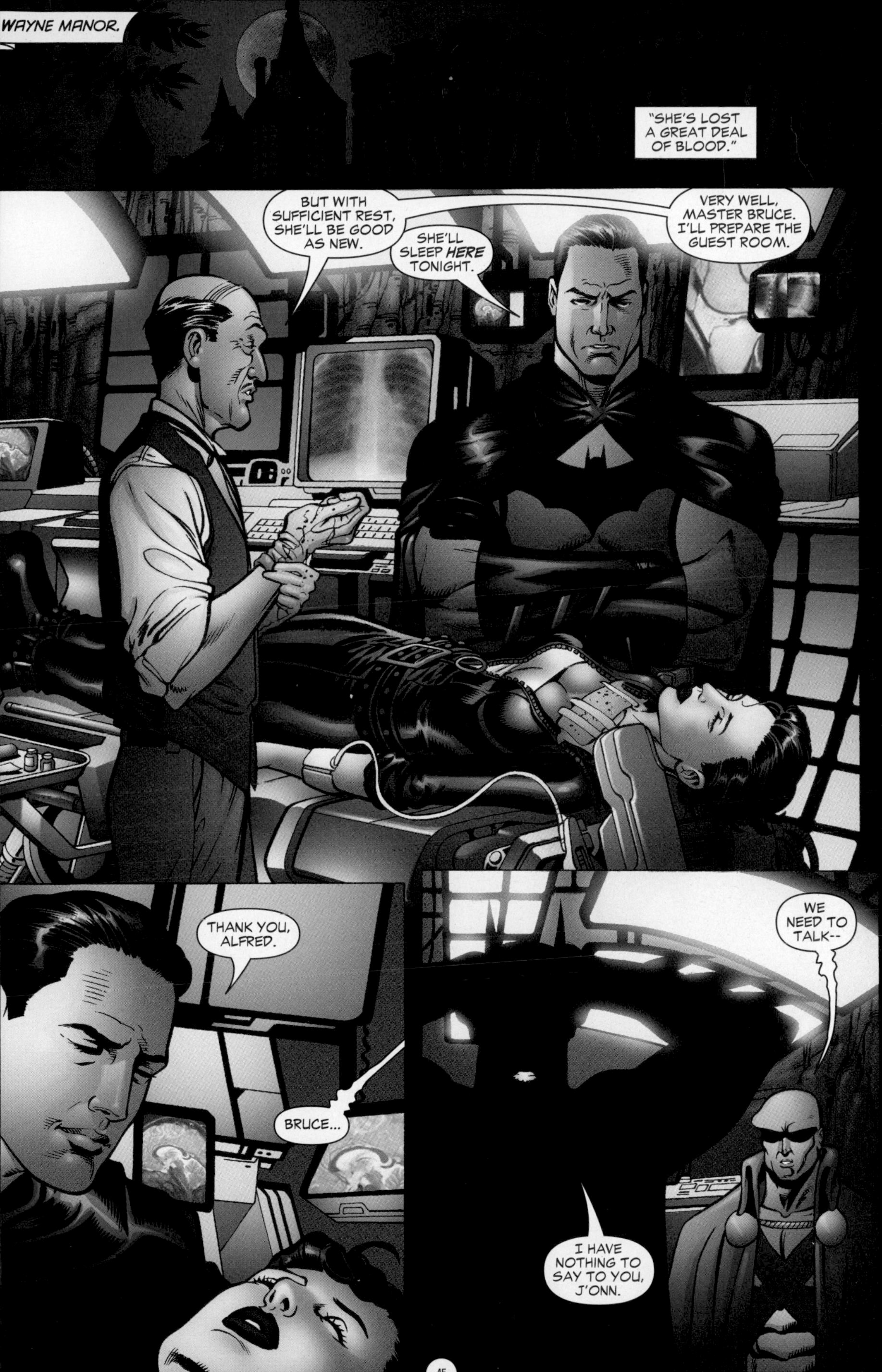

WAYNE MANOR.
"SHE'S LOST A GREAT DEAL OF BLOOD."
BUT WITH SUFFICIENT REST, SHE'LL BE GOOD AS NEW.
SHE'LL SLEEP *HERE* TONIGHT.
VERY WELL, MASTER BRUCE. I'LL PREPARE THE GUEST ROOM.
THANK YOU, ALFRED.
BRUCE...
WE NEED TO TALK--
I HAVE NOTHING TO SAY TO YOU, J'ONN.

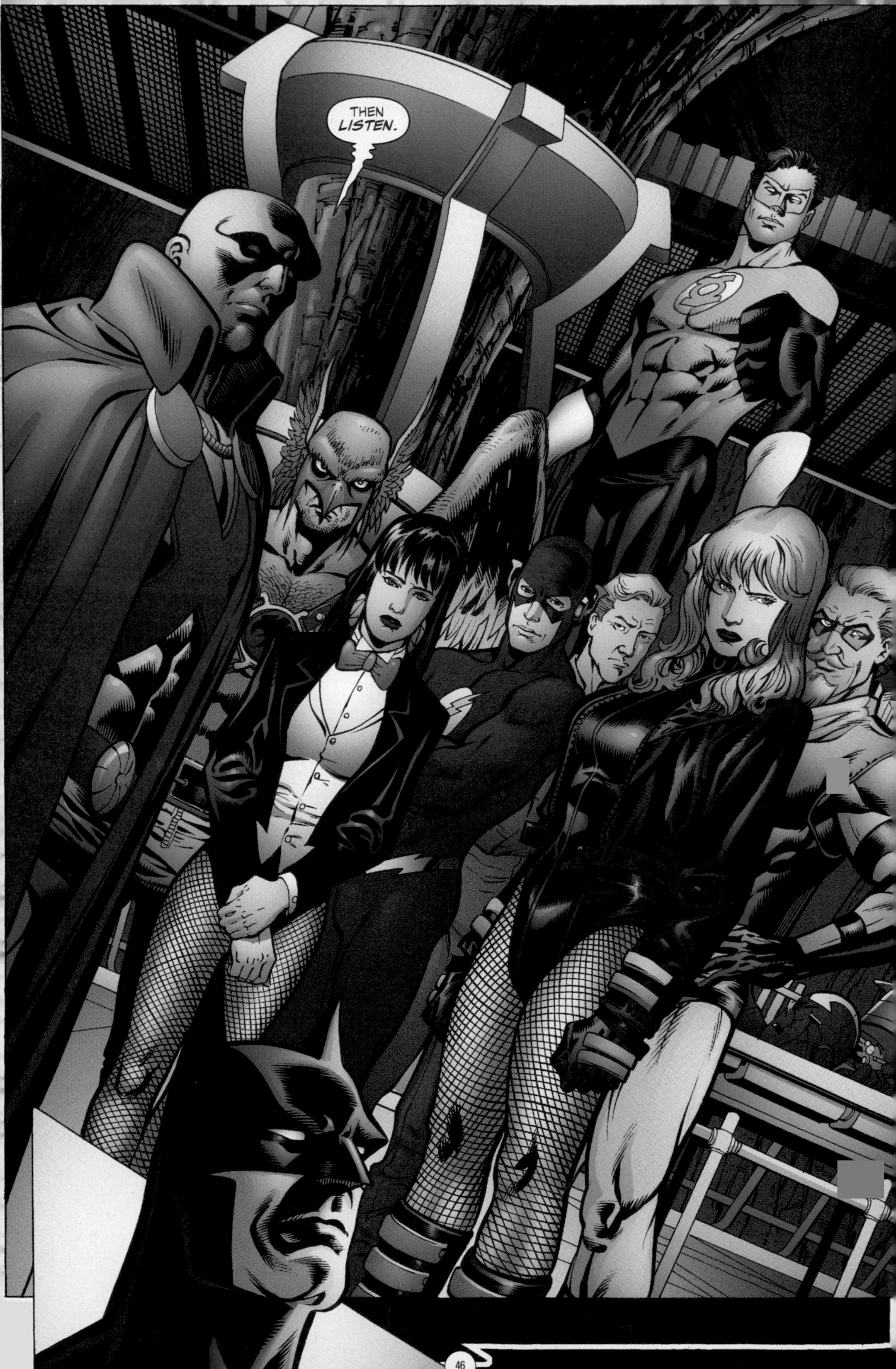
THEN LISTEN.

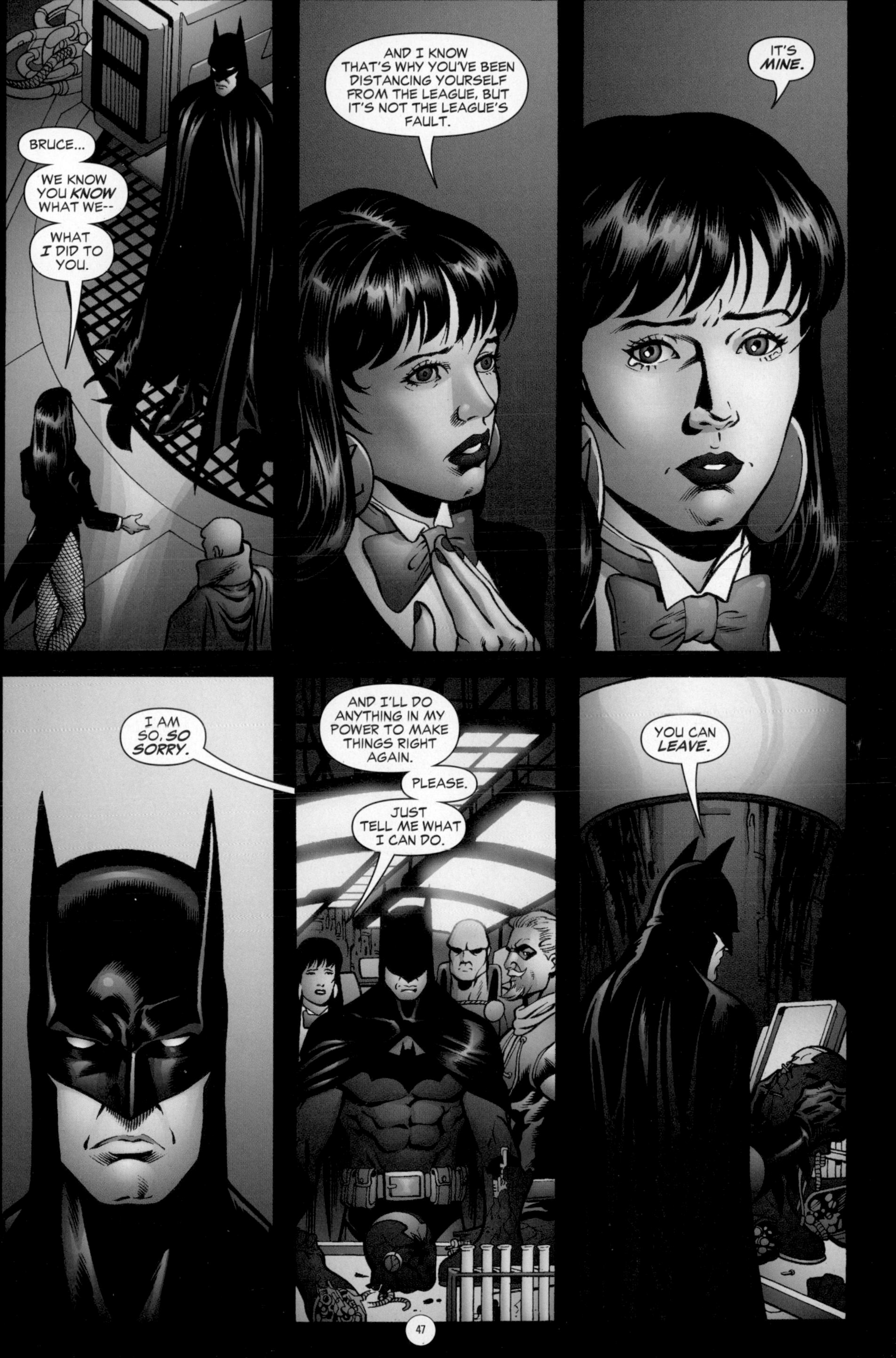
BRUCE...
WE KNOW YOU KNOW WHAT WE--
WHAT I DID TO YOU.
AND I KNOW THAT'S WHY YOU'VE BEEN DISTANCING YOURSELF FROM THE LEAGUE, BUT IT'S NOT THE LEAGUE'S FAULT.
IT'S MINE.
I AM SO, SO SORRY.
AND I'LL DO ANYTHING IN MY POWER TO MAKE THINGS RIGHT AGAIN.
PLEASE.
JUST TELL ME WHAT I CAN DO.
YOU CAN LEAVE.

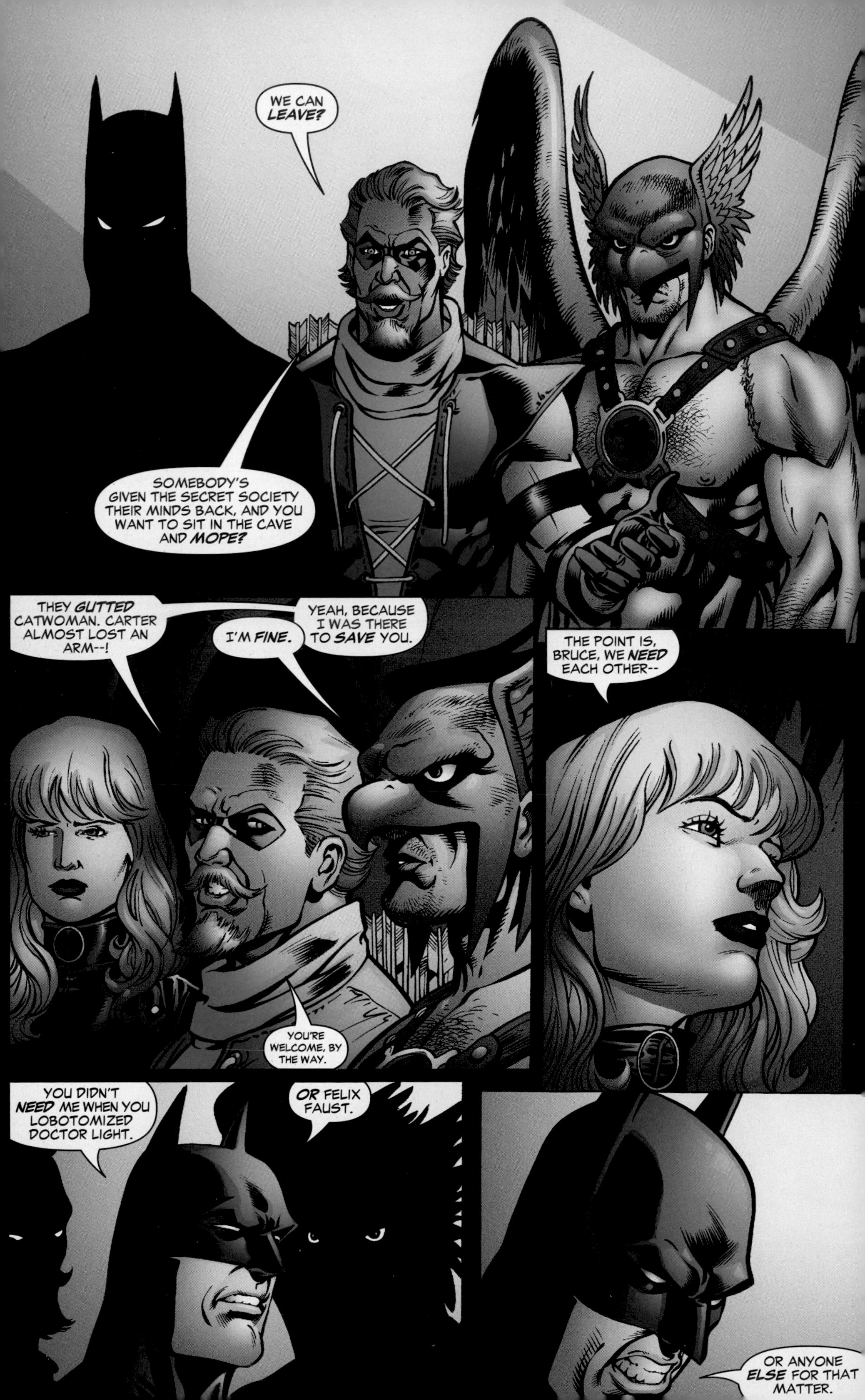
WE CAN *LEAVE?*
SOMEBODY'S GIVEN THE SECRET SOCIETY THEIR MINDS BACK, AND YOU WANT TO SIT IN THE CAVE AND *MOPE?*
THEY *GUTTED* CATWOMAN. CARTER ALMOST LOST AN ARM--!
I'M *FINE.*
YEAH, BECAUSE I WAS THERE TO *SAVE* YOU.
YOU'RE WELCOME, BY THE WAY.
THE POINT IS, BRUCE, WE *NEED* EACH OTHER--
YOU DIDN'T *NEED* ME WHEN YOU LOBOTOMIZED DOCTOR LIGHT.
OR FELIX FAUST.
OR ANYONE *ELSE* FOR THAT MATTER.

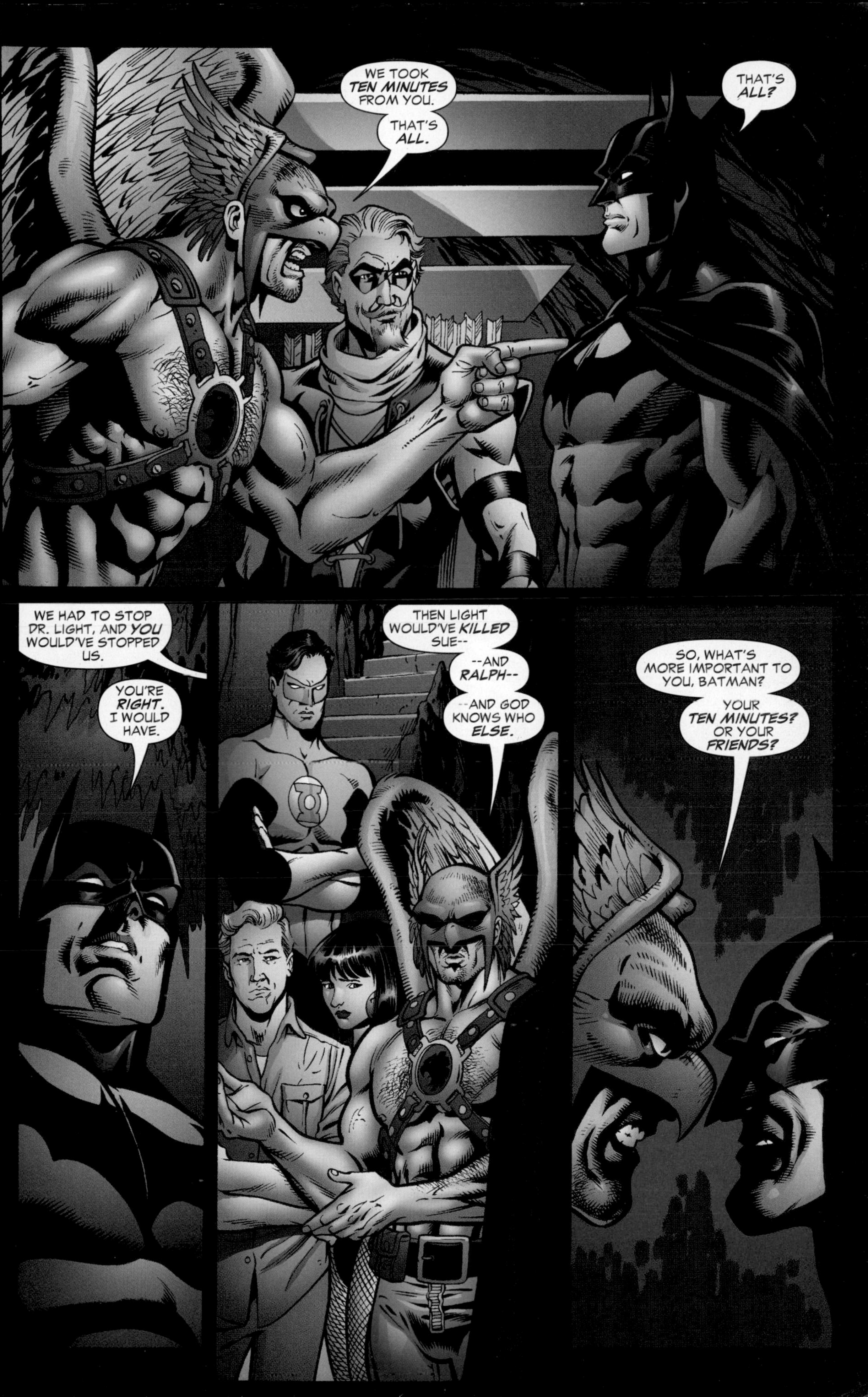
WE TOOK TEN MINUTES FROM YOU.
THAT'S ALL.
THAT'S ALL?
WE HAD TO STOP DR. LIGHT, AND YOU WOULD'VE STOPPED US.
YOU'RE RIGHT. I WOULD HAVE.
THEN LIGHT WOULD'VE KILLED SUE--
--AND RALPH--
--AND GOD KNOWS WHO ELSE.
SO, WHAT'S MORE IMPORTANT TO YOU, BATMAN?
YOUR TEN MINUTES? OR YOUR FRIENDS?

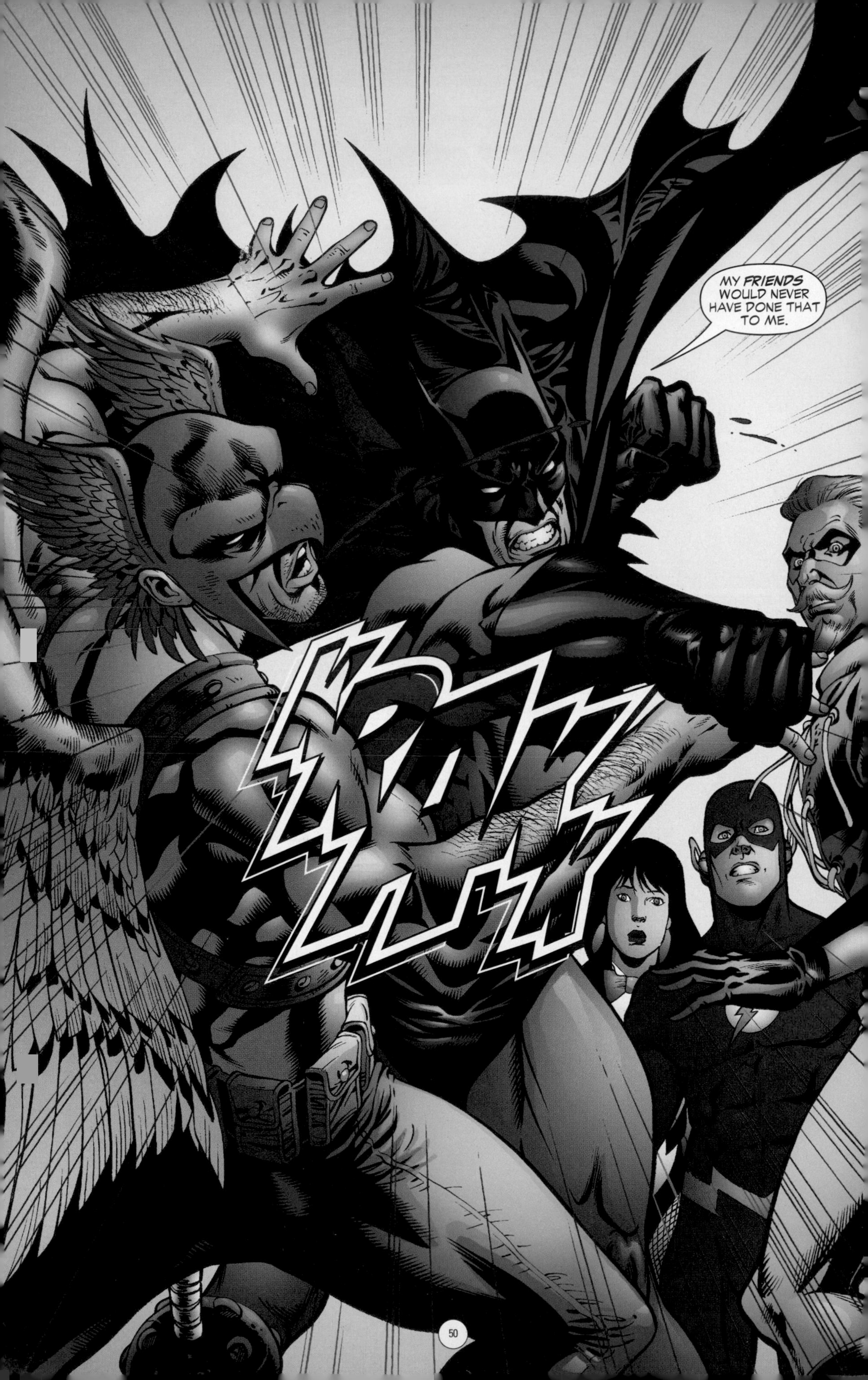
MY *FRIENDS* WOULD NEVER HAVE DONE THAT TO ME.

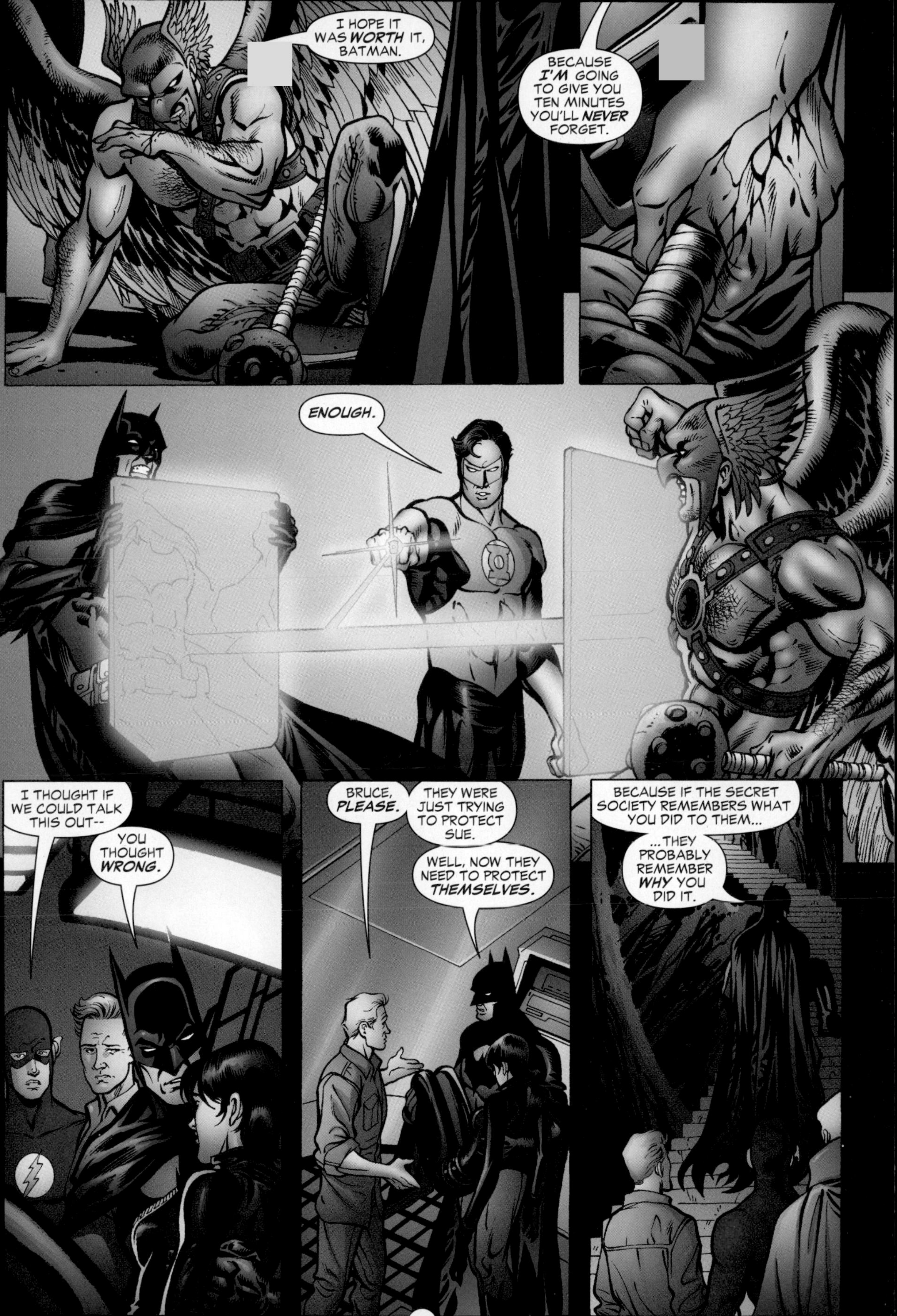
I HOPE IT WAS WORTH IT, BATMAN.
BECAUSE I'M GOING TO GIVE YOU TEN MINUTES YOU'LL NEVER FORGET.
ENOUGH.
I THOUGHT IF WE COULD TALK THIS OUT--
YOU THOUGHT WRONG.
BRUCE, PLEASE.
THEY WERE JUST TRYING TO PROTECT SUE.
WELL, NOW THEY NEED TO PROTECT THEMSELVES.
BECAUSE IF THE SECRET SOCIETY REMEMBERS WHAT YOU DID TO THEM...
...THEY PROBABLY REMEMBER WHY YOU DID IT.

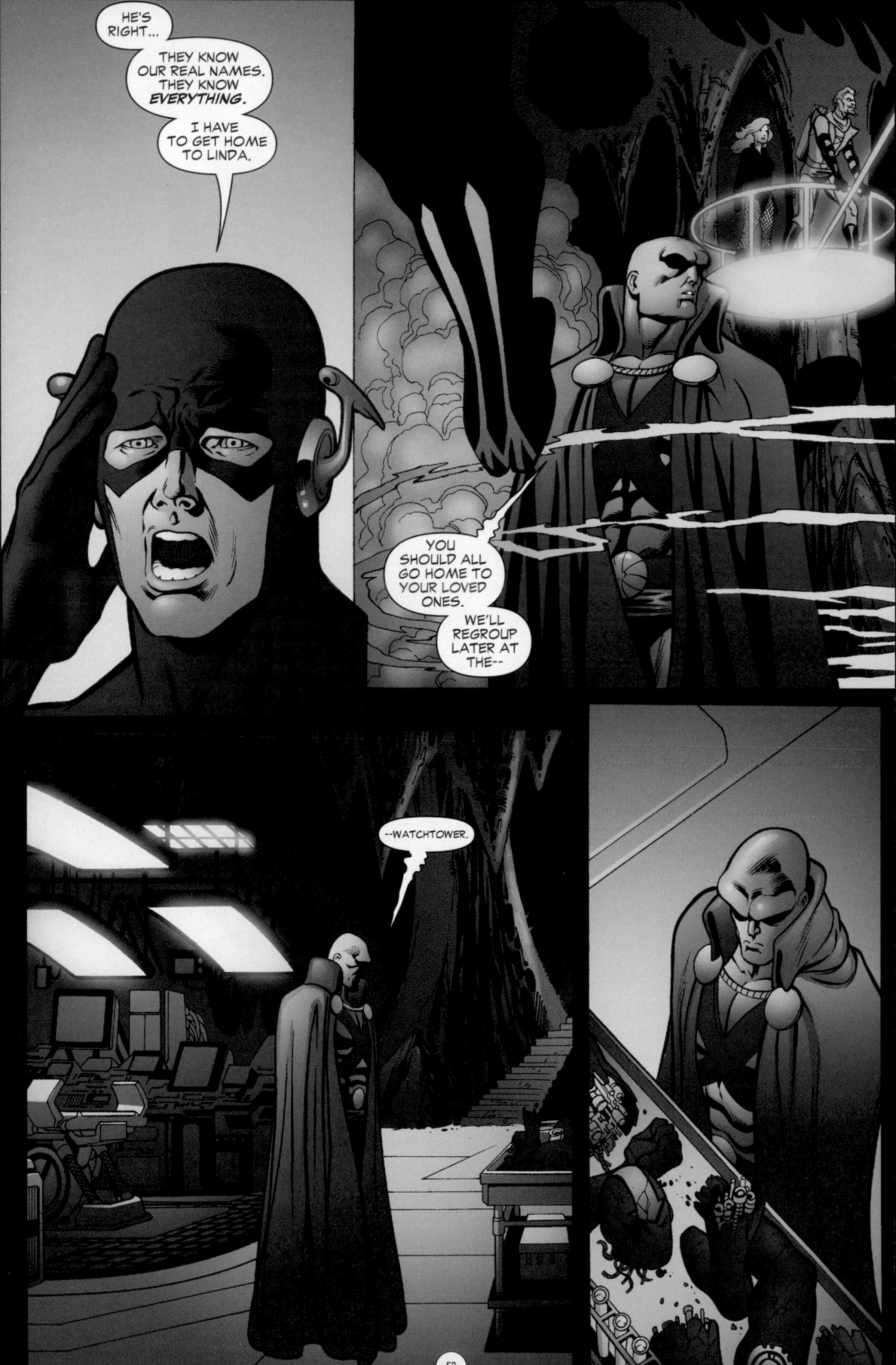

HE'S RIGHT...
THEY KNOW OUR REAL NAMES. THEY KNOW *EVERYTHING.*
I HAVE TO GET HOME TO LINDA.
YOU SHOULD ALL GO HOME TO YOUR LOVED ONES.
WE'LL REGROUP LATER AT THE--
--WATCHTOWER.

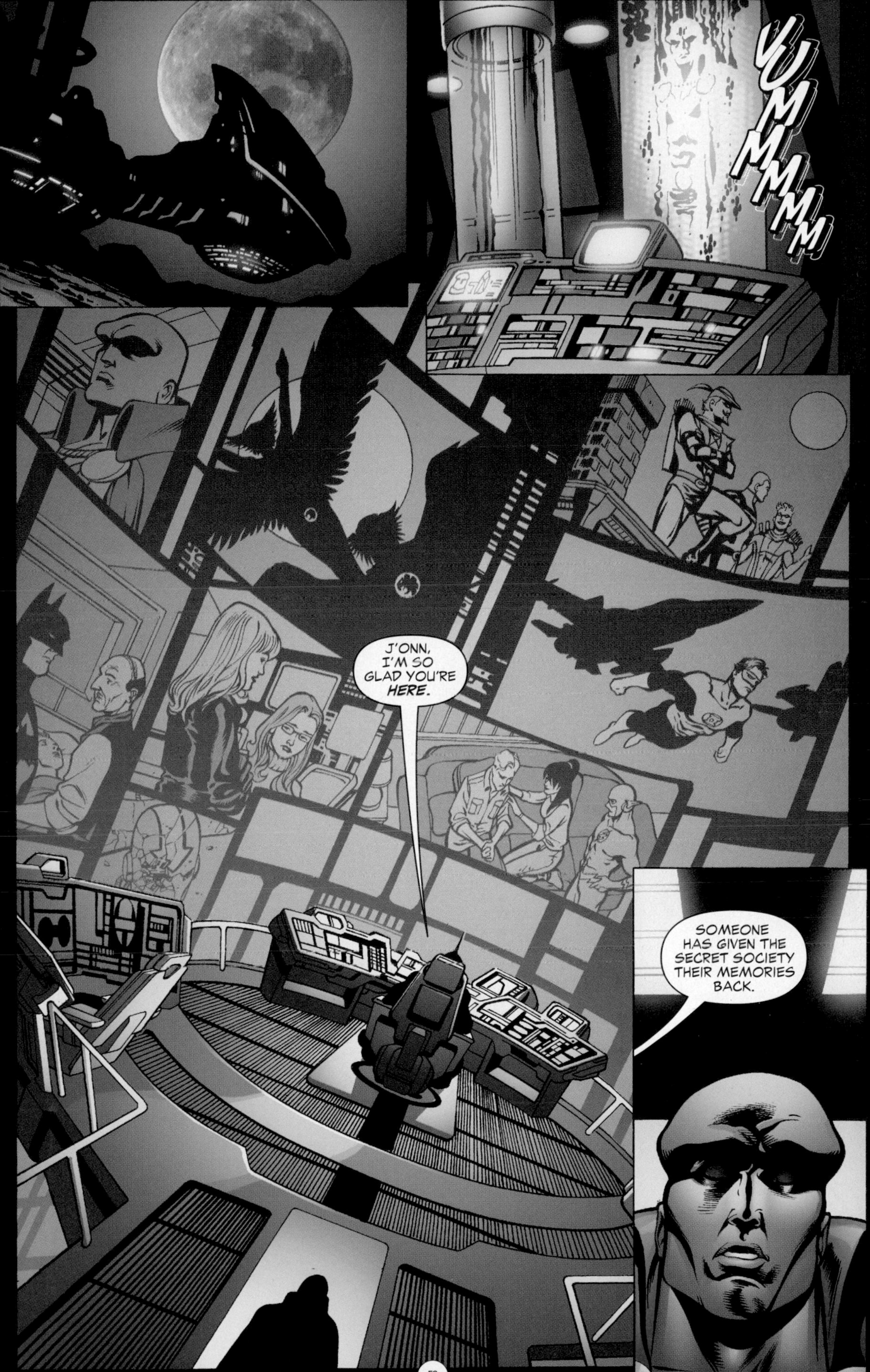
VUMMMMMM
J'ONN, I'M SO GLAD YOU'RE HERE.
SOMEONE HAS GIVEN THE SECRET SOCIETY THEIR MEMORIES BACK.

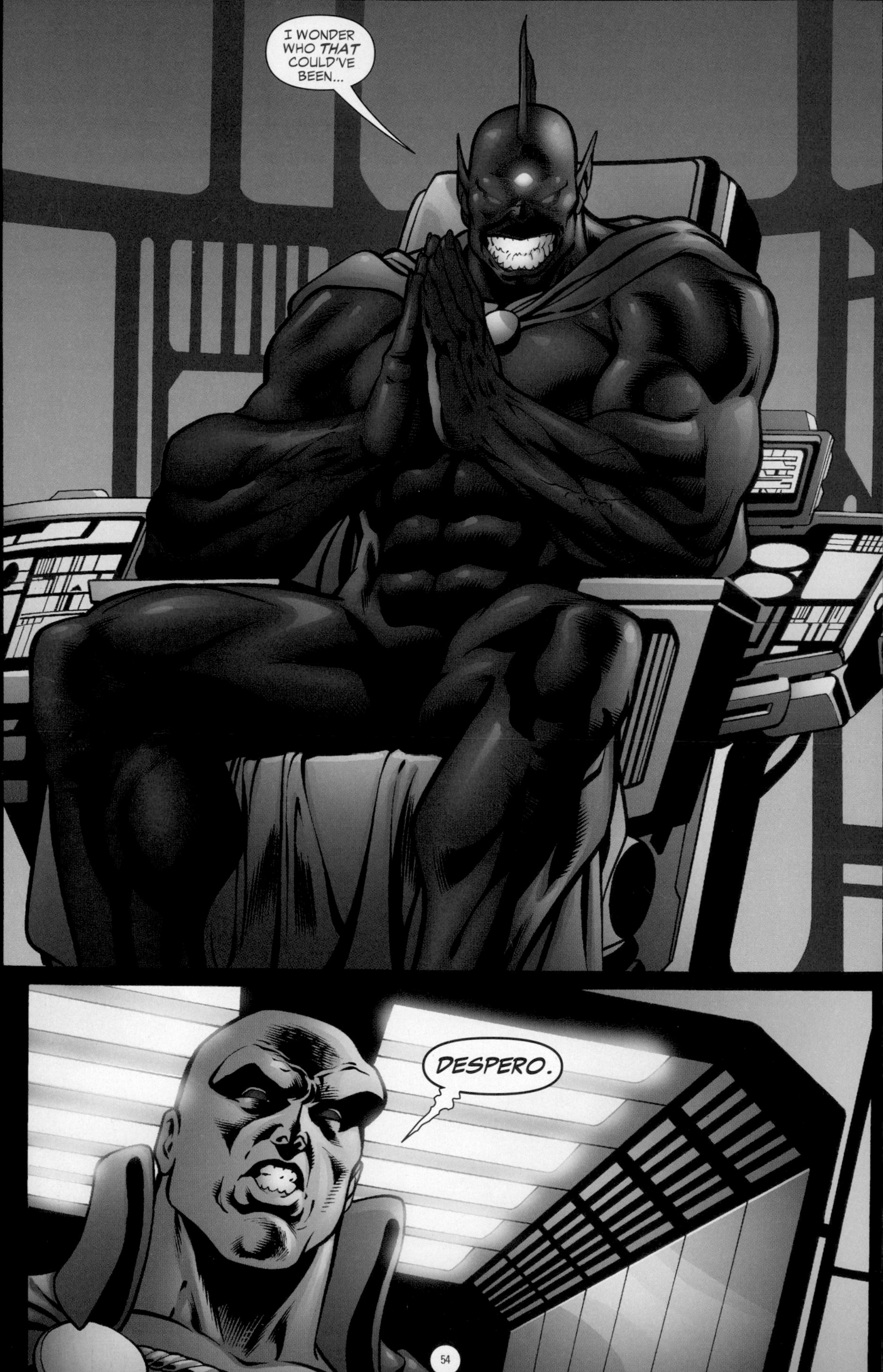
I WONDER WHO THAT COULD'VE BEEN...
DESPERO.

JLA #117
by Rags Morales & Mark Farmer

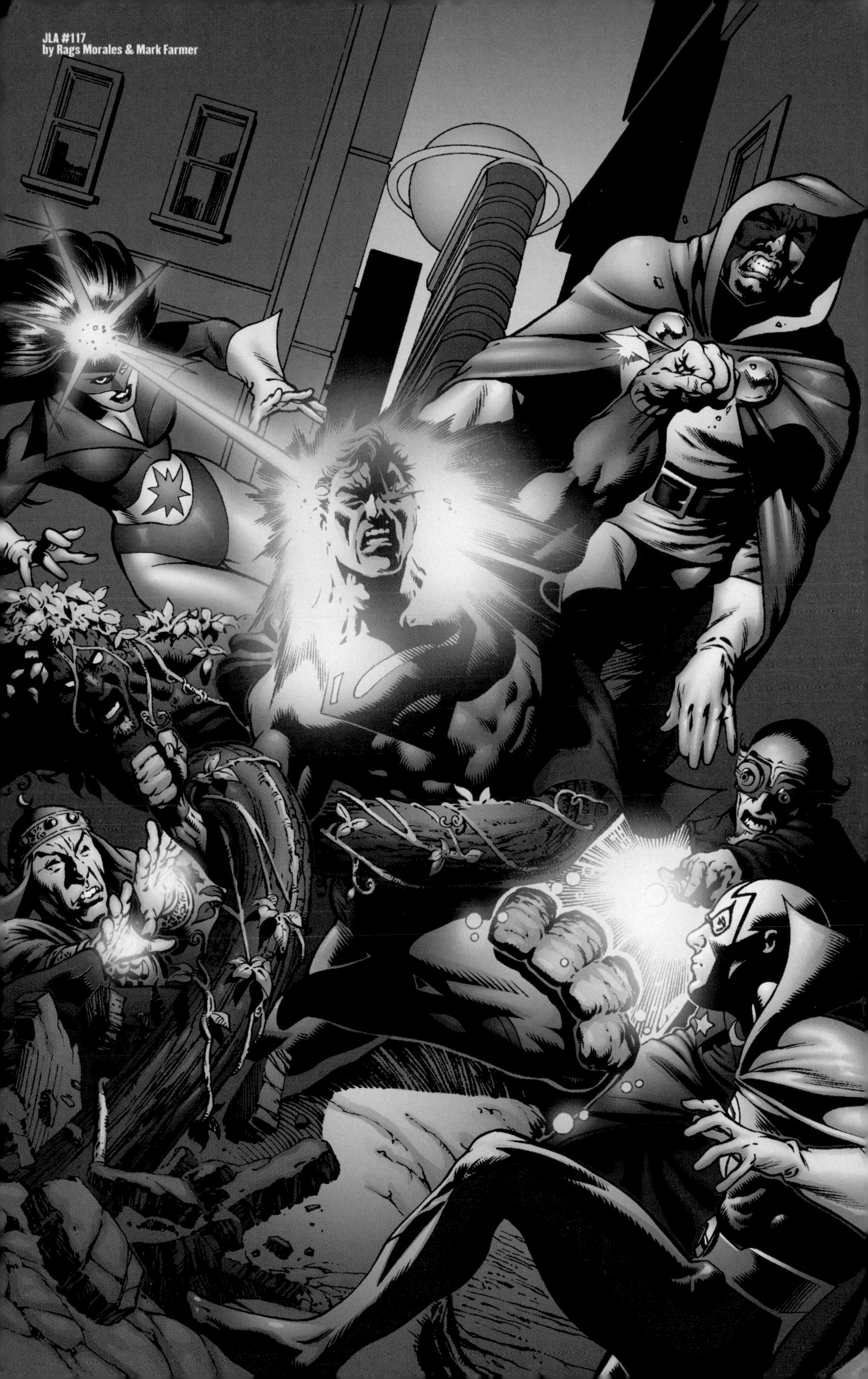

JLA

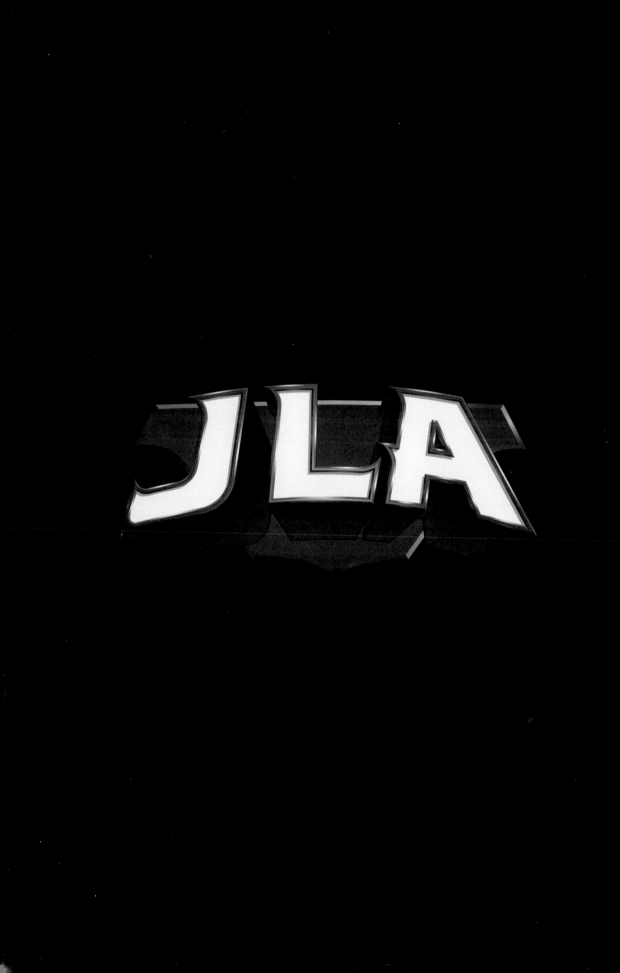

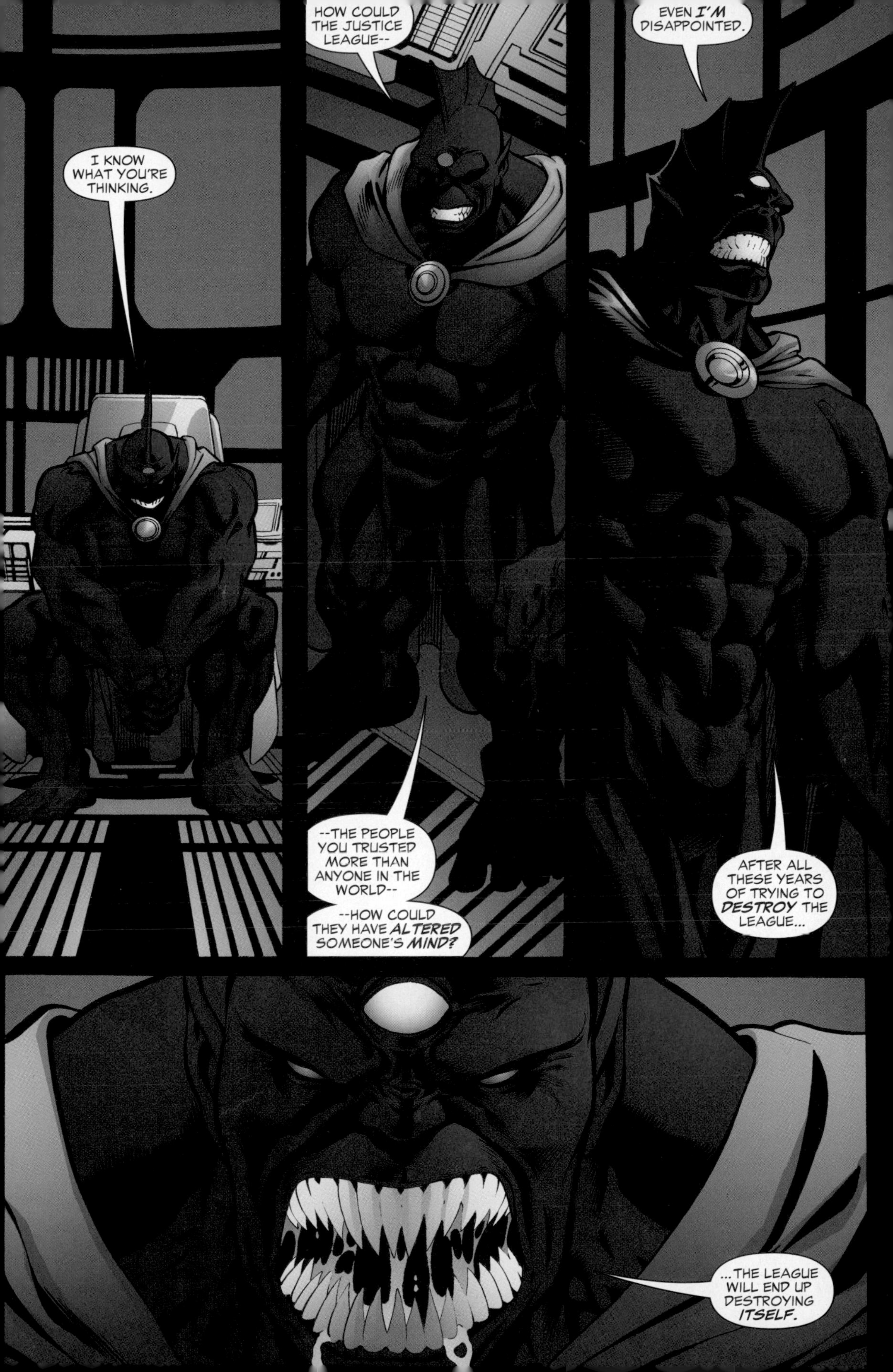
I KNOW WHAT YOU'RE THINKING.
HOW COULD THE JUSTICE LEAGUE--
--THE PEOPLE YOU TRUSTED MORE THAN ANYONE IN THE WORLD--
--HOW COULD THEY HAVE ALTERED SOMEONE'S MIND?
EVEN I'M DISAPPOINTED.
AFTER ALL THESE YEARS OF TRYING TO DESTROY THE LEAGUE...
...THE LEAGUE WILL END UP DESTROYING ITSELF.

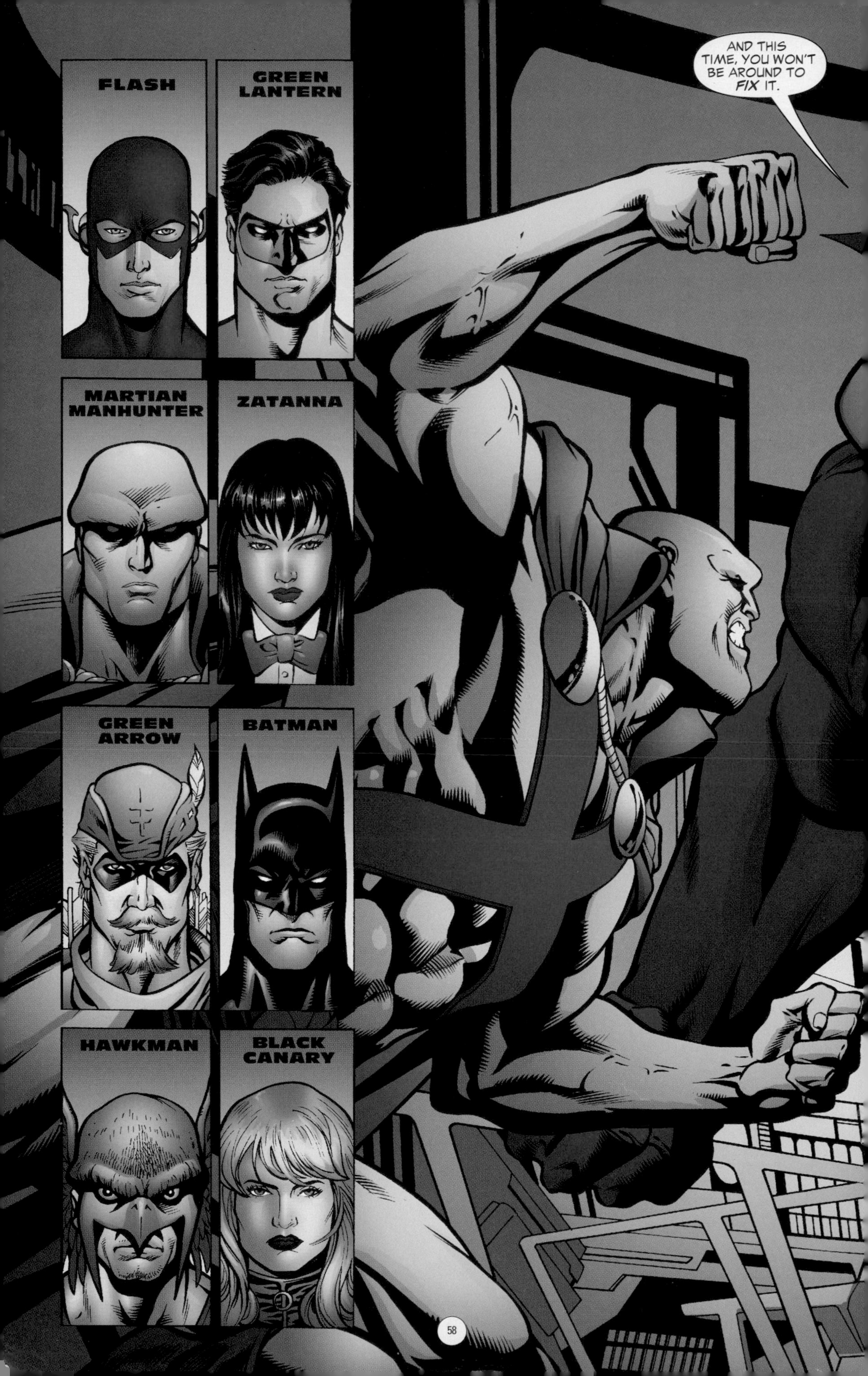
FLASH
GREEN LANTERN
MARTIAN MANHUNTER
ZATANNA
GREEN ARROW
BATMAN
HAWKMAN
BLACK CANARY
AND THIS TIME, YOU WON'T BE AROUND TO FIX IT.

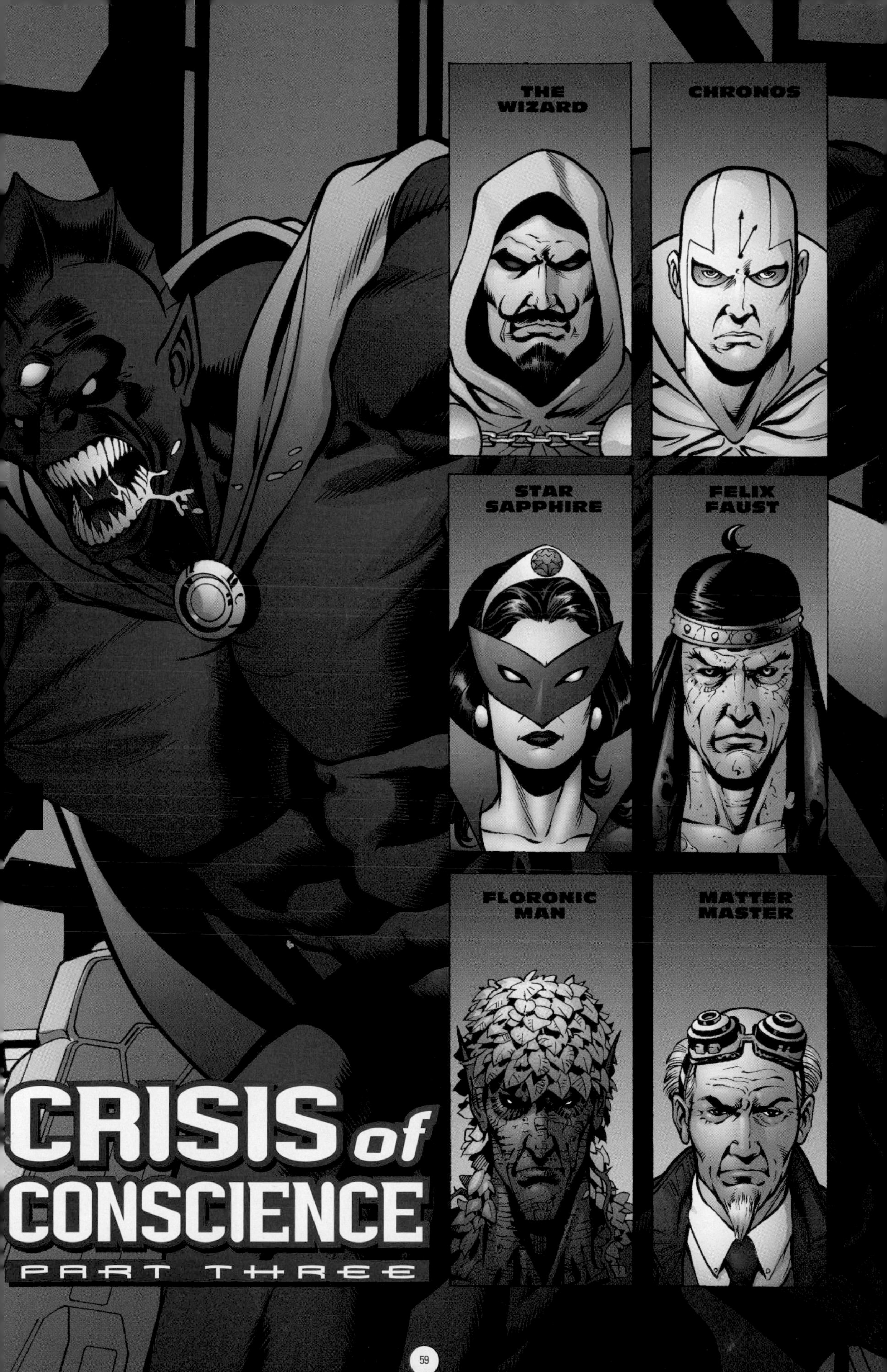

THE WIZARD
CHRONOS
STAR SAPPHIRE
FELIX FAUST
FLORONIC MAN
MATTER MASTER
CRISIS of CONSCIENCE
PART THREE

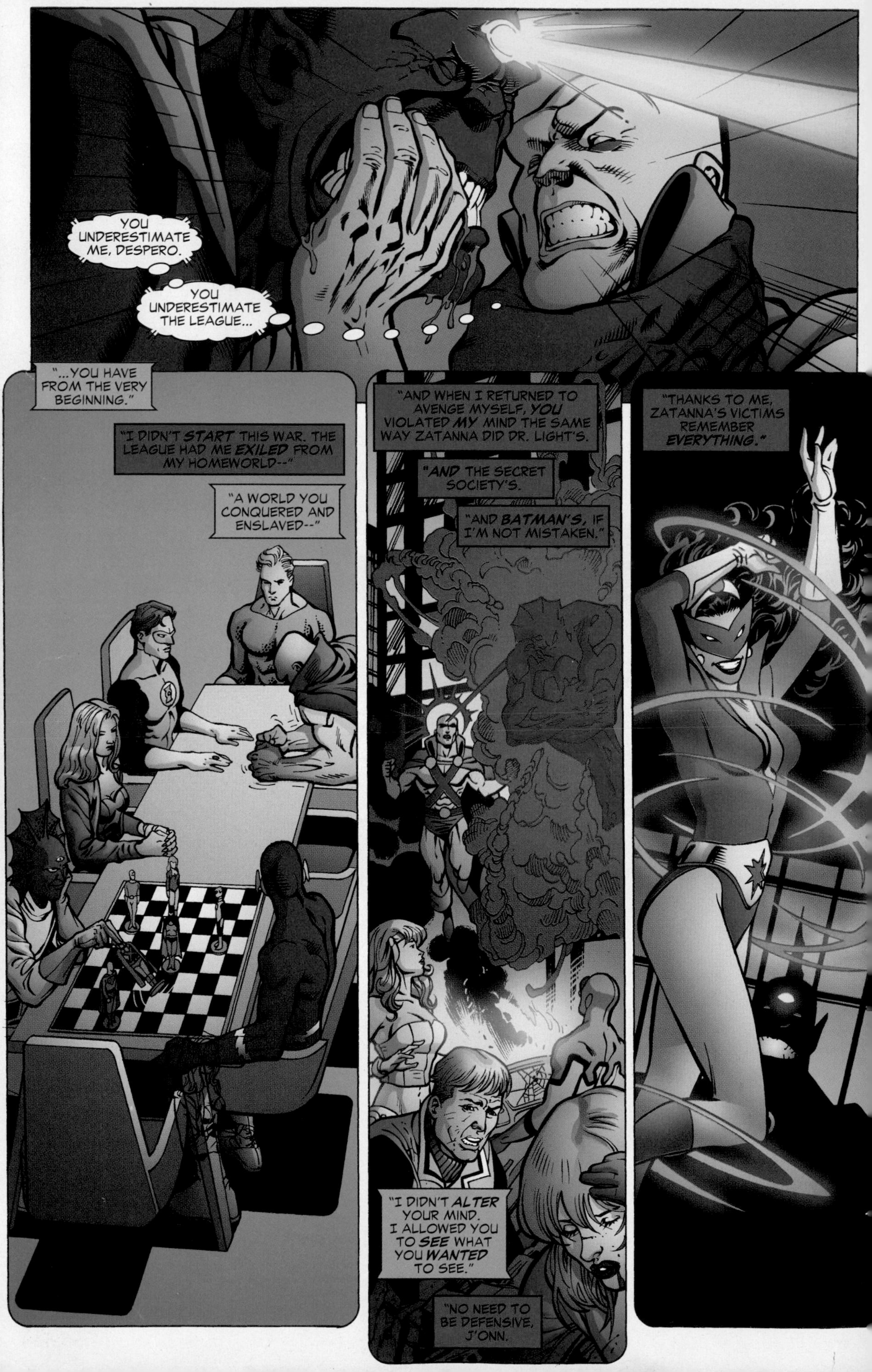
YOU UNDERESTIMATE ME, DESPERO.
YOU UNDERESTIMATE THE LEAGUE...
"...YOU HAVE FROM THE VERY BEGINNING."
"I DIDN'T START THIS WAR. THE LEAGUE HAD ME EXILED FROM MY HOMEWORLD--"
"A WORLD YOU CONQUERED AND ENSLAVED--"
"AND WHEN I RETURNED TO AVENGE MYSELF, YOU VIOLATED MY MIND THE SAME WAY ZATANNA DID DR. LIGHT'S.
"AND THE SECRET SOCIETY'S.
"AND BATMAN'S, IF I'M NOT MISTAKEN."
"I DIDN'T ALTER YOUR MIND. I ALLOWED YOU TO SEE WHAT YOU WANTED TO SEE."
"NO NEED TO BE DEFENSIVE, J'ONN.
"THANKS TO ME, ZATANNA'S VICTIMS REMEMBER EVERYTHING."

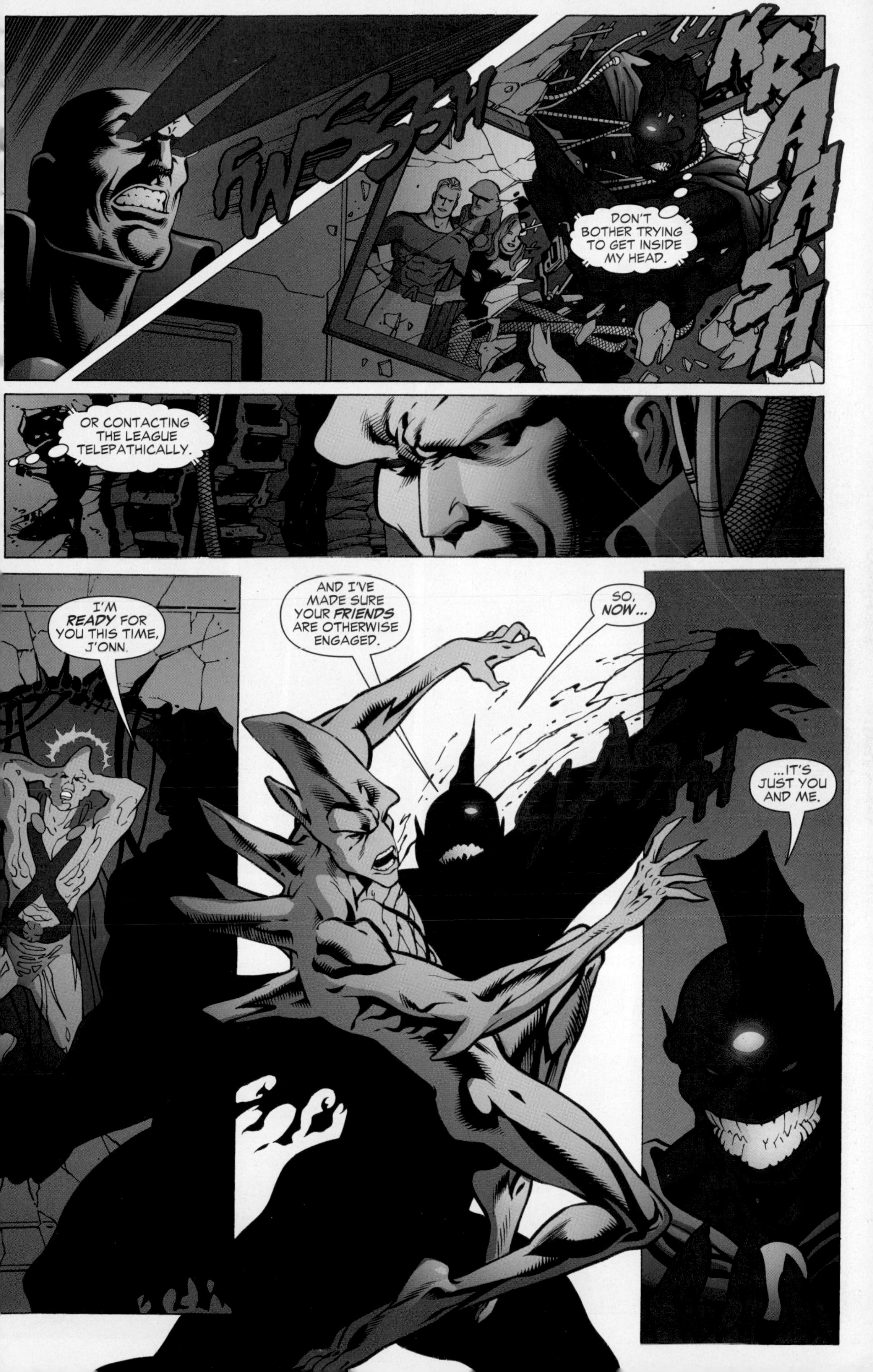
FWSSSH
KRAASH
DON'T BOTHER TRYING TO GET INSIDE MY HEAD.
OR CONTACTING THE LEAGUE TELEPATHICALLY.
I'M READY FOR YOU THIS TIME, J'ONN.
AND I'VE MADE SURE YOUR FRIENDS ARE OTHERWISE ENGAGED.
SO, NOW...
...IT'S JUST YOU AND ME.

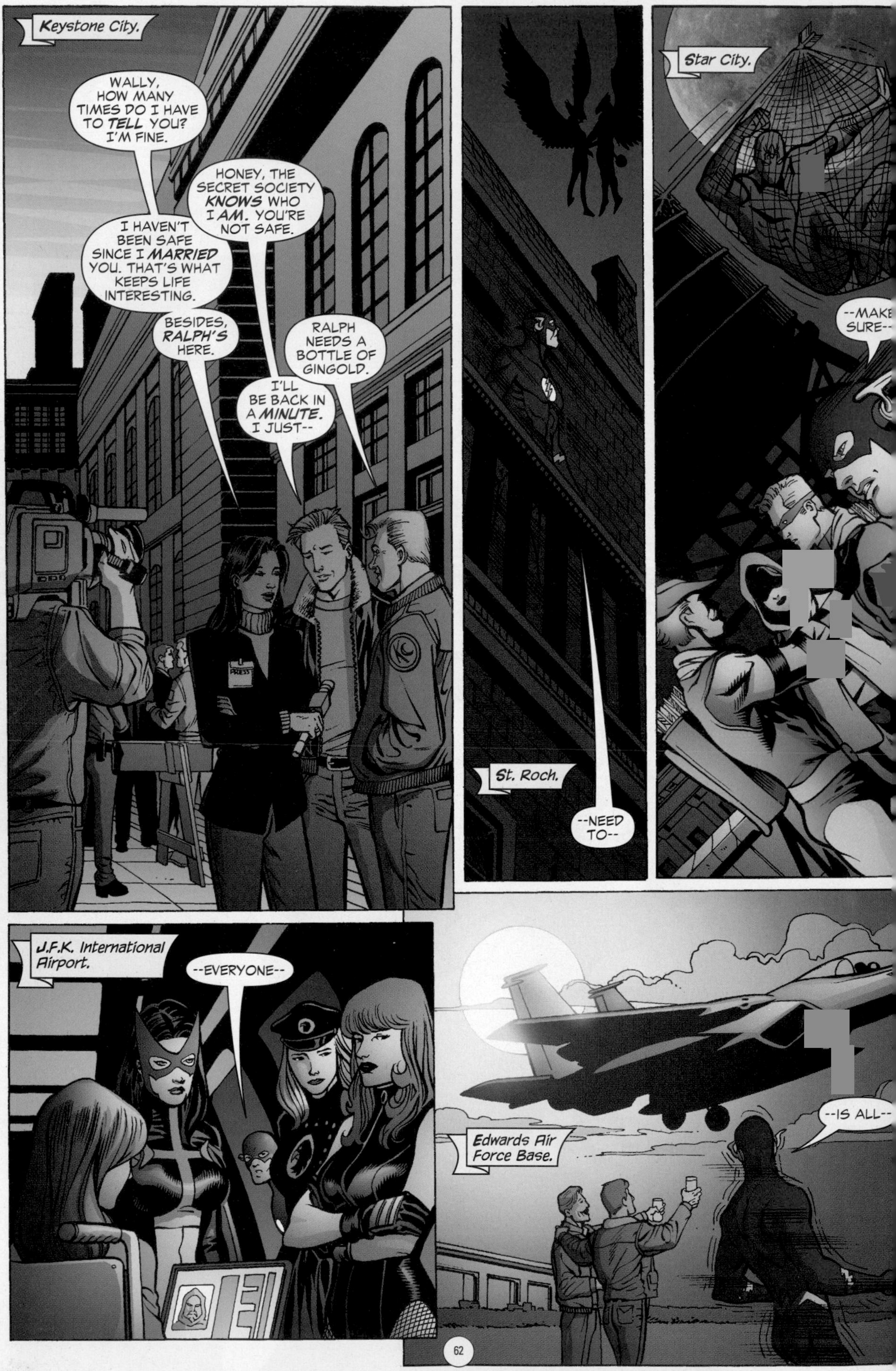
Keystone City.
WALLY, HOW MANY TIMES DO I HAVE TO TELL YOU? I'M FINE.
HONEY, THE SECRET SOCIETY KNOWS WHO I AM. YOU'RE NOT SAFE.
I HAVEN'T BEEN SAFE SINCE I MARRIED YOU. THAT'S WHAT KEEPS LIFE INTERESTING.
BESIDES, RALPH'S HERE.
RALPH NEEDS A BOTTLE OF GINGOLD.
I'LL BE BACK IN A MINUTE. I JUST--
St. Roch.
--NEED TO--
Star City.
--MAKE SURE--
J.F.K. International Airport.
--EVERYONE--
Edwards Air Force Base.
--IS ALL--

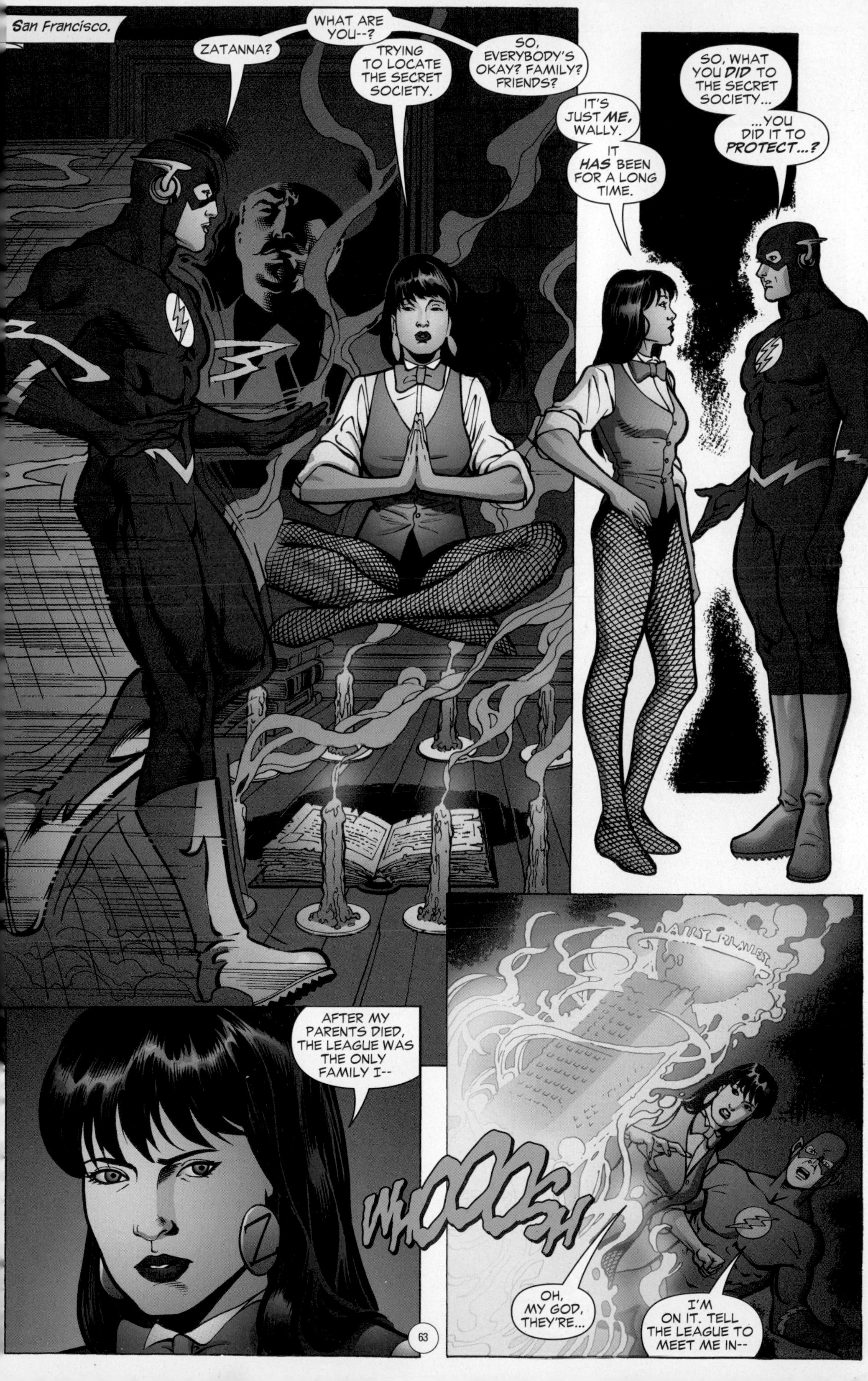
San Francisco.
ZATANNA?
WHAT ARE YOU--?
TRYING TO LOCATE THE SECRET SOCIETY.
SO, EVERYBODY'S OKAY? FAMILY? FRIENDS?
IT'S JUST ME, WALLY.
IT HAS BEEN FOR A LONG TIME.
SO, WHAT YOU DID TO THE SECRET SOCIETY...
...YOU DID IT TO PROTECT...?
AFTER MY PARENTS DIED, THE LEAGUE WAS THE ONLY FAMILY I--
WHOOOSH
OH, MY GOD, THEY'RE...
I'M ON IT. TELL THE LEAGUE TO MEET ME IN--

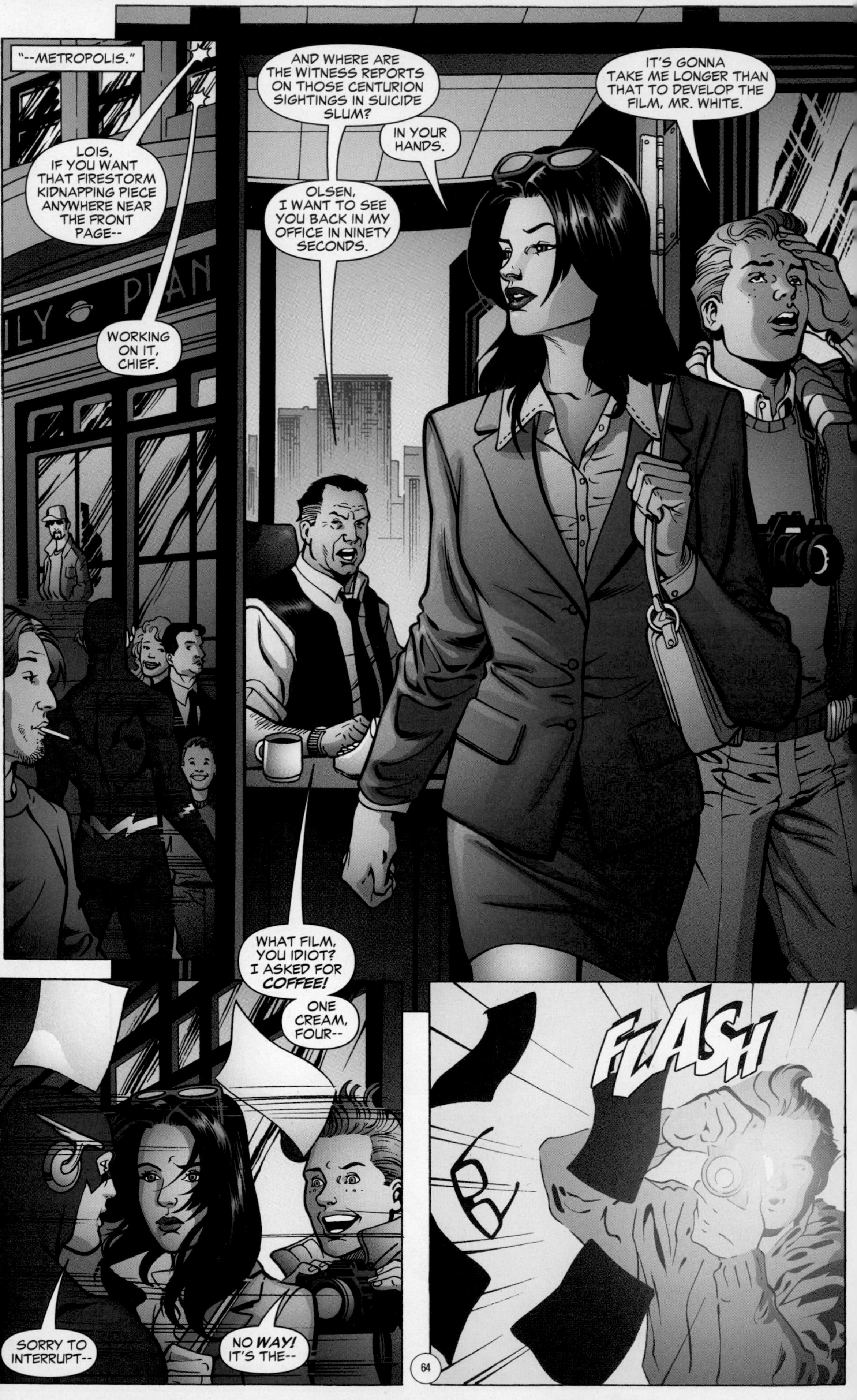
"--METROPOLIS."
LOIS, IF YOU WANT THAT FIRESTORM KIDNAPPING PIECE ANYWHERE NEAR THE FRONT PAGE--
WORKING ON IT, CHIEF.
AND WHERE ARE THE WITNESS REPORTS ON THOSE CENTURION SIGHTINGS IN SUICIDE SLUM?
IN YOUR HANDS.
OLSEN, I WANT TO SEE YOU BACK IN MY OFFICE IN NINETY SECONDS.
IT'S GONNA TAKE ME LONGER THAN THAT TO DEVELOP THE FILM, MR. WHITE.
WHAT FILM, YOU IDIOT? I ASKED FOR *COFFEE!*
ONE CREAM, FOUR--
SORRY TO INTERRUPT--
NO *WAY!* IT'S THE--
FLASH

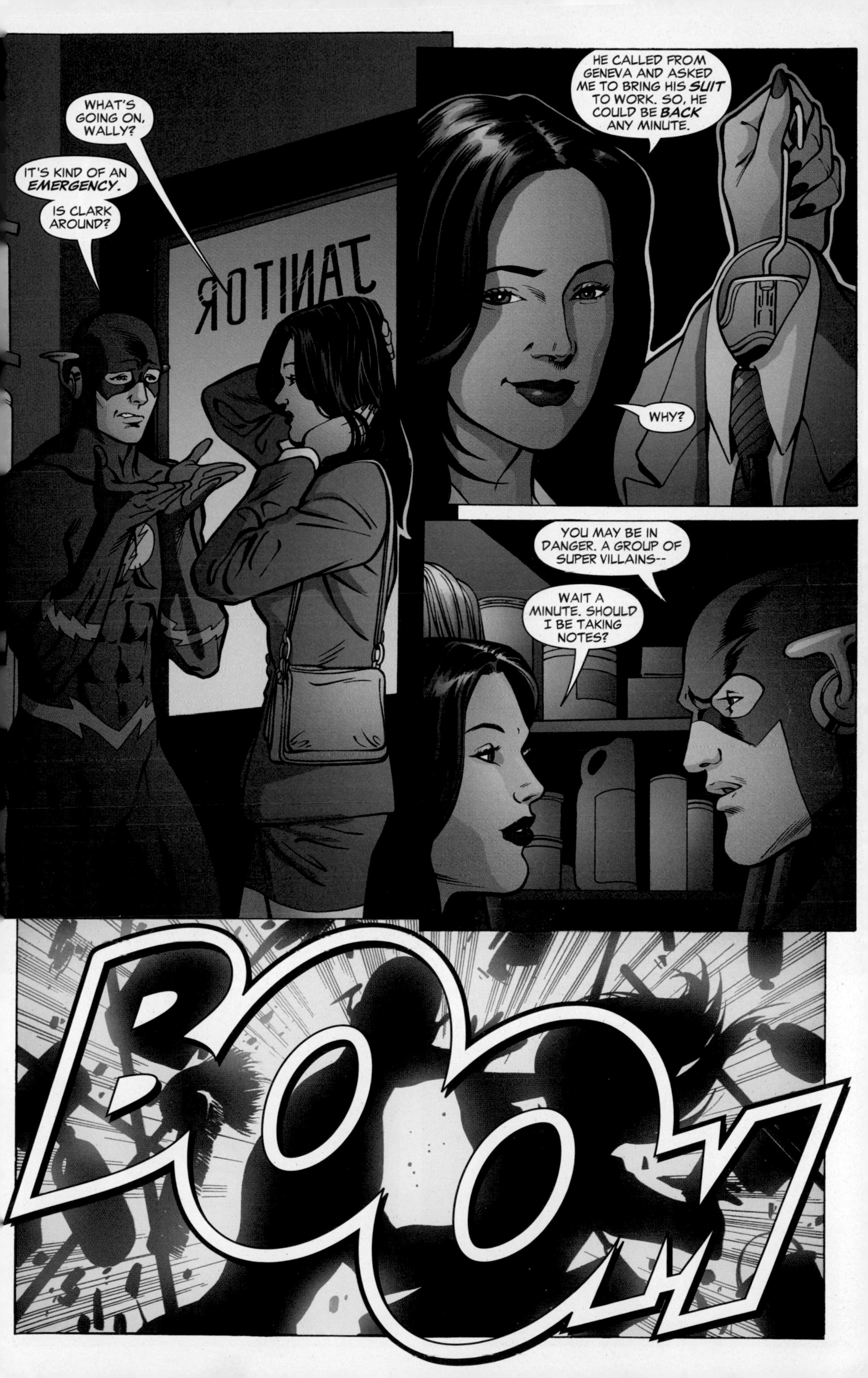
WHAT'S GOING ON, WALLY?
IT'S KIND OF AN EMERGENCY.
IS CLARK AROUND?
JANITOR
HE CALLED FROM GENEVA AND ASKED ME TO BRING HIS SUIT TO WORK. SO, HE COULD BE BACK ANY MINUTE.
WHY?
YOU MAY BE IN DANGER. A GROUP OF SUPER VILLAINS--
WAIT A MINUTE. SHOULD I BE TAKING NOTES?
BOOM

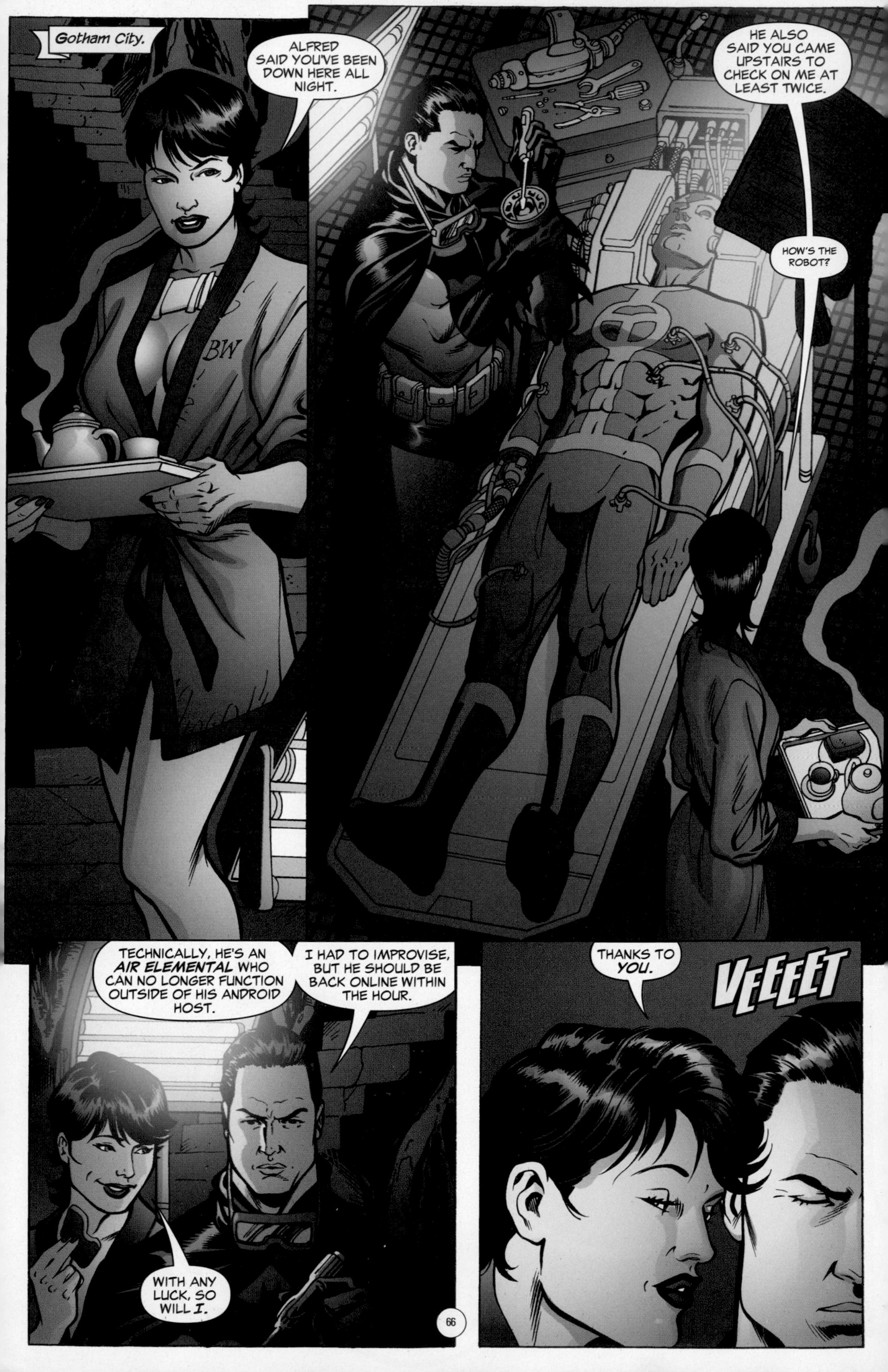
Gotham City.
ALFRED SAID YOU'VE BEEN DOWN HERE ALL NIGHT.
HE ALSO SAID YOU CAME UPSTAIRS TO CHECK ON ME AT LEAST TWICE.
HOW'S THE ROBOT?
TECHNICALLY, HE'S AN AIR ELEMENTAL WHO CAN NO LONGER FUNCTION OUTSIDE OF HIS ANDROID HOST.
I HAD TO IMPROVISE, BUT HE SHOULD BE BACK ONLINE WITHIN THE HOUR.
WITH ANY LUCK, SO WILL I.
THANKS TO YOU.
VEEEET

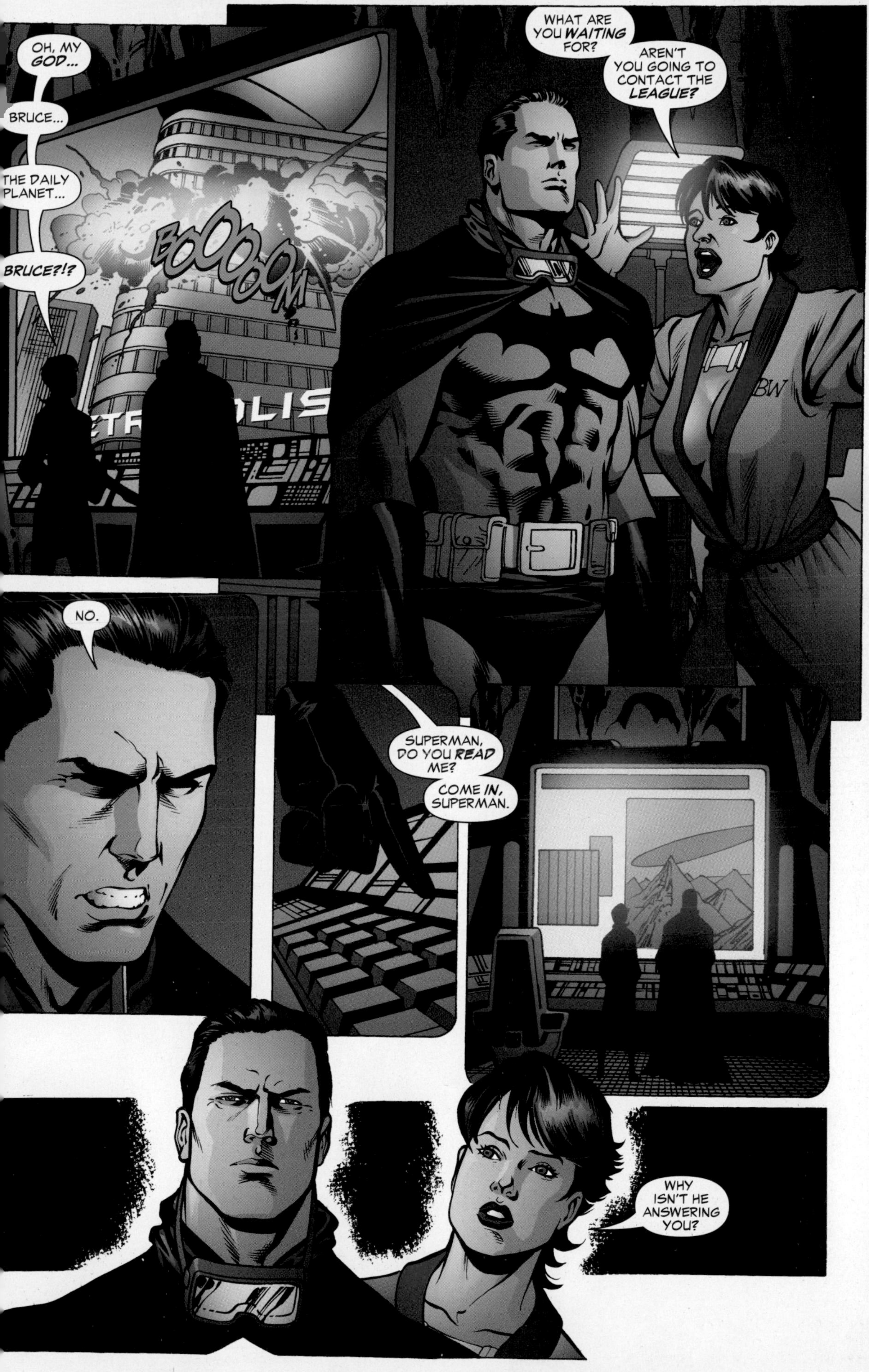
OH, MY GOD...
BRUCE...
THE DAILY PLANET...
BRUCE?!?
BOOOOOOM
ETR OLIS
WHAT ARE YOU WAITING FOR?
AREN'T YOU GOING TO CONTACT THE LEAGUE?
BW
NO.
SUPERMAN, DO YOU READ ME?
COME IN, SUPERMAN.
WHY ISN'T HE ANSWERING YOU?

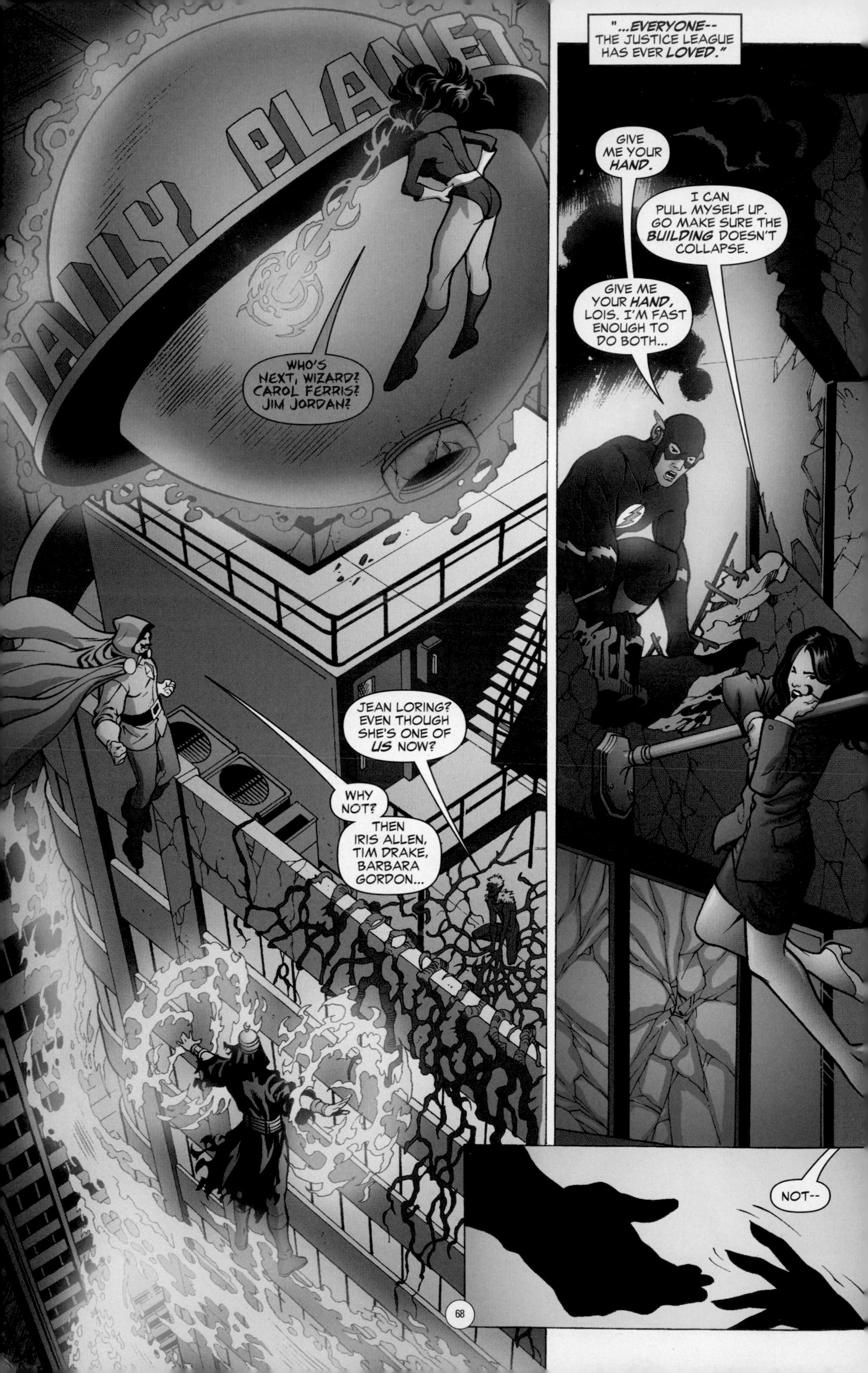

DAILY PLANET
WHO'S NEXT, WIZARD? CAROL FERRIS? JIM JORDAN?
JEAN LORING? EVEN THOUGH SHE'S ONE OF US NOW?
WHY NOT?
THEN IRIS ALLEN, TIM DRAKE, BARBARA GORDON...
"...EVERYONE-- THE JUSTICE LEAGUE HAS EVER LOVED."
GIVE ME YOUR HAND.
I CAN PULL MYSELF UP. GO MAKE SURE THE BUILDING DOESN'T COLLAPSE.
GIVE ME YOUR HAND, LOIS. I'M FAST ENOUGH TO DO BOTH...
NOT--

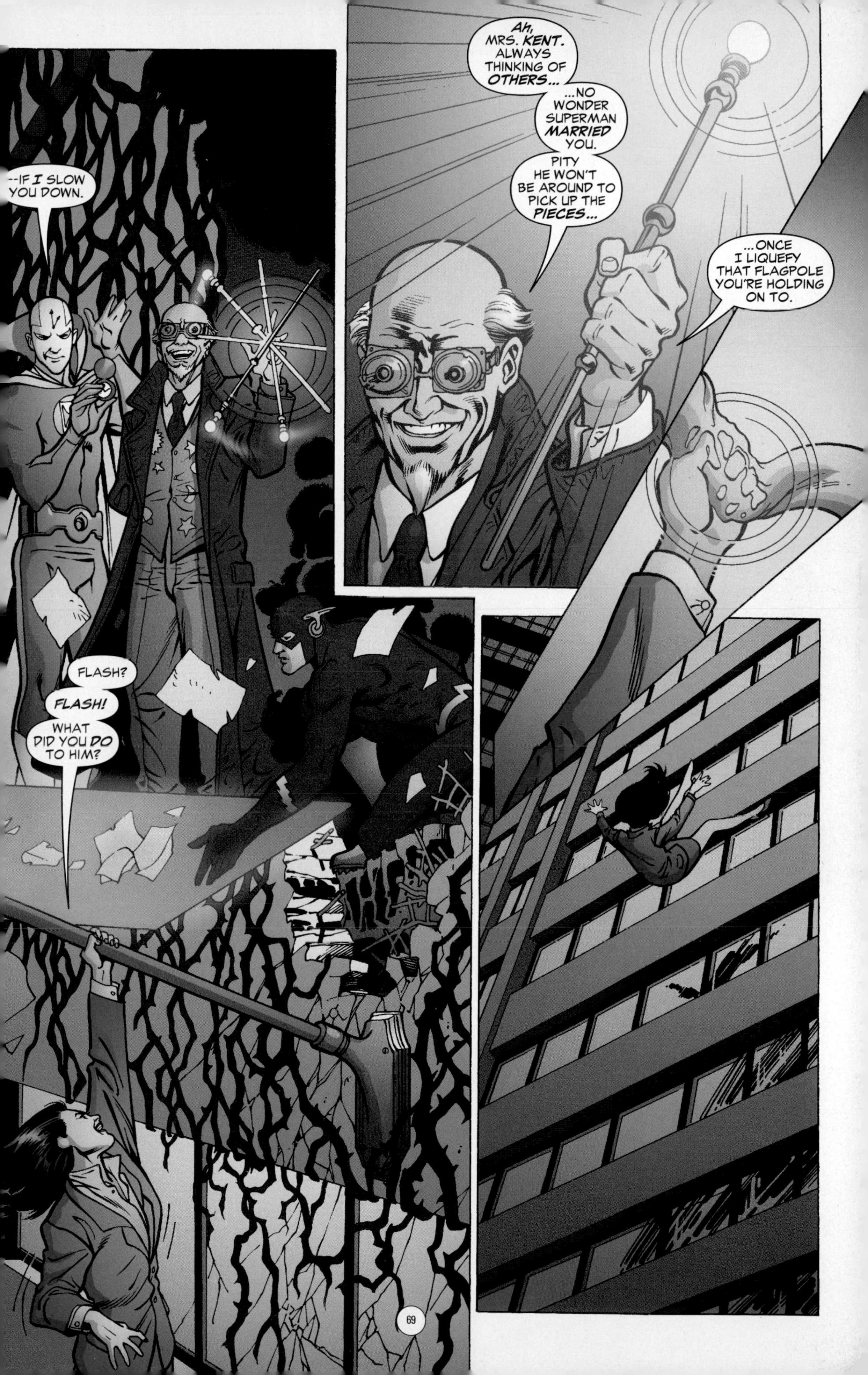
--IF I SLOW YOU DOWN.
Ah, MRS. KENT. ALWAYS THINKING OF OTHERS...
...NO WONDER SUPERMAN MARRIED YOU.
PITY HE WON'T BE AROUND TO PICK UP THE PIECES...
...ONCE I LIQUEFY THAT FLAGPOLE YOU'RE HOLDING ON TO.
FLASH?
FLASH!
WHAT DID YOU DO TO HIM?

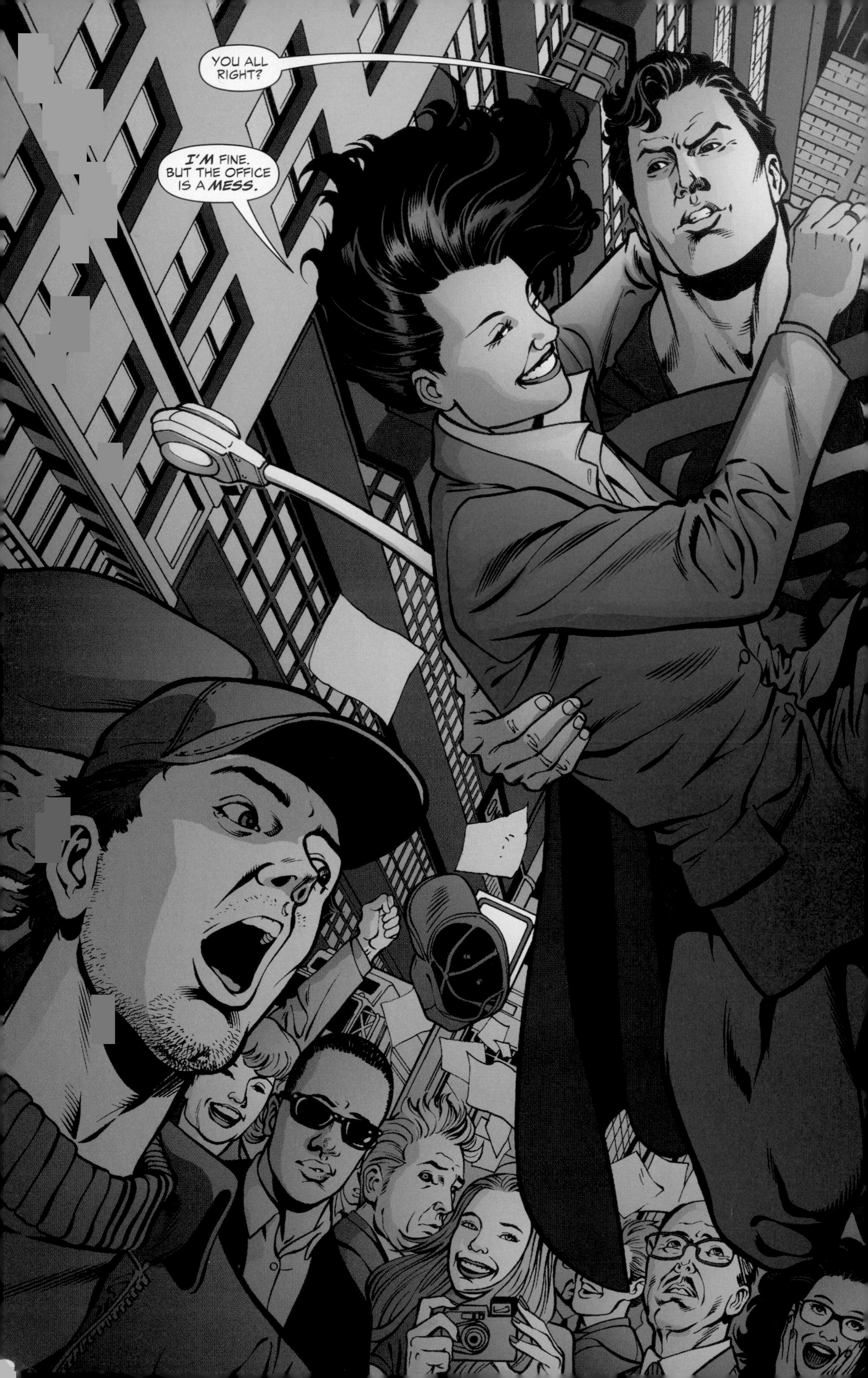
YOU ALL RIGHT?
I'M FINE. BUT THE OFFICE IS A MESS.

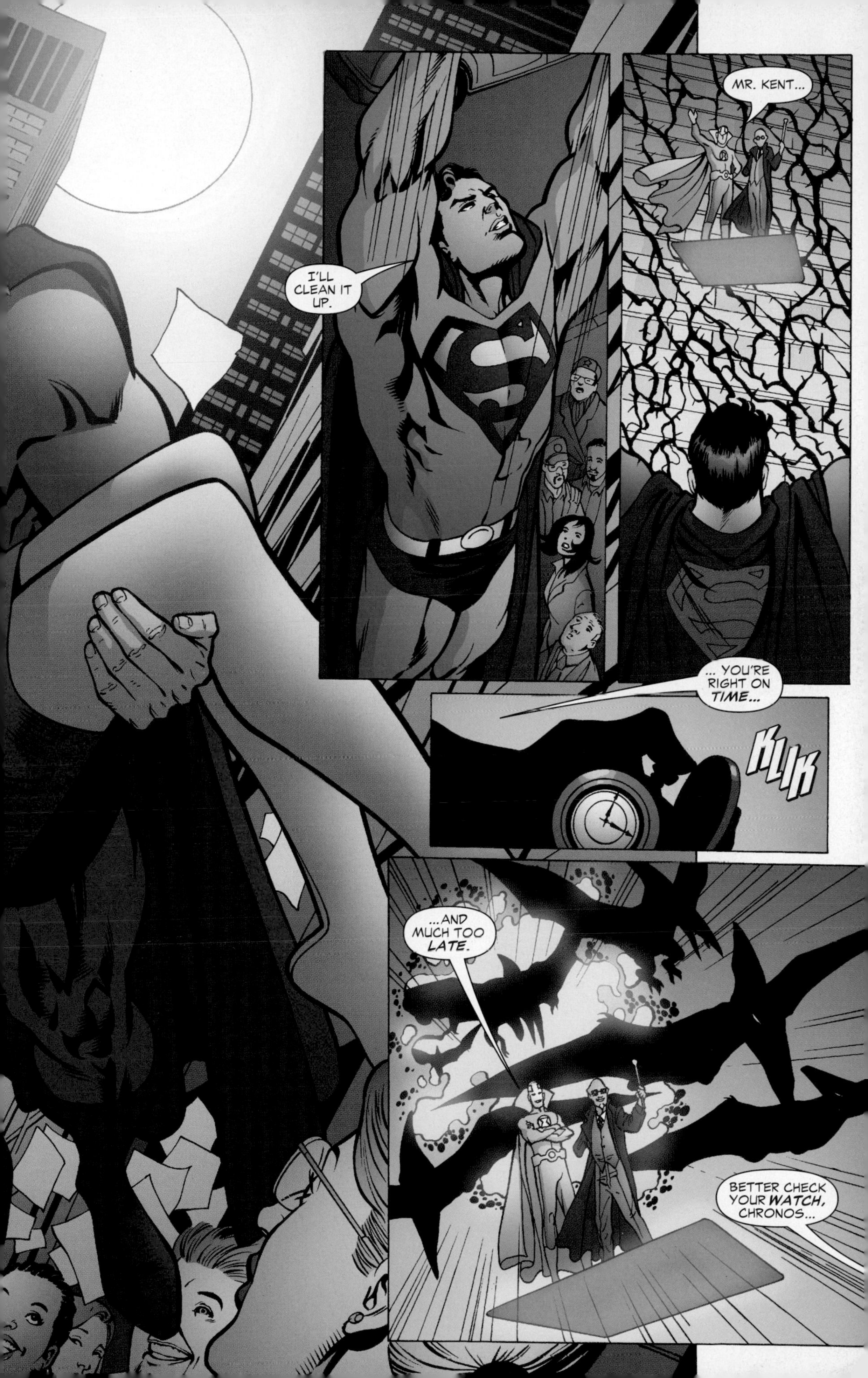
I'LL CLEAN IT UP.
MR. KENT...
... YOU'RE RIGHT ON TIME...
KLIK
...AND MUCH TOO LATE.
BETTER CHECK YOUR WATCH, CHRONOS...

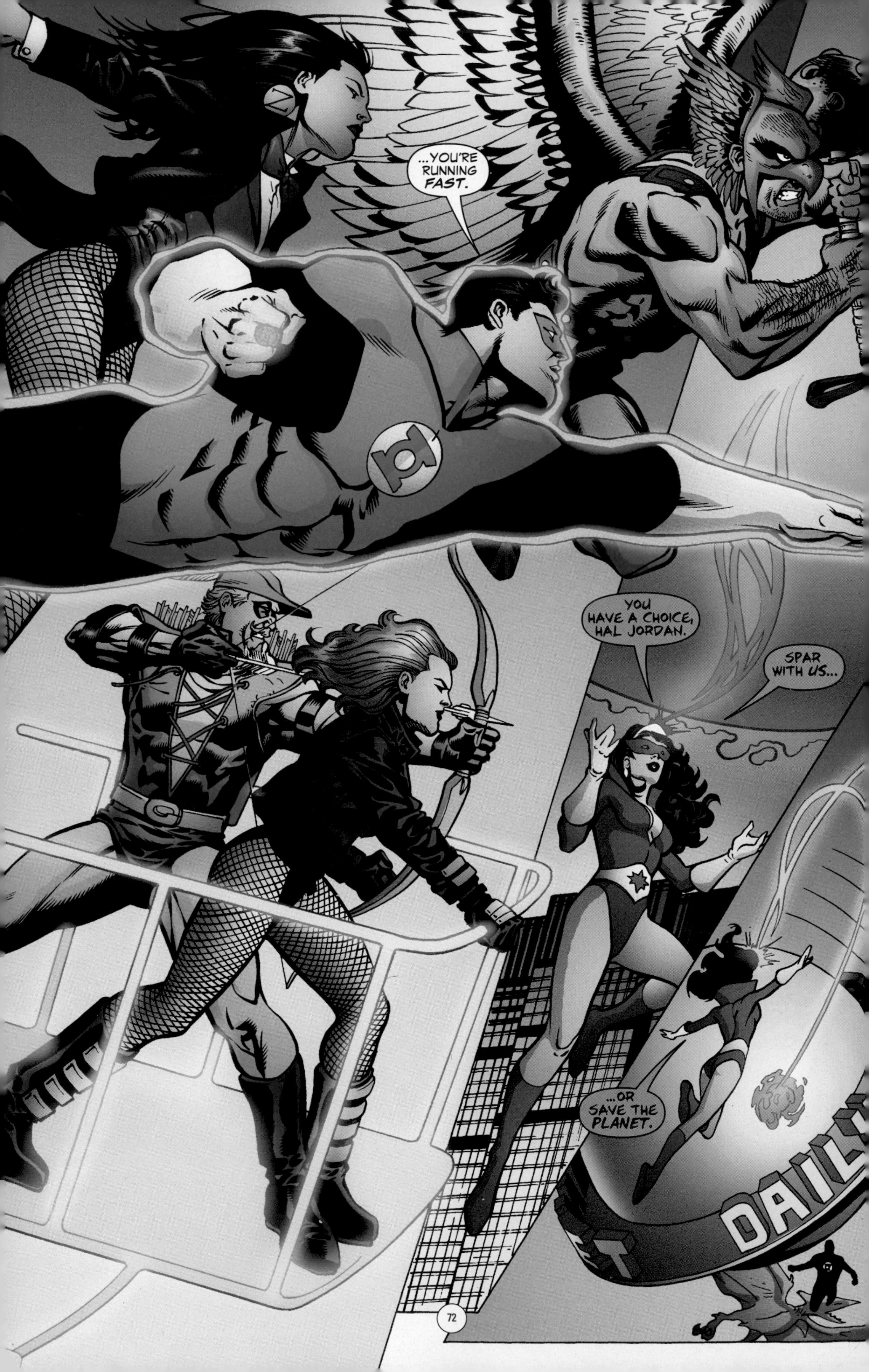
...YOU'RE RUNNING FAST.
YOU HAVE A CHOICE, HAL JORDAN.
SPAR WITH US...
...OR SAVE THE PLANET.
DAIL

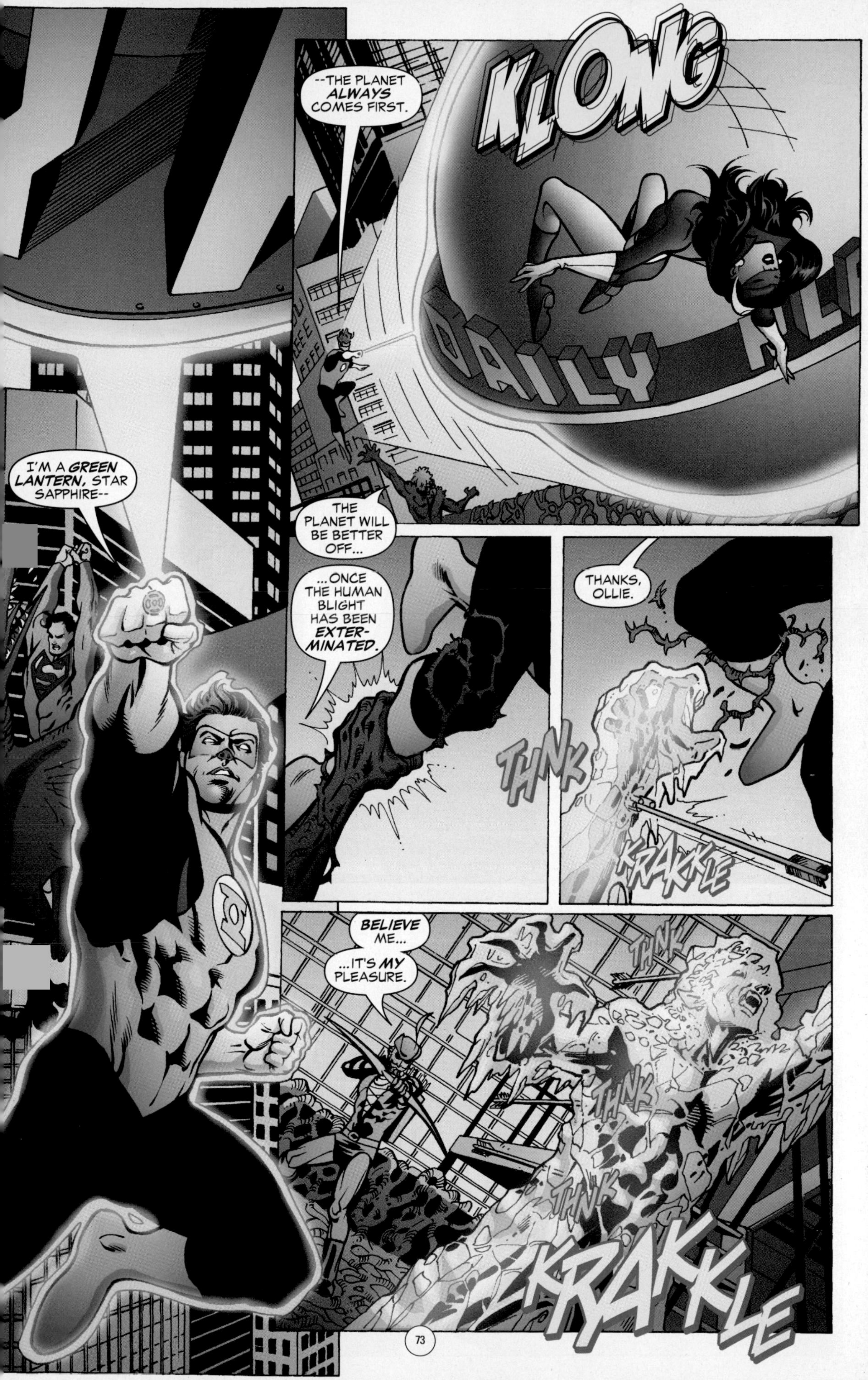
--THE PLANET ALWAYS COMES FIRST.
KLONG
DAILY
I'M A GREEN LANTERN, STAR SAPPHIRE--
THE PLANET WILL BE BETTER OFF...
...ONCE THE HUMAN BLIGHT HAS BEEN EXTER-MINATED.
THANKS, OLLIE.
THNK
KRAKKLE
BELIEVE ME...
...IT'S MY PLEASURE.
THNK
THNK
THNK
KRAKKLE

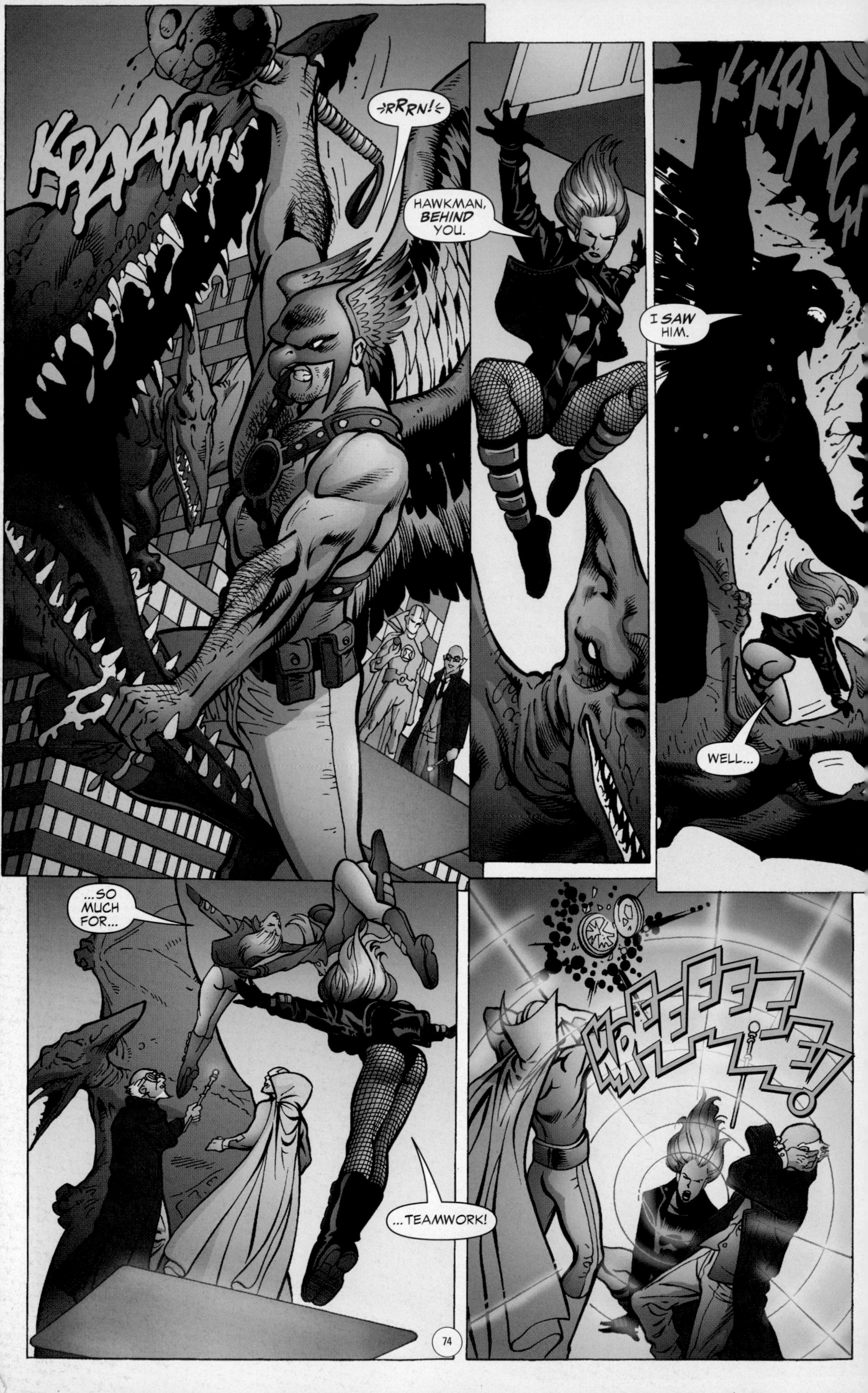
KRAANN
RRRN!
HAWKMAN, BEHIND YOU.
K'KRA
I SAW HIM.
WELL...
...SO MUCH FOR...
...TEAMWORK!
KREEEEEE!

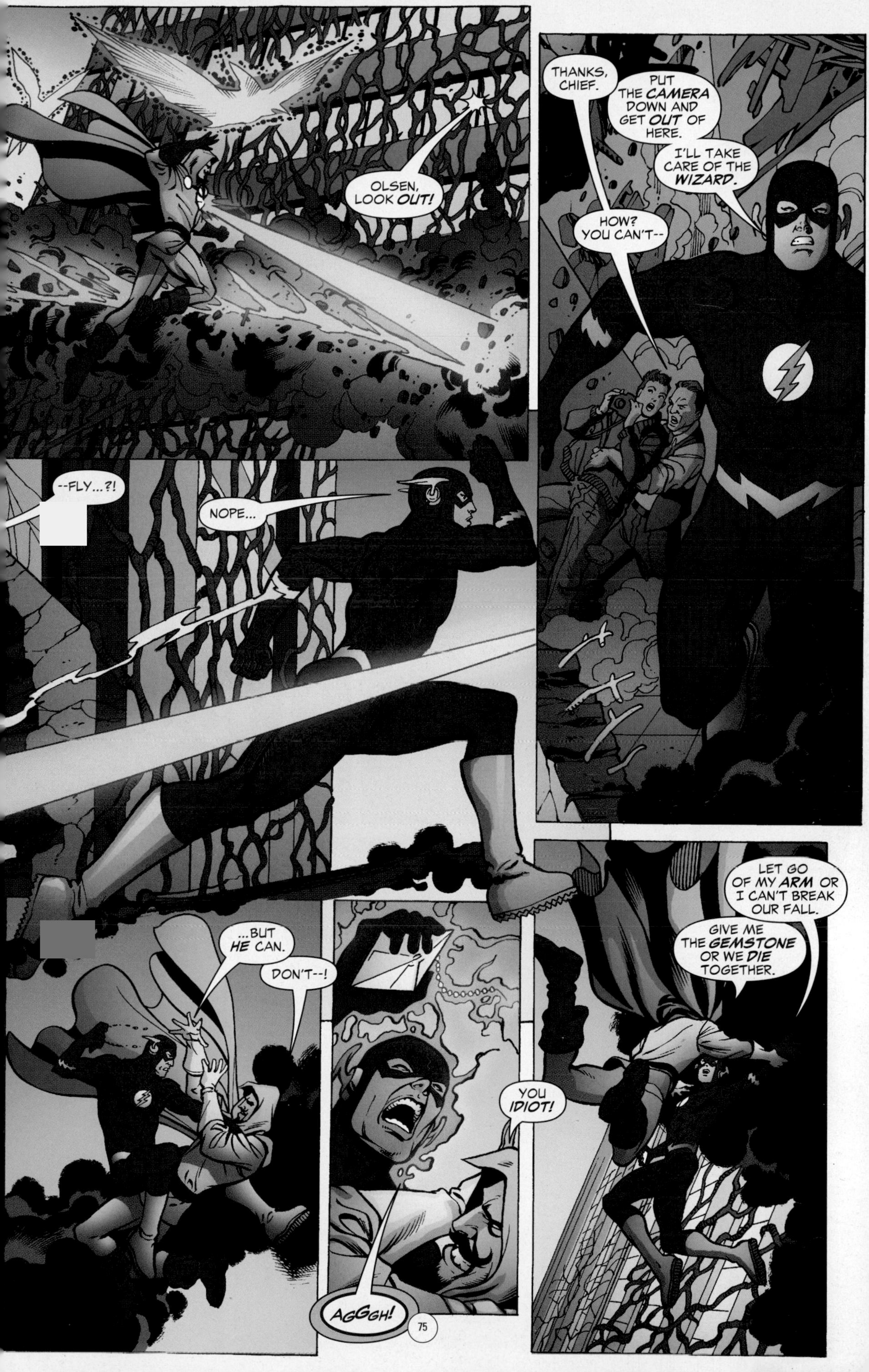

OLSEN, LOOK OUT!
THANKS, CHIEF.
PUT THE CAMERA DOWN AND GET OUT OF HERE.
I'LL TAKE CARE OF THE WIZARD.
HOW? YOU CAN'T--
--FLY...?!
NOPE...
...BUT HE CAN.
DON'T--!
YOU IDIOT!
AGGGH!
LET GO OF MY ARM OR I CAN'T BREAK OUR FALL.
GIVE ME THE GEMSTONE OR WE DIE TOGETHER.

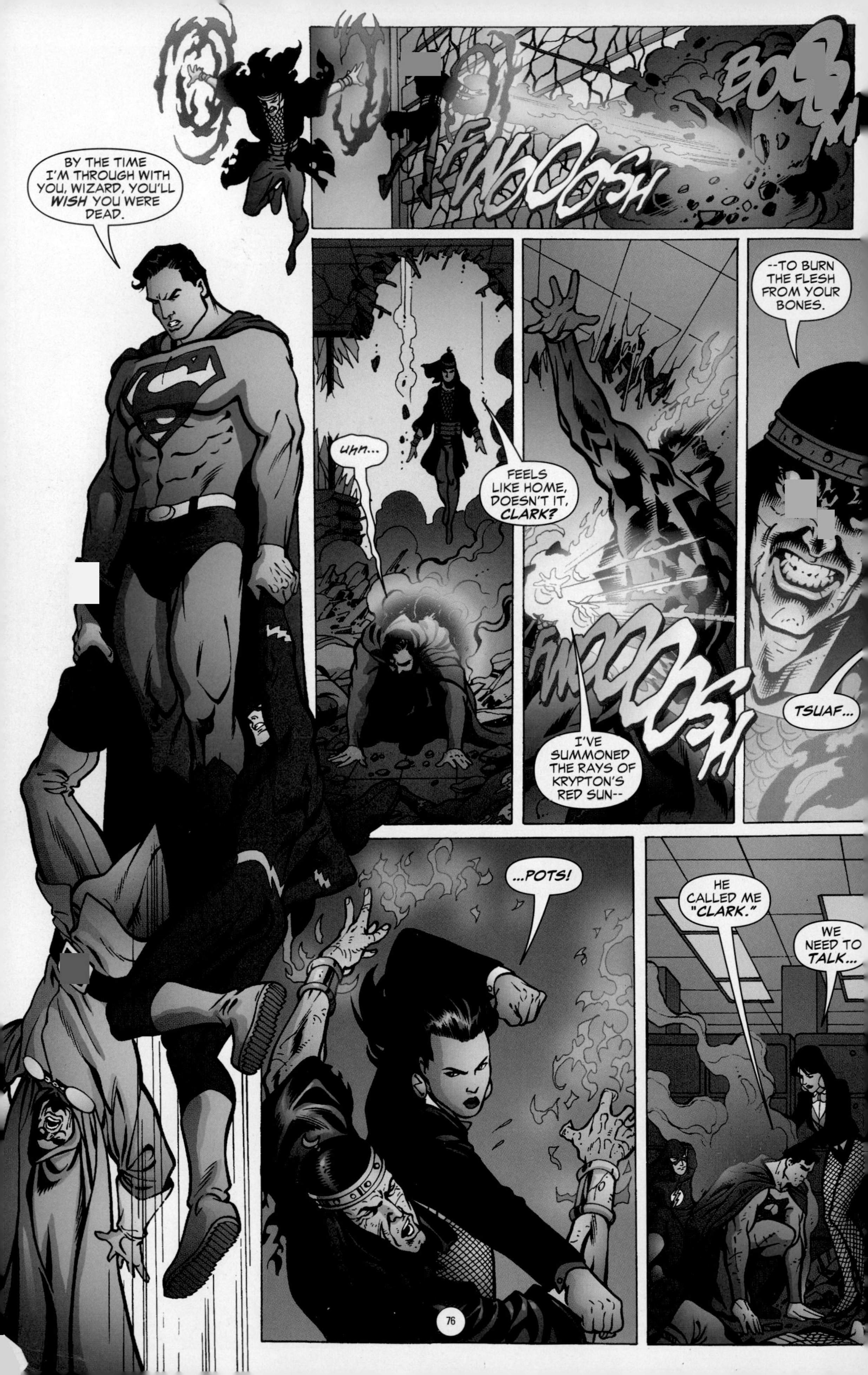
BY THE TIME I'M THROUGH WITH YOU, WIZARD, YOU'LL *WISH* YOU WERE DEAD.
FWOOOSH
unn...
FEELS LIKE HOME, DOESN'T IT, *CLARK?*
I'VE SUMMONED THE RAYS OF KRYPTON'S RED SUN--
FWOOOOOSH
--TO BURN THE FLESH FROM YOUR BONES.
TSUAF...
...POTS!
HE CALLED ME *"CLARK."*
WE NEED TO *TALK...*

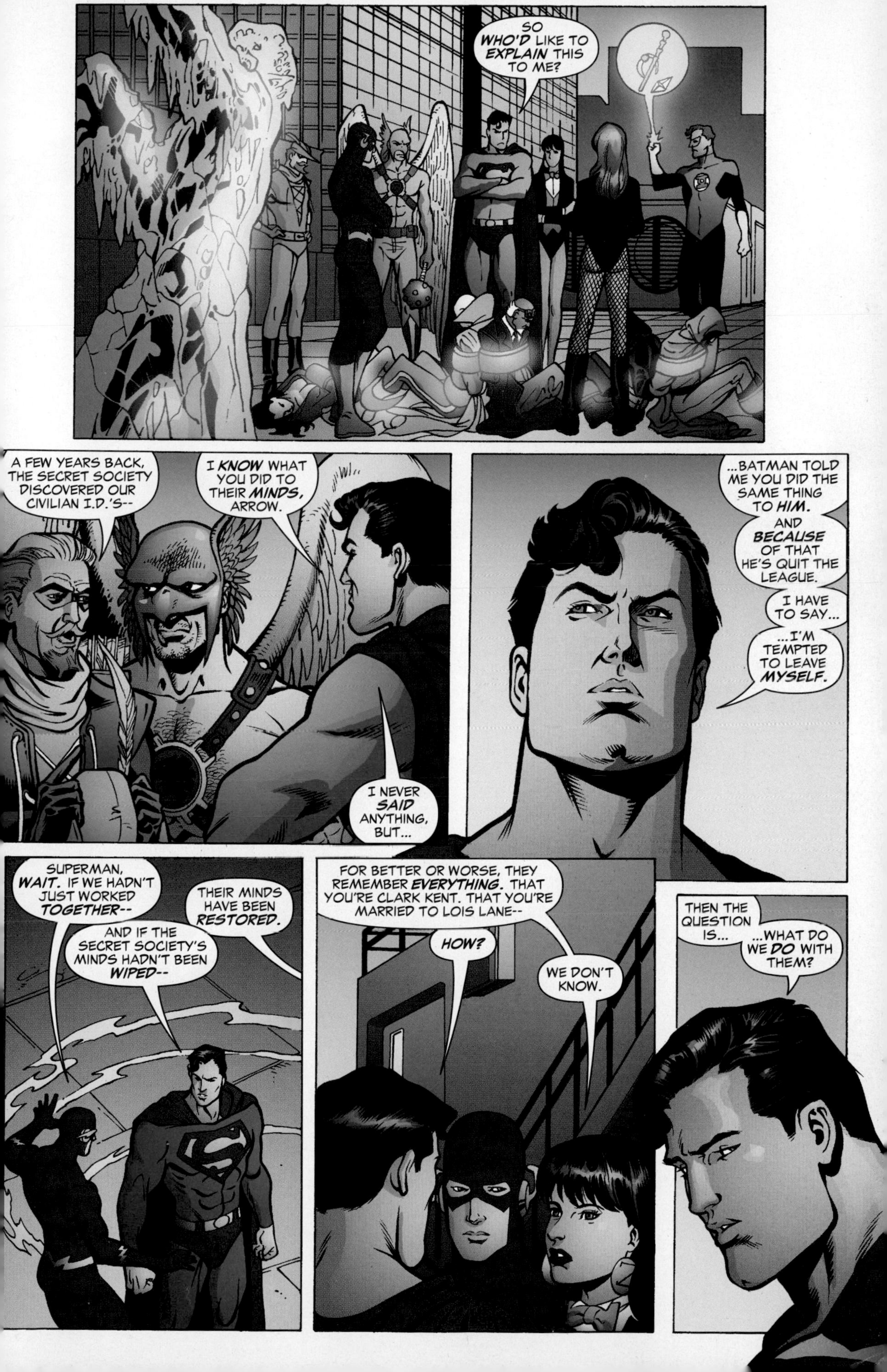
SO WHO'D LIKE TO EXPLAIN THIS TO ME?
A FEW YEARS BACK, THE SECRET SOCIETY DISCOVERED OUR CIVILIAN I.D.'S--
I KNOW WHAT YOU DID TO THEIR MINDS, ARROW.
I NEVER SAID ANYTHING, BUT...
...BATMAN TOLD ME YOU DID THE SAME THING TO HIM.
AND BECAUSE OF THAT HE'S QUIT THE LEAGUE.
I HAVE TO SAY...
...I'M TEMPTED TO LEAVE MYSELF.
SUPERMAN, WAIT. IF WE HADN'T JUST WORKED TOGETHER--
AND IF THE SECRET SOCIETY'S MINDS HADN'T BEEN WIPED--
THEIR MINDS HAVE BEEN RESTORED.
FOR BETTER OR WORSE, THEY REMEMBER EVERYTHING. THAT YOU'RE CLARK KENT. THAT YOU'RE MARRIED TO LOIS LANE--
HOW?
WE DON'T KNOW.
THEN THE QUESTION IS...
...WHAT DO WE DO WITH THEM?

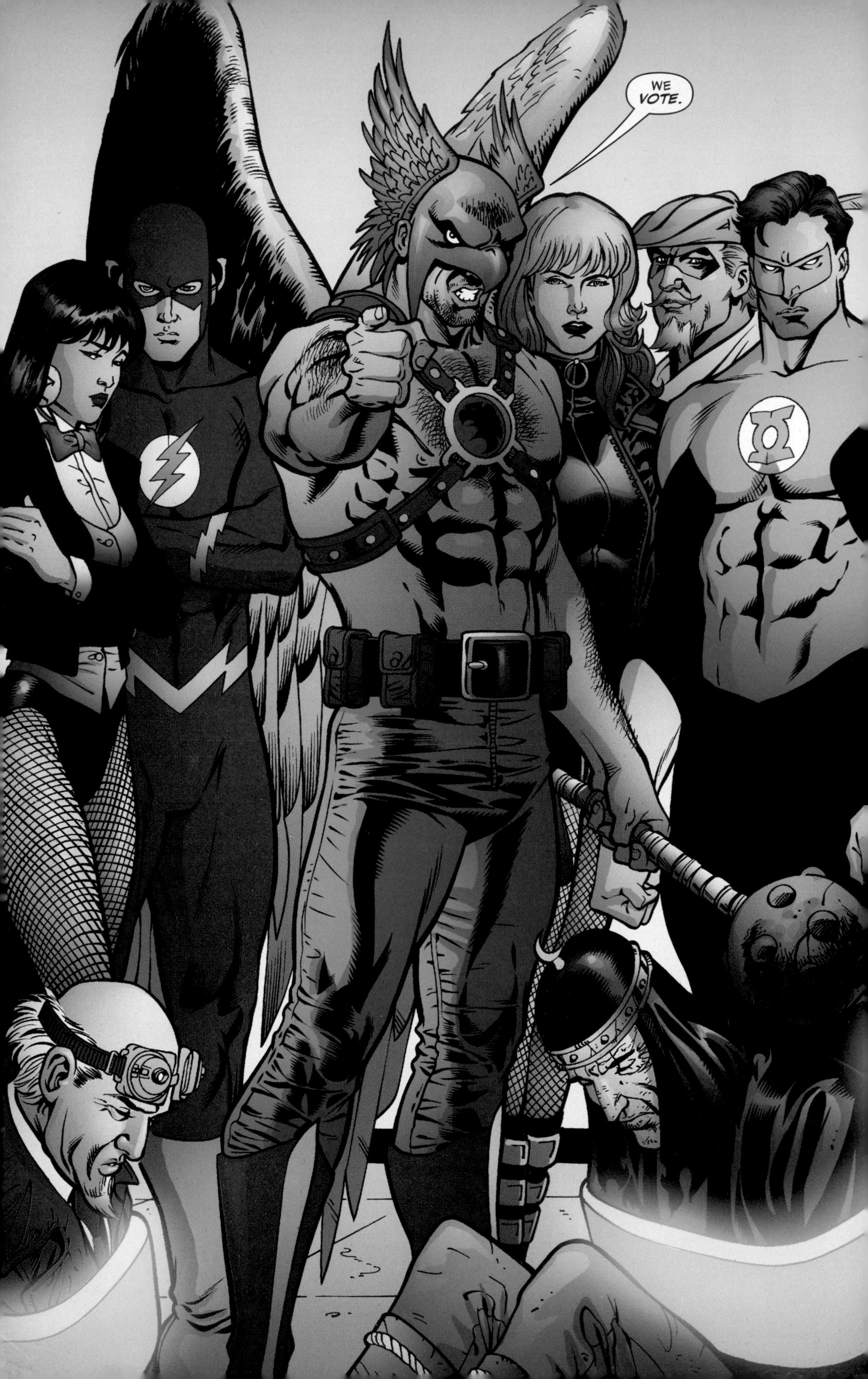
WE VOTE.

JLA #118
by Rags Morales & Mark Farmer

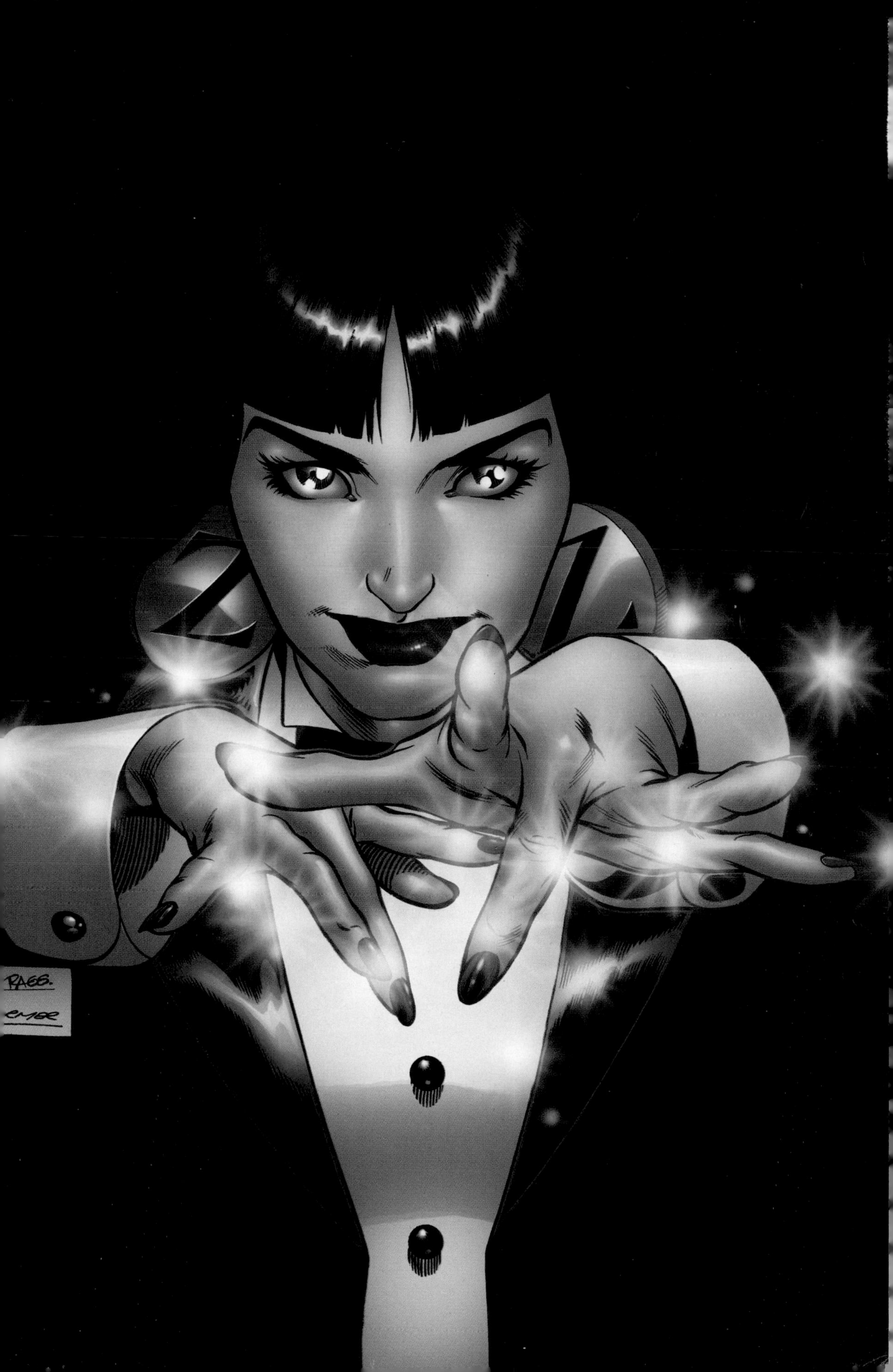
RAGS.

JLA

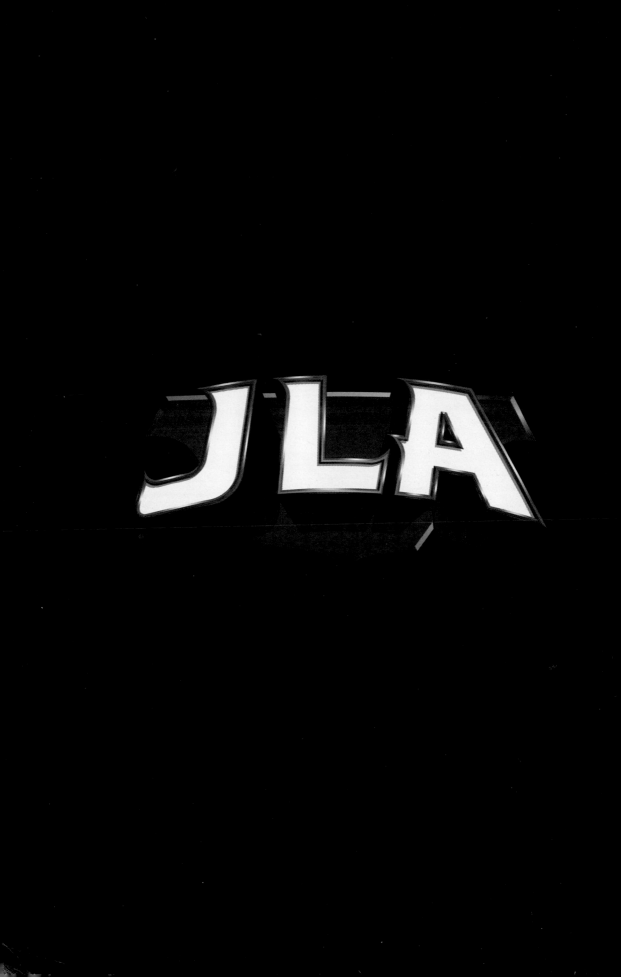

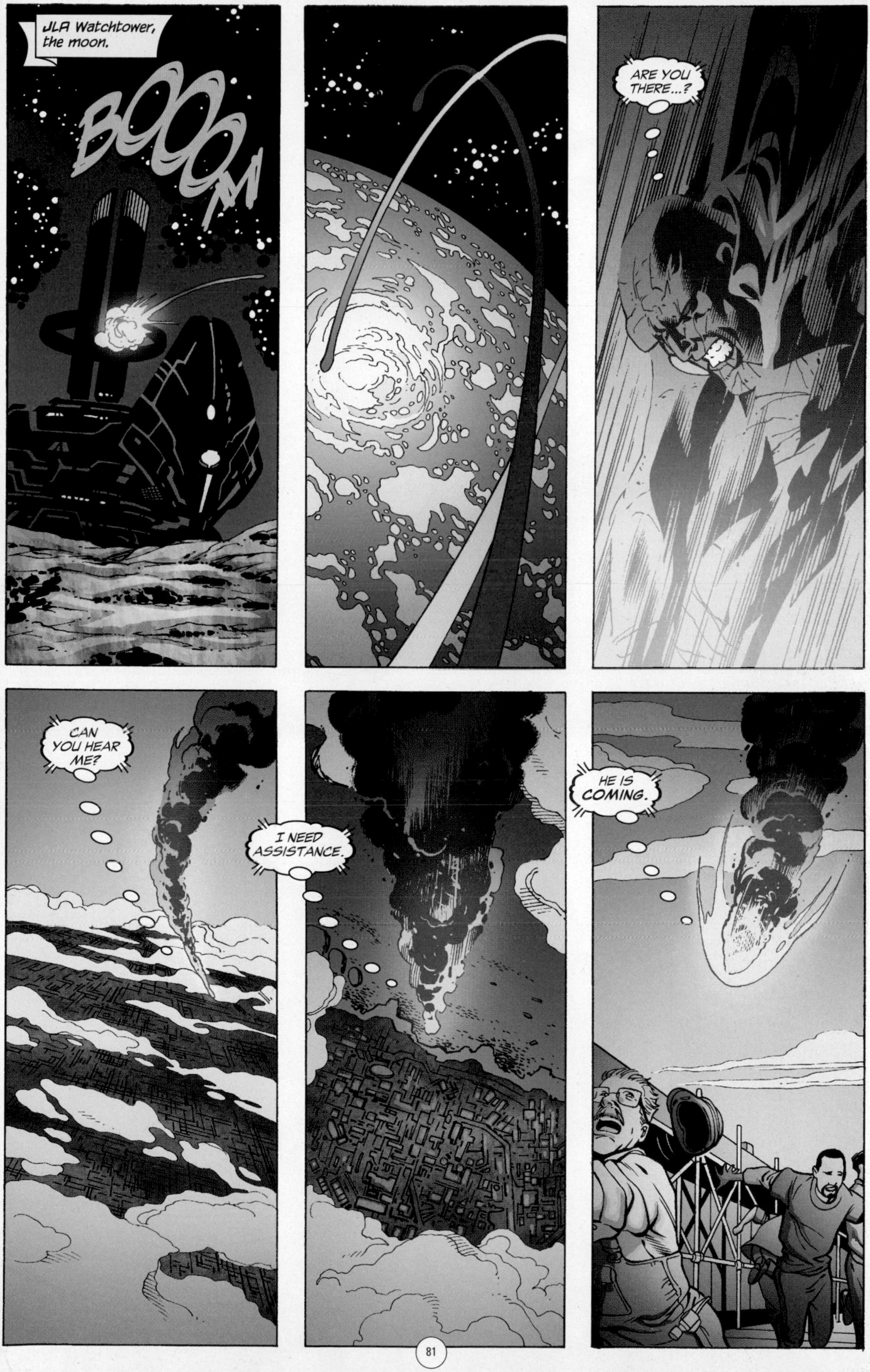
JLA Watchtower, the moon.
BOOOM
ARE YOU THERE...?
CAN YOU HEAR ME?
I NEED ASSISTANCE.
HE IS COMING.

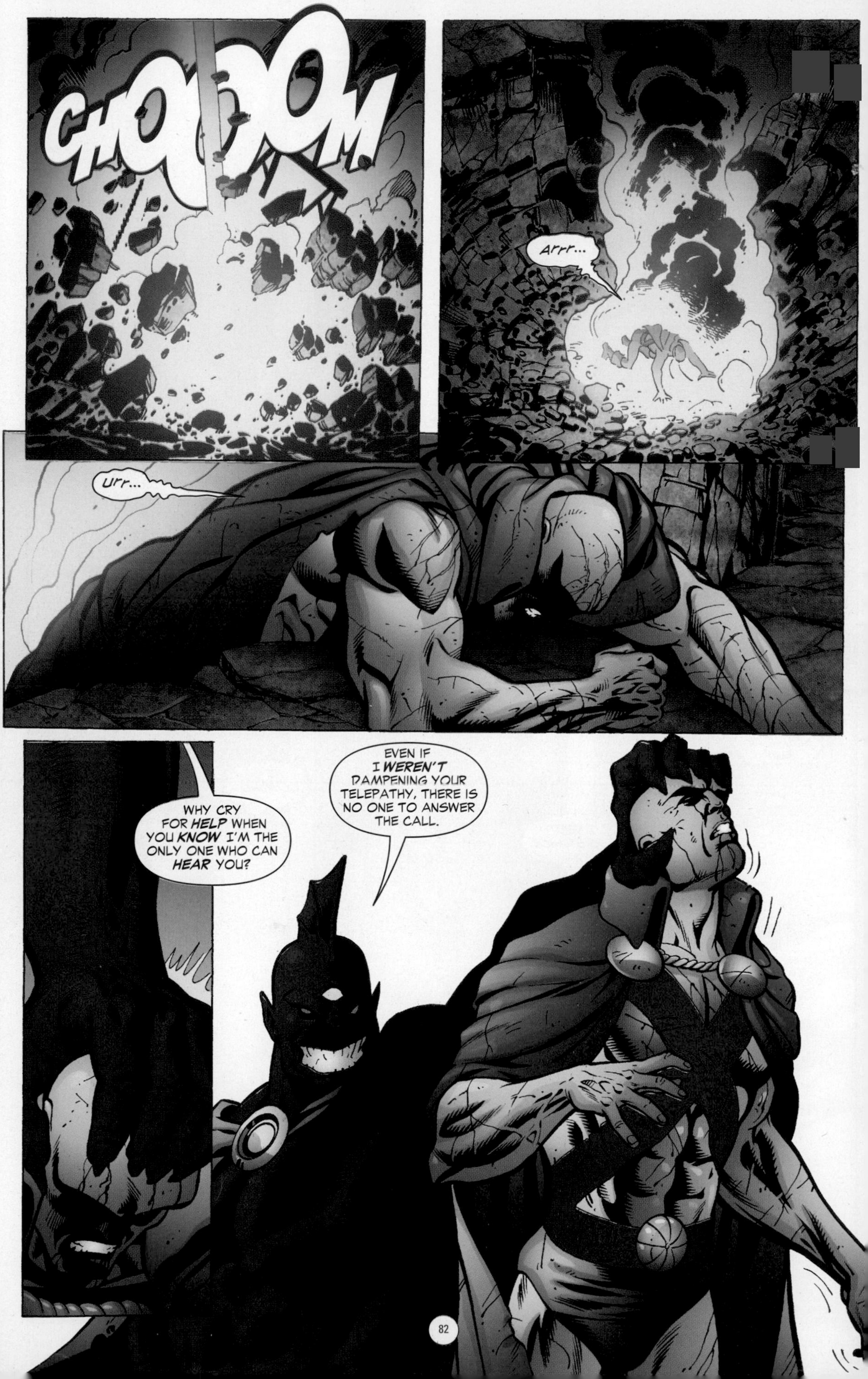
CHOOOM
Arrr...
urr...
WHY CRY FOR HELP WHEN YOU KNOW I'M THE ONLY ONE WHO CAN HEAR YOU?
EVEN IF I WEREN'T DAMPENING YOUR TELEPATHY, THERE IS NO ONE TO ANSWER THE CALL.

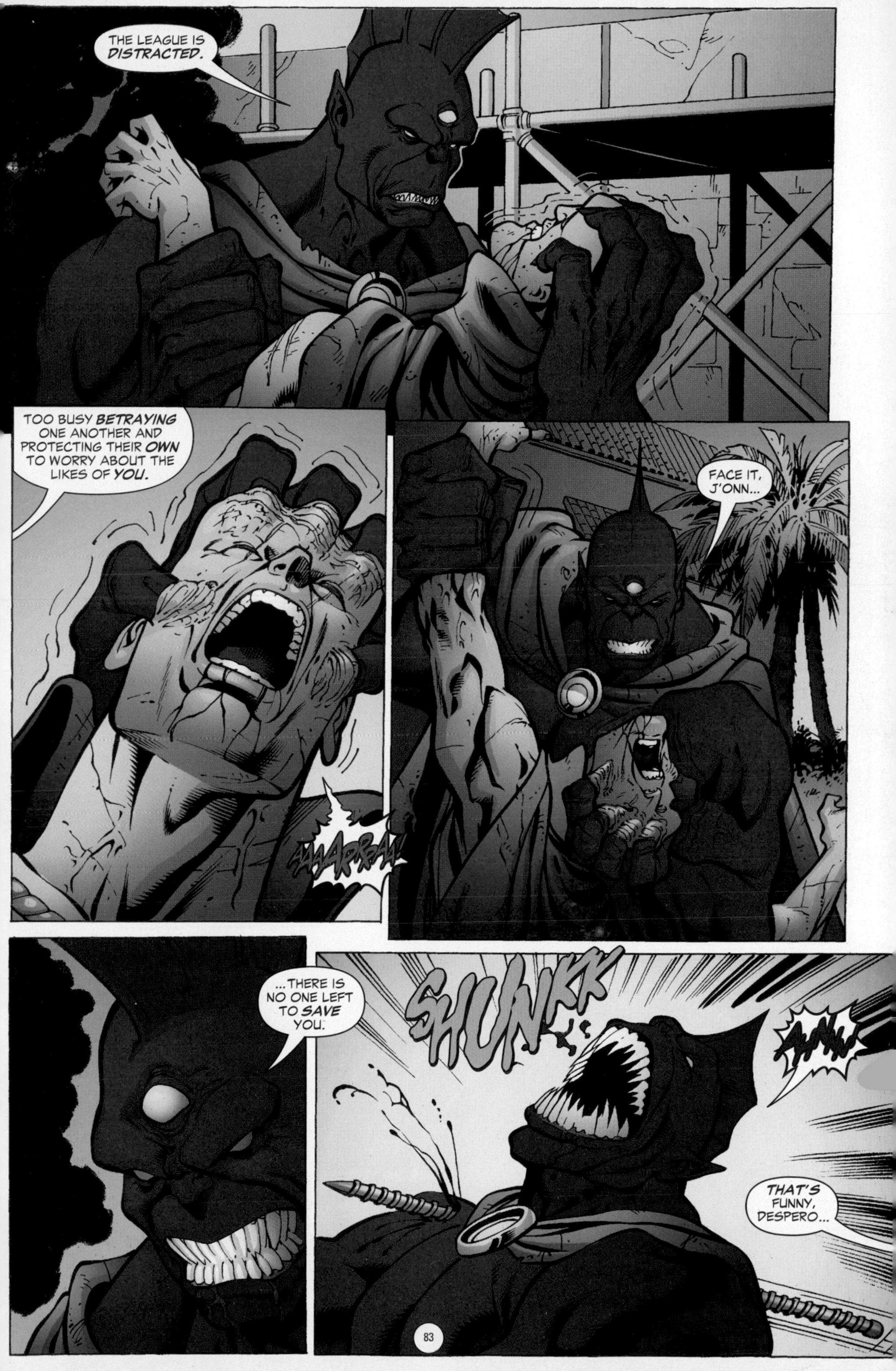
THE LEAGUE IS *DISTRACTED.*
TOO BUSY *BETRAYING* ONE ANOTHER AND PROTECTING THEIR *OWN* TO WORRY ABOUT THE LIKES OF *YOU.*
AAAARRRAA!
FACE IT, J'ONN...
...THERE IS NO ONE LEFT TO *SAVE* YOU.
SHUNKK
AWW
THAT'S FUNNY, DESPERO...

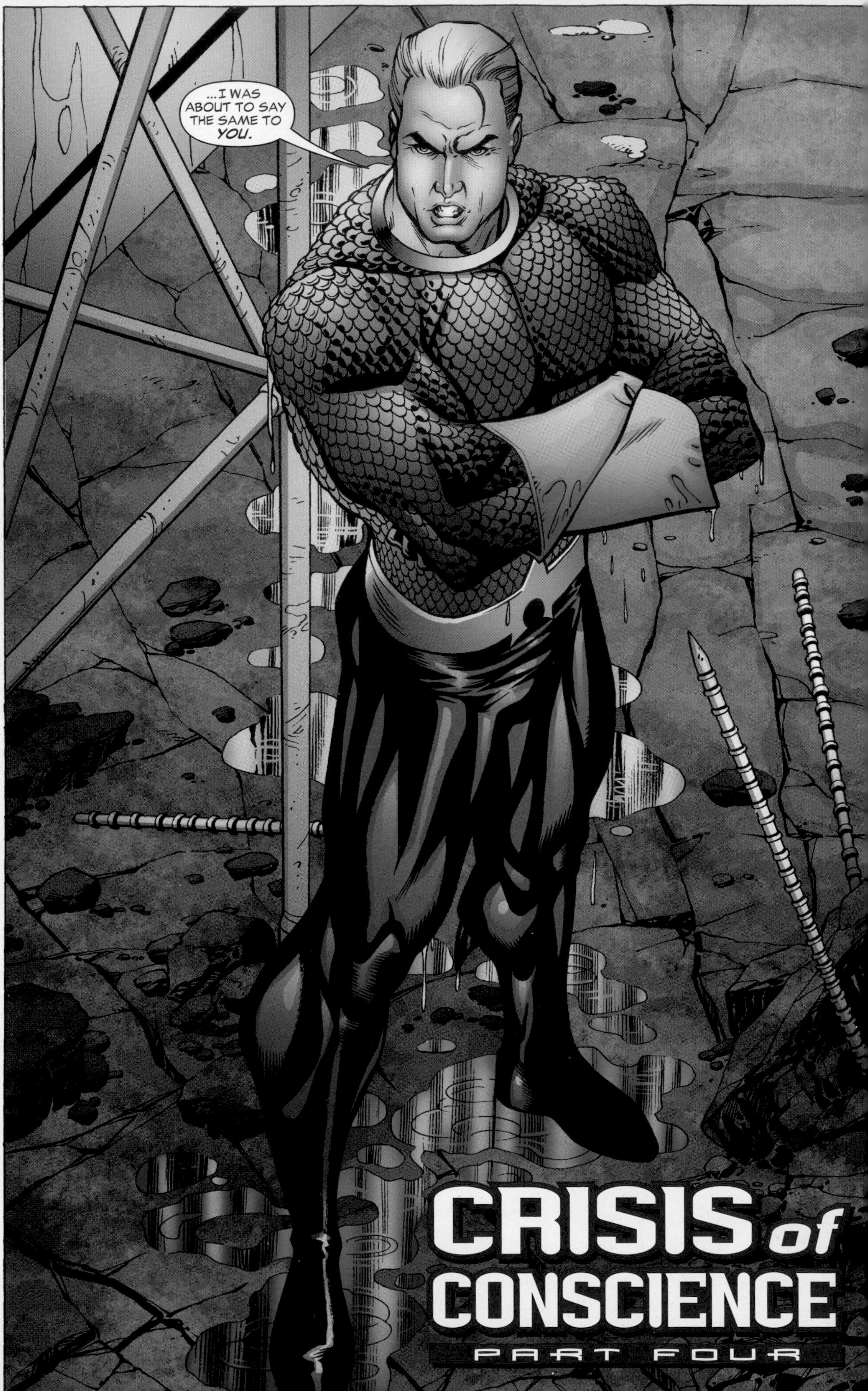
...I WAS ABOUT TO SAY THE SAME TO YOU.
CRISIS of CONSCIENCE
PART FOUR

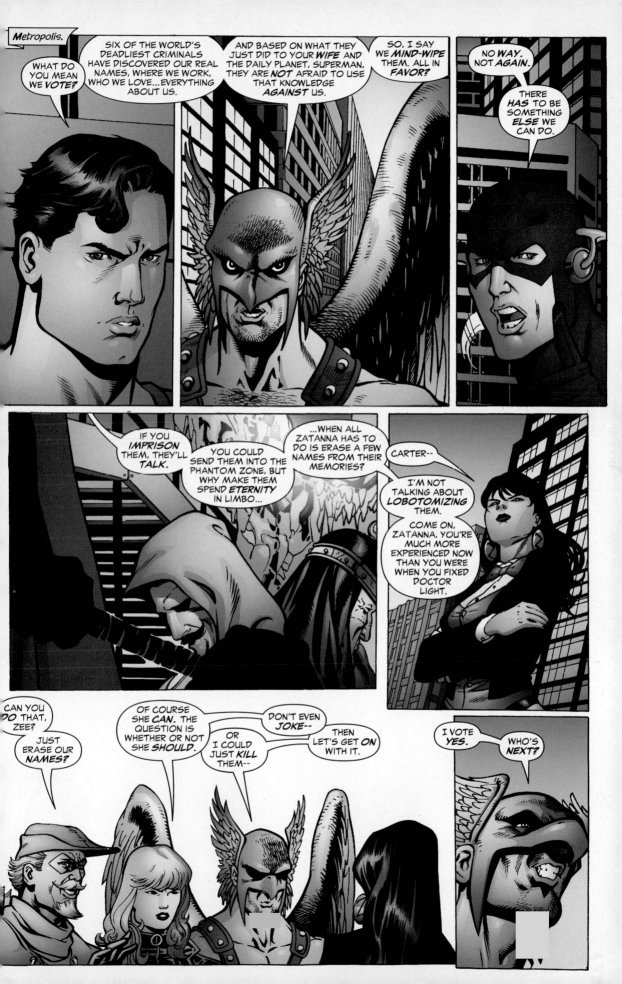

Metropolis.

WHAT DO YOU MEAN WE *VOTE*?

SIX OF THE WORLD'S DEADLIEST CRIMINALS HAVE DISCOVERED OUR REAL NAMES, WHERE WE WORK, WHO WE LOVE...EVERYTHING ABOUT US.

AND BASED ON WHAT THEY JUST DID TO YOUR *WIFE* AND THE DAILY PLANET, SUPERMAN, THEY ARE *NOT* AFRAID TO USE THAT KNOWLEDGE *AGAINST* US.

SO, I SAY WE *MIND-WIPE* THEM. ALL IN *FAVOR*?

NO *WAY*. NOT *AGAIN*.

THERE *HAS* TO BE SOMETHING *ELSE* WE CAN DO.

IF YOU *IMPRISON* THEM, THEY'LL *TALK*.

YOU COULD SEND THEM INTO THE PHANTOM ZONE, BUT WHY MAKE THEM SPEND *ETERNITY* IN LIMBO...

...WHEN ALL ZATANNA HAS TO DO IS ERASE A FEW NAMES FROM THEIR MEMORIES?

CARTER--

I'M NOT TALKING ABOUT *LOBOTOMIZING* THEM. COME ON, ZATANNA, YOU'RE MUCH MORE EXPERIENCED NOW THAN YOU WERE WHEN YOU FIXED DOCTOR LIGHT.

CAN YOU *DO* THAT, ZEE? JUST ERASE OUR *NAMES*?

OF COURSE SHE *CAN*. THE QUESTION IS WHETHER OR NOT SHE *SHOULD*.

OR I COULD JUST *KILL* THEM--

DON'T EVEN *JOKE*--

THEN LET'S GET *ON* WITH IT.

I VOTE YES.

WHO'S *NEXT*?

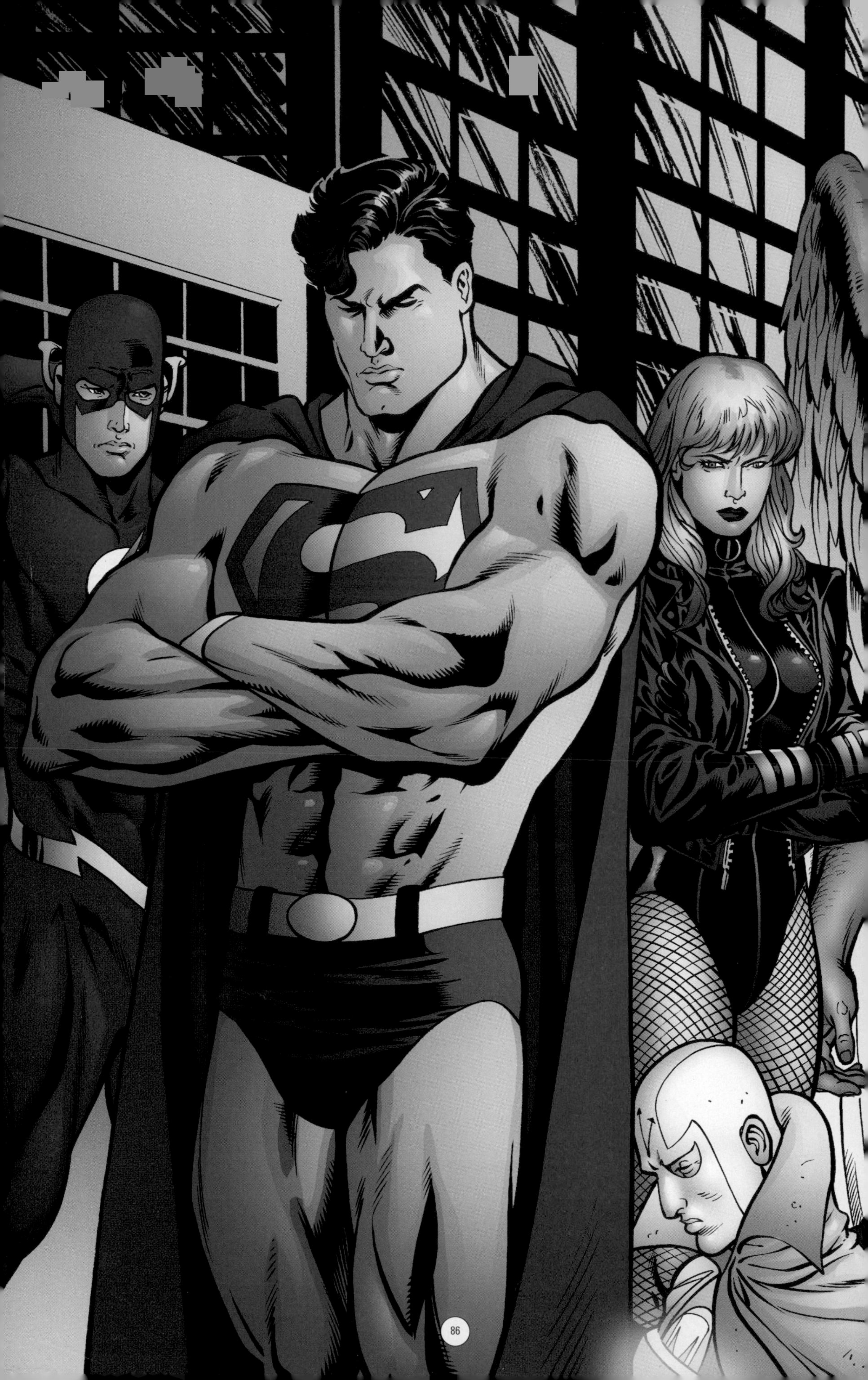

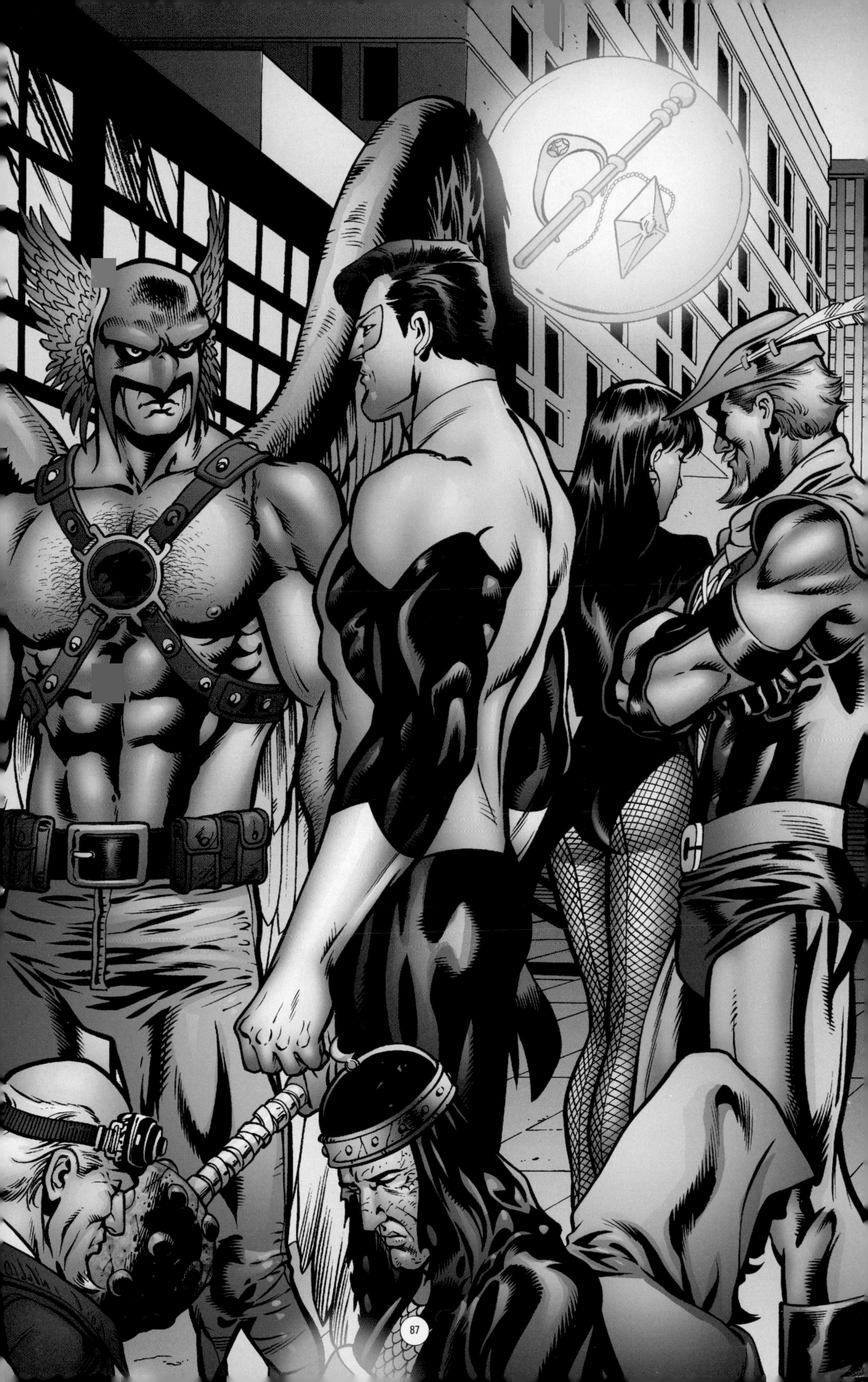

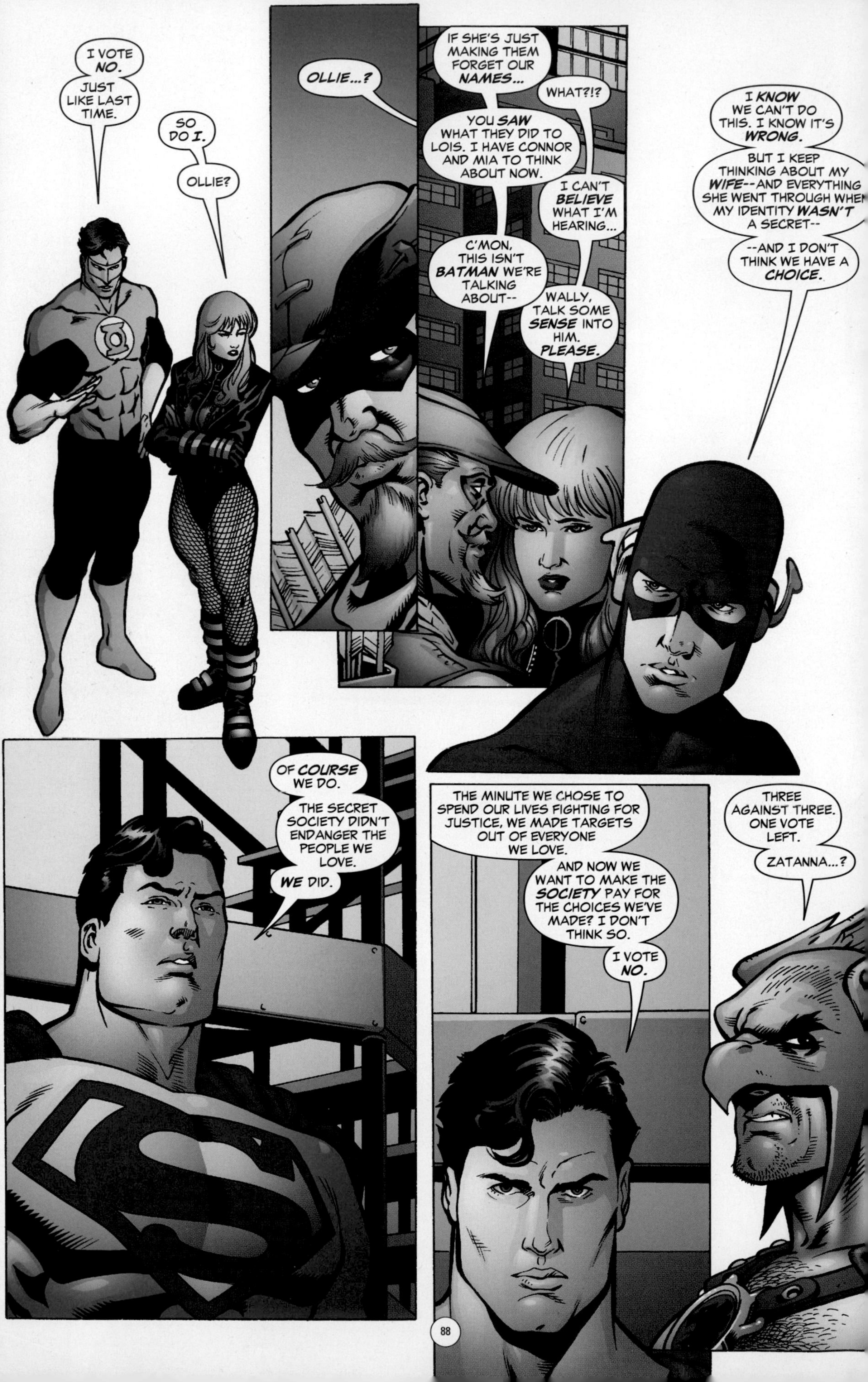

I VOTE NO. JUST LIKE LAST TIME.
SO DO I.
OLLIE?
OLLIE...?
IF SHE'S JUST MAKING THEM FORGET OUR NAMES...
WHAT?!?
YOU SAW WHAT THEY DID TO LOIS. I HAVE CONNOR AND MIA TO THINK ABOUT NOW.
I CAN'T BELIEVE WHAT I'M HEARING...
C'MON, THIS ISN'T BATMAN WE'RE TALKING ABOUT--
WALLY, TALK SOME SENSE INTO HIM. PLEASE.
I KNOW WE CAN'T DO THIS. I KNOW IT'S WRONG.
BUT I KEEP THINKING ABOUT MY WIFE--AND EVERYTHING SHE WENT THROUGH WHEN MY IDENTITY WASN'T A SECRET--
--AND I DON'T THINK WE HAVE A CHOICE.
OF COURSE WE DO.
THE SECRET SOCIETY DIDN'T ENDANGER THE PEOPLE WE LOVE.
WE DID.
THE MINUTE WE CHOSE TO SPEND OUR LIVES FIGHTING FOR JUSTICE, WE MADE TARGETS OUT OF EVERYONE WE LOVE.
AND NOW WE WANT TO MAKE THE SOCIETY PAY FOR THE CHOICES WE'VE MADE? I DON'T THINK SO.
I VOTE NO.
THREE AGAINST THREE. ONE VOTE LEFT.
ZATANNA...?

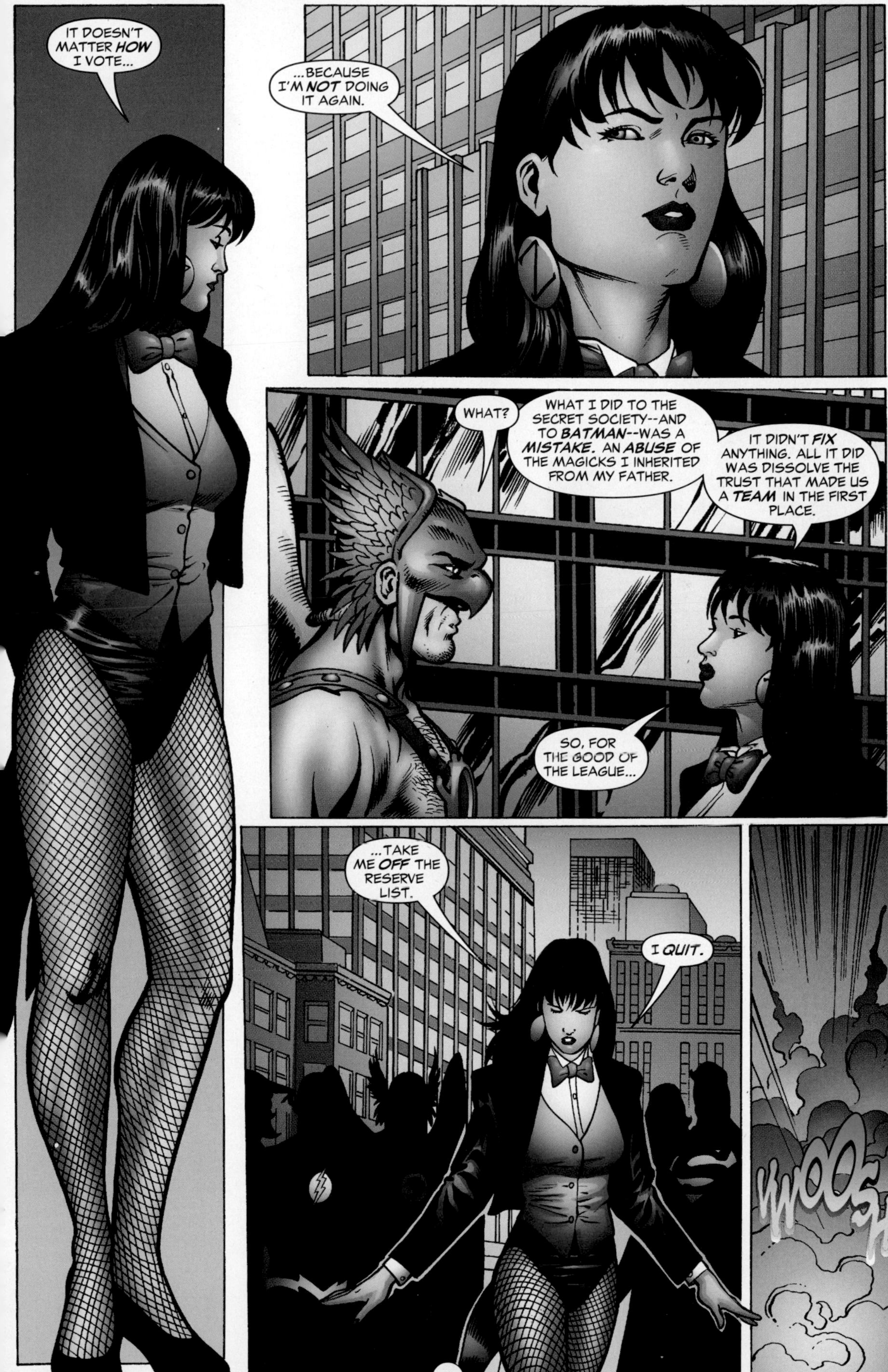
IT DOESN'T MATTER HOW I VOTE...
...BECAUSE I'M NOT DOING IT AGAIN.
WHAT?
WHAT I DID TO THE SECRET SOCIETY--AND TO BATMAN--WAS A MISTAKE. AN ABUSE OF THE MAGICKS I INHERITED FROM MY FATHER.
IT DIDN'T FIX ANYTHING. ALL IT DID WAS DISSOLVE THE TRUST THAT MADE US A TEAM IN THE FIRST PLACE.
SO, FOR THE GOOD OF THE LEAGUE...
...TAKE ME OFF THE RESERVE LIST.
I QUIT.
WOOSH

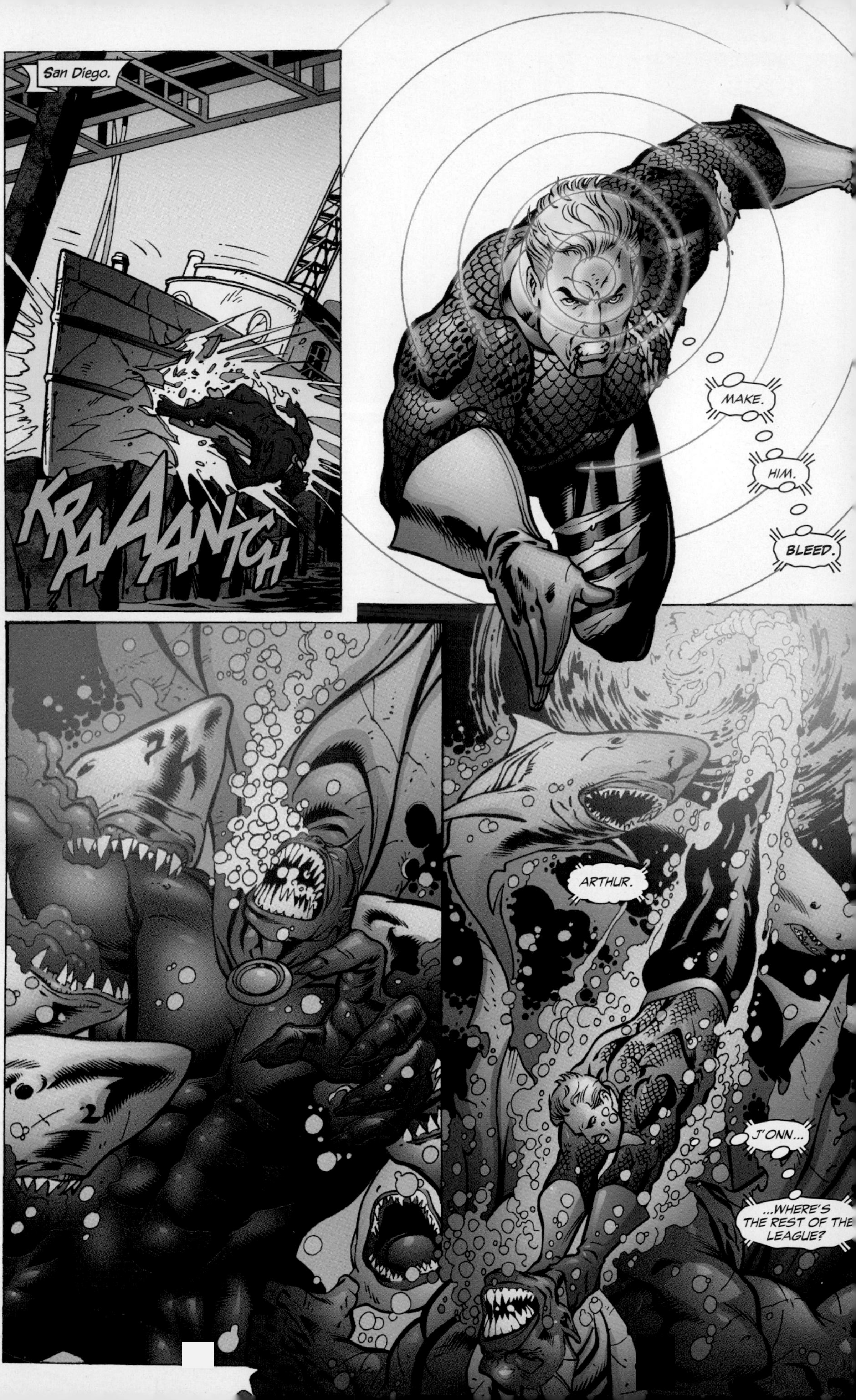
San Diego.
KRAAANTCH
MAKE.
HIM.
BLEED.
ARTHUR.
J'ONN...
...WHERE'S THE REST OF THE LEAGUE?

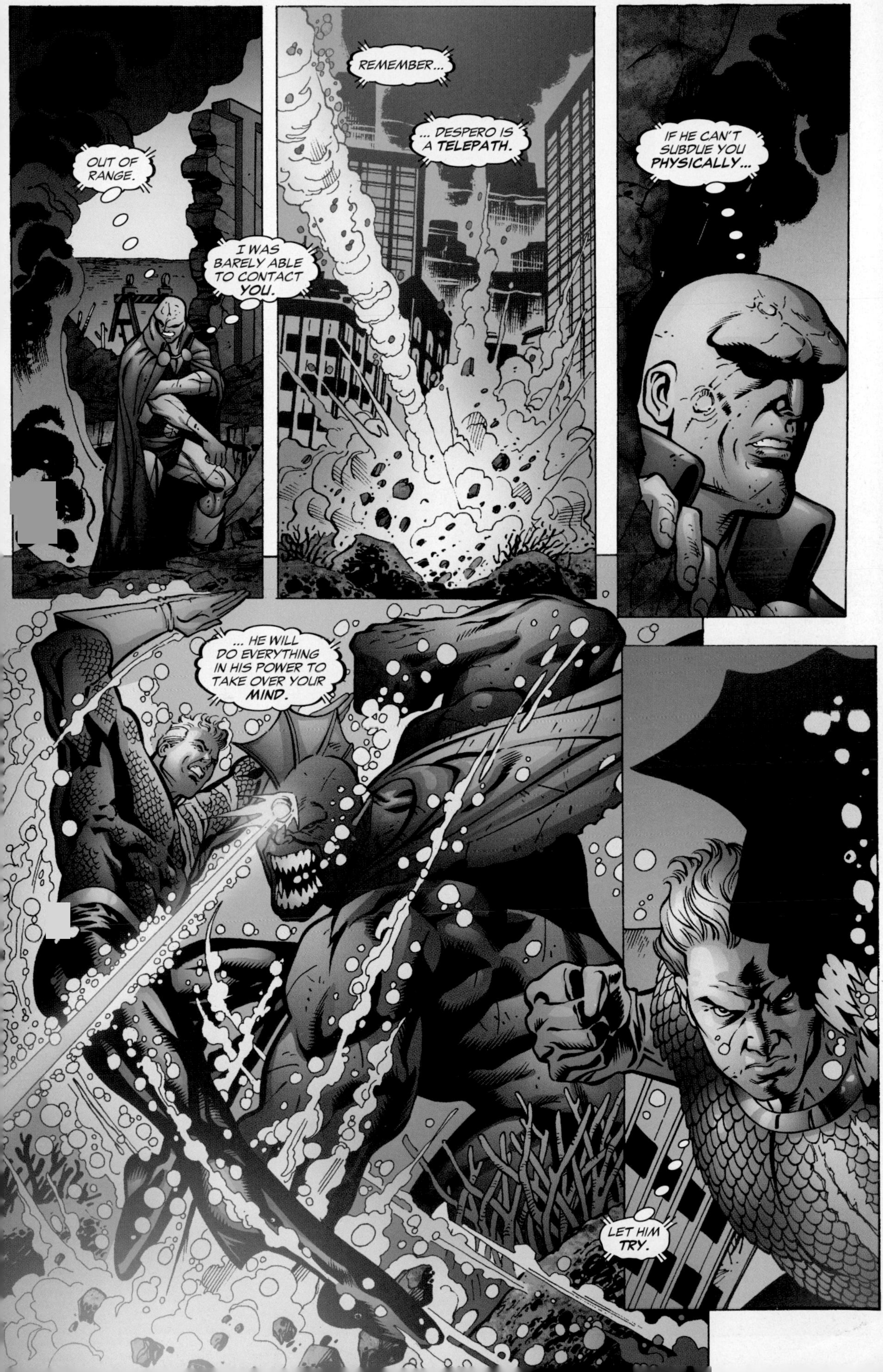
OUT OF RANGE.
I WAS BARELY ABLE TO CONTACT YOU.
REMEMBER...
... DESPERO IS A TELEPATH.
IF HE CAN'T SUBDUE YOU PHYSICALLY...
... HE WILL DO EVERYTHING IN HIS POWER TO TAKE OVER YOUR MIND.
LET HIM TRY.

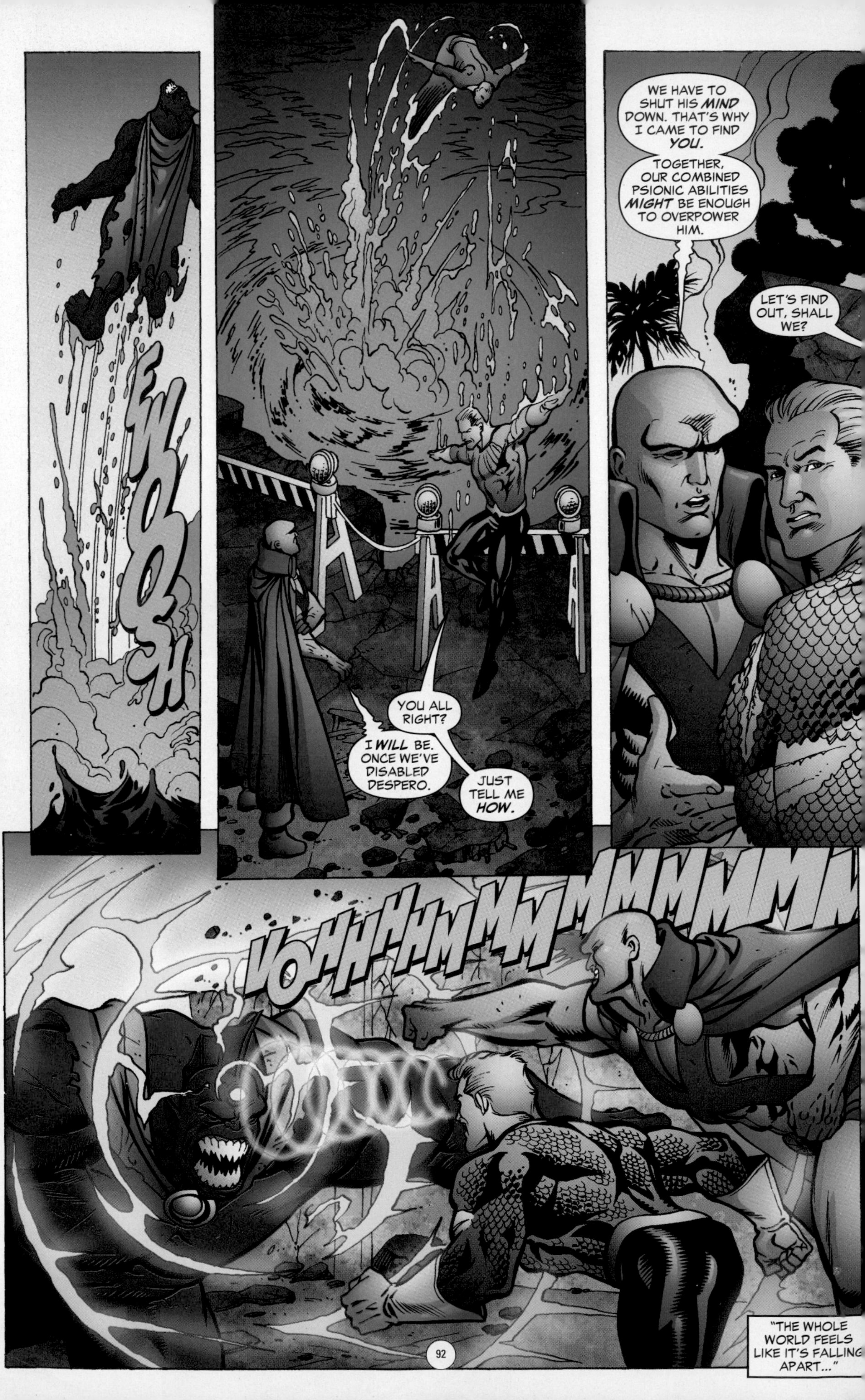

EWOOSH
YOU ALL RIGHT?
I WILL BE. ONCE WE'VE DISABLED DESPERO.
JUST TELL ME HOW.
WE HAVE TO SHUT HIS MIND DOWN. THAT'S WHY I CAME TO FIND YOU.
TOGETHER, OUR COMBINED PSIONIC ABILITIES MIGHT BE ENOUGH TO OVERPOWER HIM.
LET'S FIND OUT, SHALL WE?
VOHHHHMMMMMMMMMMMMM
"THE WHOLE WORLD FEELS LIKE IT'S FALLING APART..."

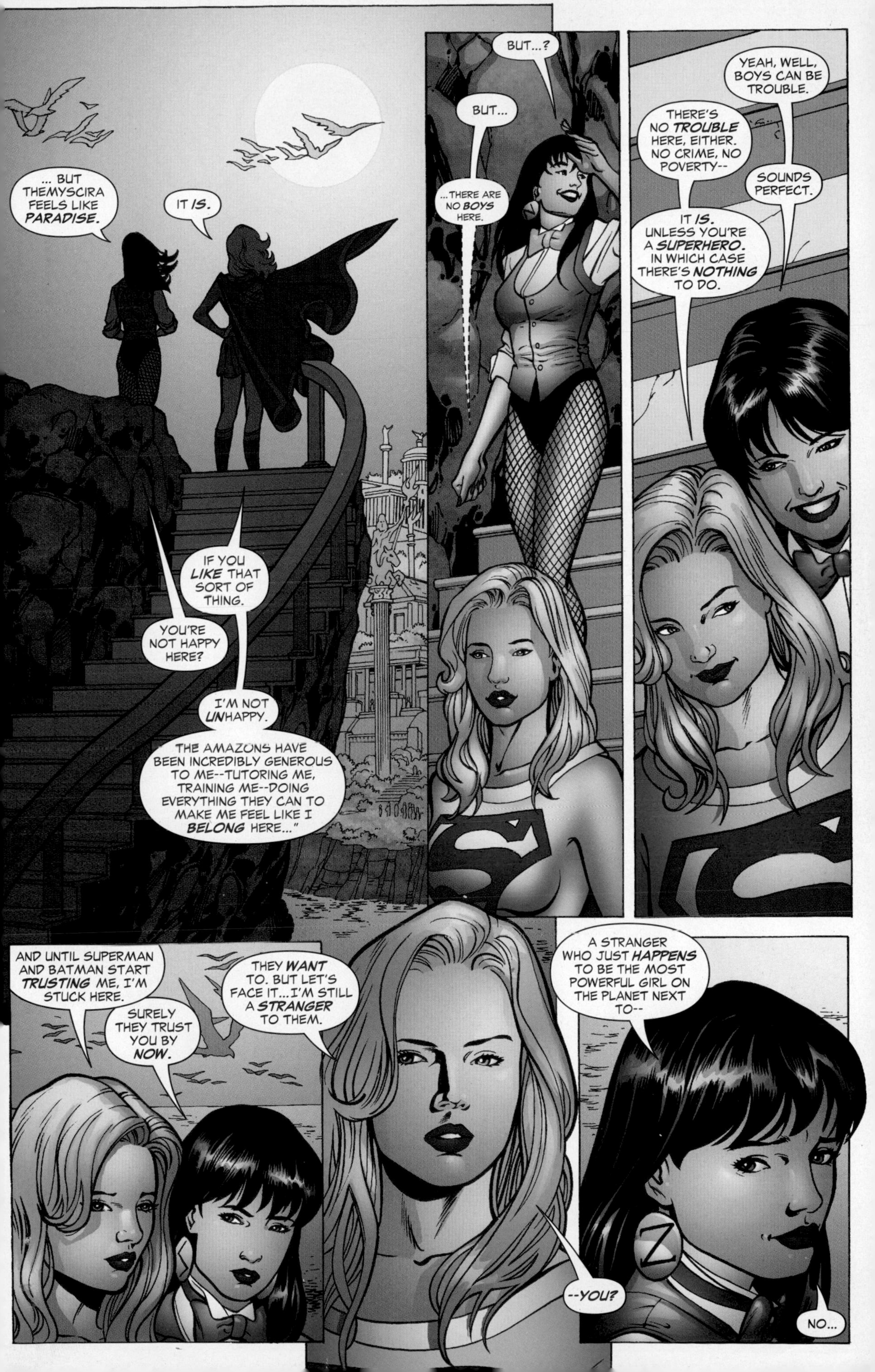
... BUT THEMYSCIRA FEELS LIKE PARADISE.
IT IS.
IF YOU LIKE THAT SORT OF THING.
YOU'RE NOT HAPPY HERE?
I'M NOT UNHAPPY.
THE AMAZONS HAVE BEEN INCREDIBLY GENEROUS TO ME--TUTORING ME, TRAINING ME--DOING EVERYTHING THEY CAN TO MAKE ME FEEL LIKE I BELONG HERE..."
BUT...
...THERE ARE NO BOYS HERE.
BUT...?
YEAH, WELL, BOYS CAN BE TROUBLE.
THERE'S NO TROUBLE HERE, EITHER. NO CRIME, NO POVERTY--
SOUNDS PERFECT.
IT IS. UNLESS YOU'RE A SUPERHERO. IN WHICH CASE THERE'S NOTHING TO DO.
AND UNTIL SUPERMAN AND BATMAN START TRUSTING ME, I'M STUCK HERE.
SURELY THEY TRUST YOU BY NOW.
THEY WANT TO. BUT LET'S FACE IT...I'M STILL A STRANGER TO THEM.
A STRANGER WHO JUST HAPPENS TO BE THE MOST POWERFUL GIRL ON THE PLANET NEXT TO--
--YOU?
NO...

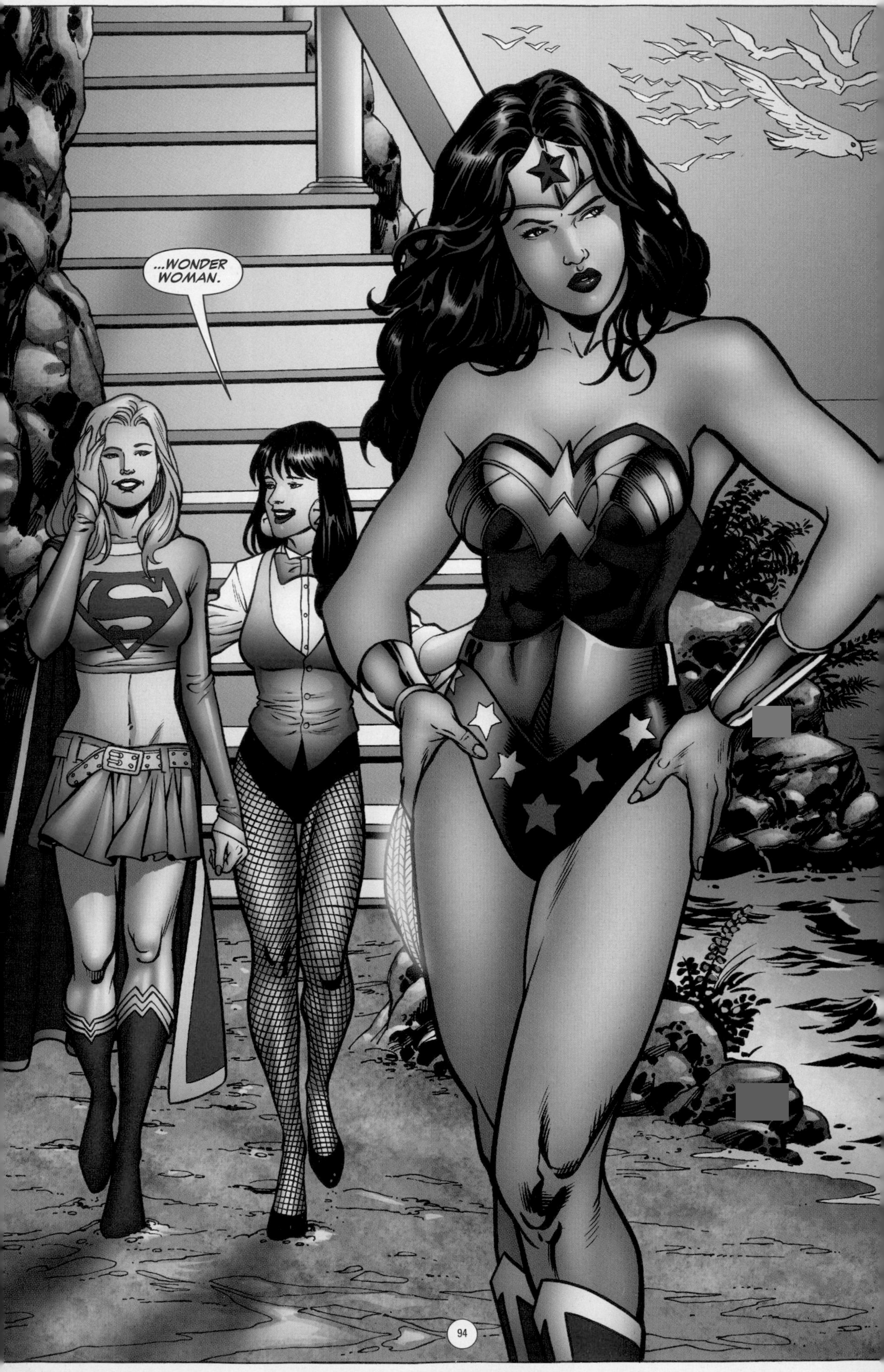
...WONDER WOMAN.

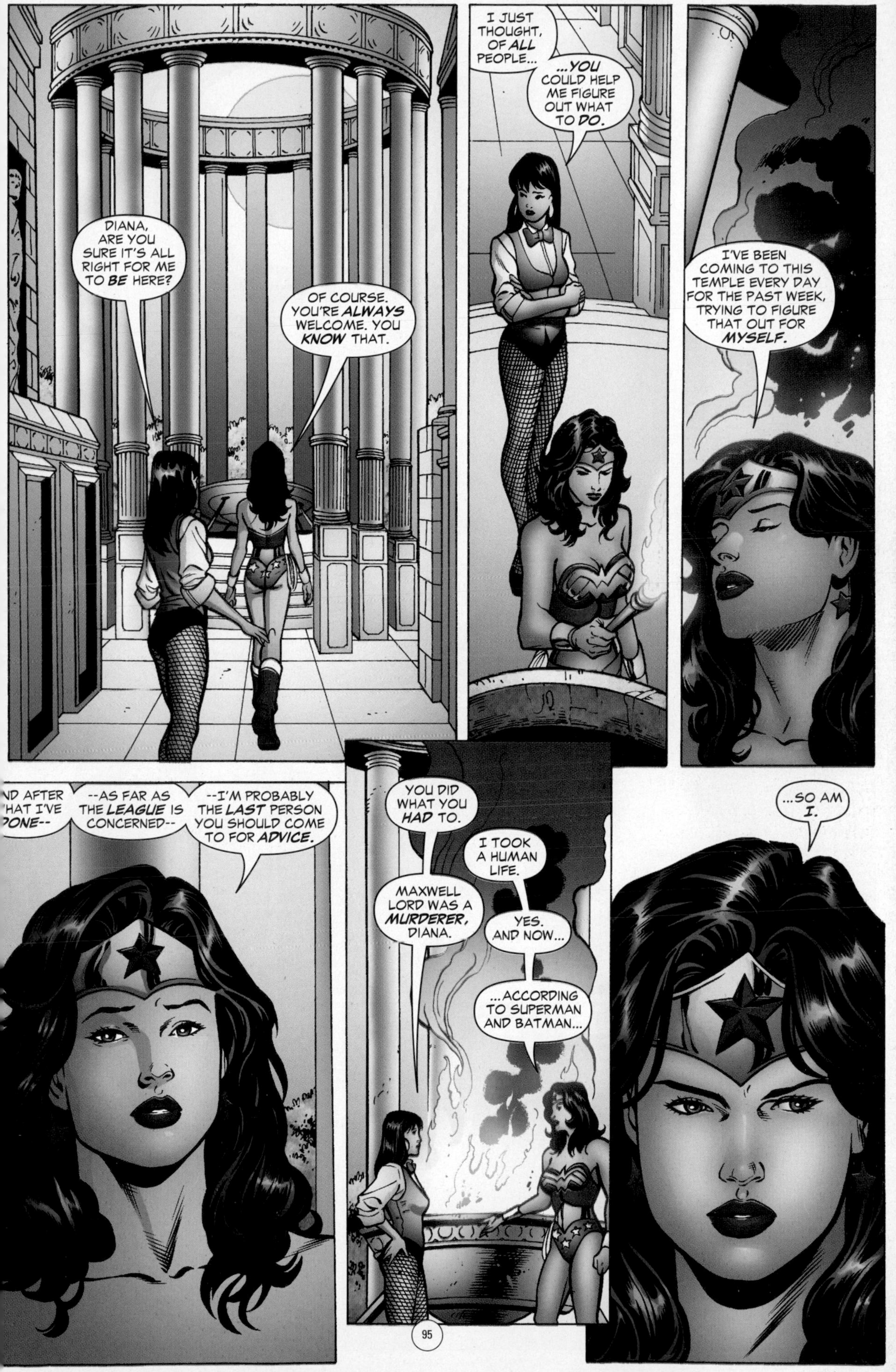

DIANA, ARE YOU SURE IT'S ALL RIGHT FOR ME TO *BE* HERE?
OF COURSE. YOU'RE *ALWAYS* WELCOME. YOU *KNOW* THAT.
I JUST THOUGHT, OF *ALL* PEOPLE...
...*YOU* COULD HELP ME FIGURE OUT WHAT TO *DO*.
I'VE BEEN COMING TO THIS TEMPLE EVERY DAY FOR THE PAST WEEK, TRYING TO FIGURE THAT OUT FOR *MYSELF*.
ND AFTER HAT I'VE *DONE*--
--AS FAR AS THE *LEAGUE* IS CONCERNED--
--I'M PROBABLY THE *LAST* PERSON YOU SHOULD COME TO FOR *ADVICE*.
YOU DID WHAT YOU *HAD* TO.
I TOOK A HUMAN LIFE.
MAXWELL LORD WAS A *MURDERER*, DIANA.
YES. AND NOW...
...ACCORDING TO SUPERMAN AND BATMAN...
...SO AM *I*.

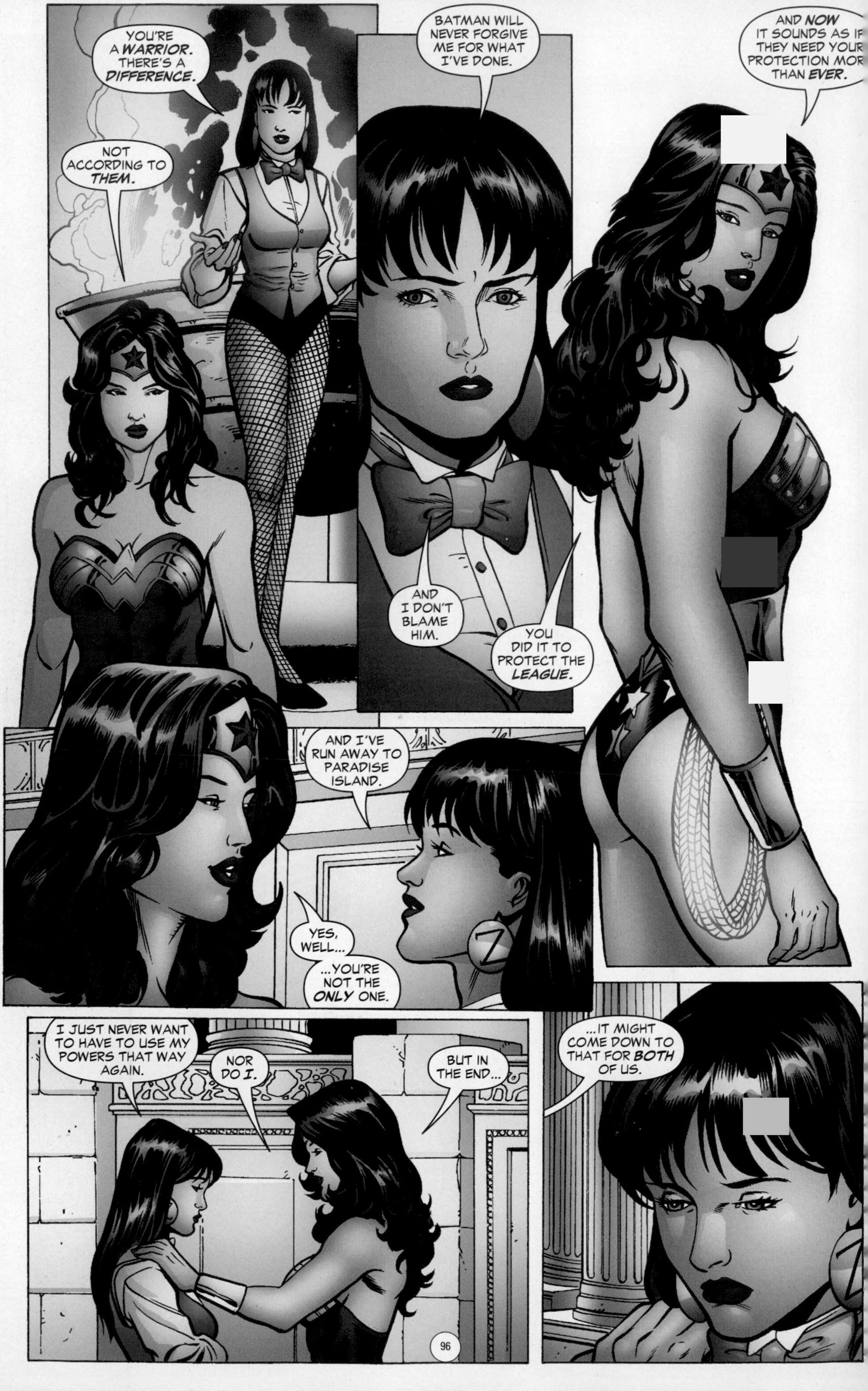

YOU'RE A WARRIOR. THERE'S A DIFFERENCE.
NOT ACCORDING TO THEM.
BATMAN WILL NEVER FORGIVE ME FOR WHAT I'VE DONE.
AND I DON'T BLAME HIM.
YOU DID IT TO PROTECT THE LEAGUE.
AND NOW IT SOUNDS AS IF THEY NEED YOUR PROTECTION MOR THAN EVER.
AND I'VE RUN AWAY TO PARADISE ISLAND.
YES, WELL...
...YOU'RE NOT THE ONLY ONE.
I JUST NEVER WANT TO HAVE TO USE MY POWERS THAT WAY AGAIN.
NOR DO I.
BUT IN THE END...
...IT MIGHT COME DOWN TO THAT FOR BOTH OF US.

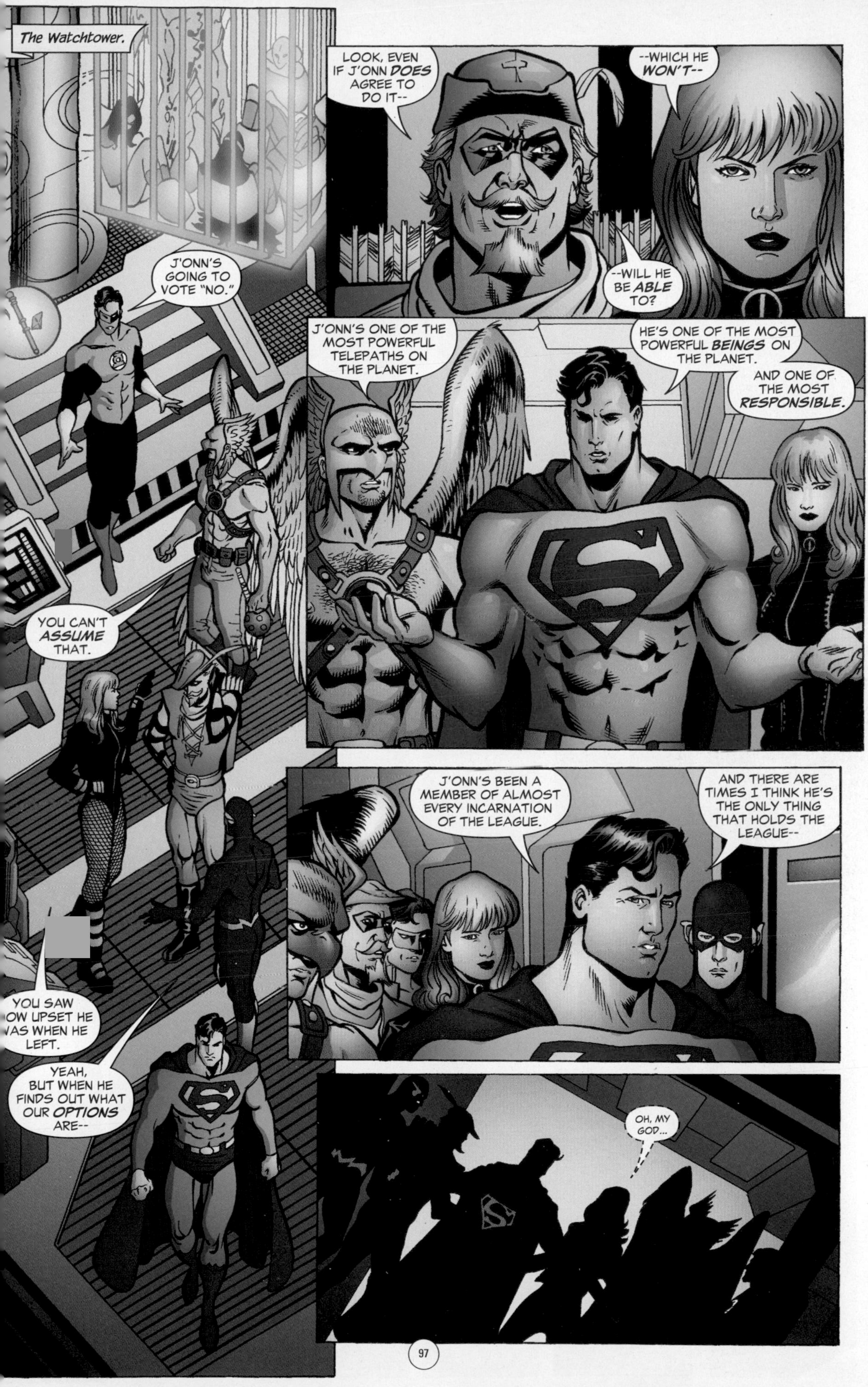
The Watchtower.
LOOK, EVEN IF J'ONN DOES AGREE TO DO IT--
--WHICH HE WON'T--
--WILL HE BE ABLE TO?
J'ONN'S GOING TO VOTE "NO."
J'ONN'S ONE OF THE MOST POWERFUL TELEPATHS ON THE PLANET.
HE'S ONE OF THE MOST POWERFUL BEINGS ON THE PLANET.
AND ONE OF THE MOST RESPONSIBLE.
YOU CAN'T ASSUME THAT.
J'ONN'S BEEN A MEMBER OF ALMOST EVERY INCARNATION OF THE LEAGUE.
AND THERE ARE TIMES I THINK HE'S THE ONLY THING THAT HOLDS THE LEAGUE--
YOU SAW OW UPSET HE VAS WHEN HE LEFT.
YEAH, BUT WHEN HE FINDS OUT WHAT OUR OPTIONS ARE--
OH, MY GOD...

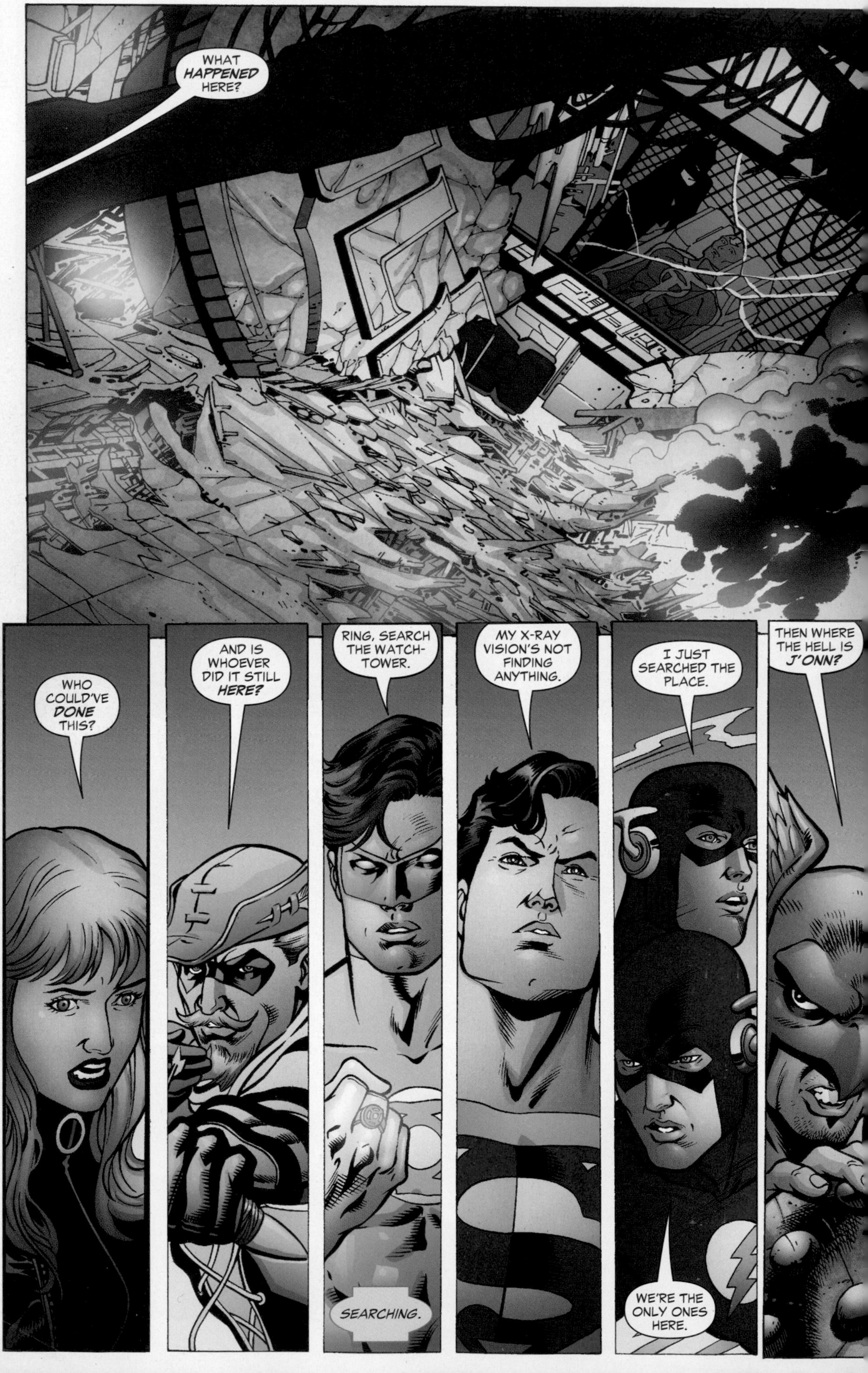
WHAT *HAPPENED* HERE?
WHO COULD'VE *DONE* THIS?
AND IS WHOEVER DID IT STILL *HERE?*
RING, SEARCH THE WATCH-TOWER.
SEARCHING.
MY X-RAY VISION'S NOT FINDING ANYTHING.
I JUST SEARCHED THE PLACE.
WE'RE THE ONLY ONES HERE.
THEN WHERE THE HELL IS *J'ONN?*

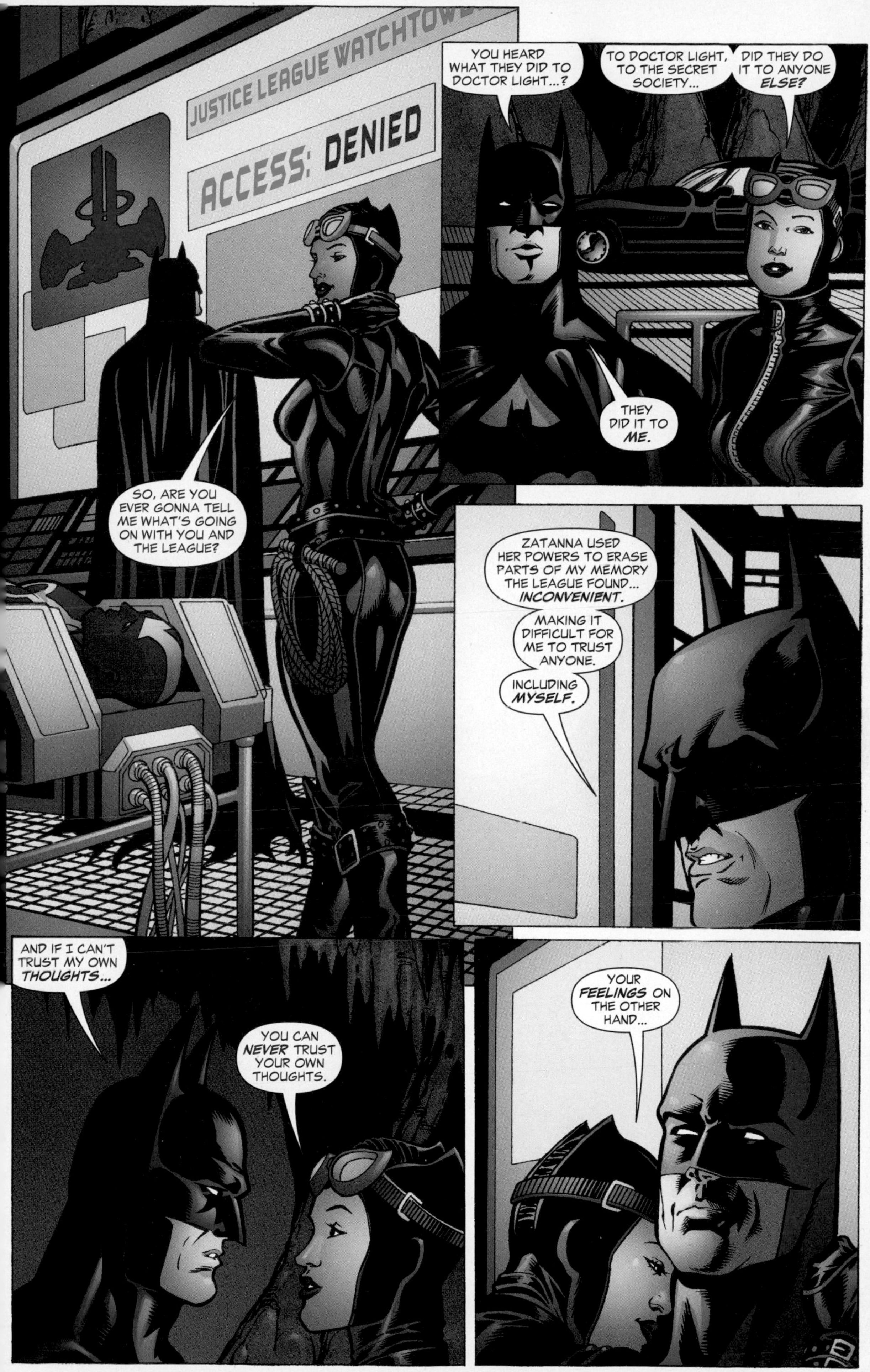
JUSTICE LEAGUE WATCHTOW
ACCESS: DENIED
SO, ARE YOU EVER GONNA TELL ME WHAT'S GOING ON WITH YOU AND THE LEAGUE?
YOU HEARD WHAT THEY DID TO DOCTOR LIGHT...?
TO DOCTOR LIGHT, TO THE SECRET SOCIETY...
DID THEY DO IT TO ANYONE ELSE?
THEY DID IT TO ME.
ZATANNA USED HER POWERS TO ERASE PARTS OF MY MEMORY THE LEAGUE FOUND... INCONVENIENT.
MAKING IT DIFFICULT FOR ME TO TRUST ANYONE.
INCLUDING MYSELF.
AND IF I CAN'T TRUST MY OWN THOUGHTS...
YOU CAN NEVER TRUST YOUR OWN THOUGHTS.
YOUR FEELINGS ON THE OTHER HAND...

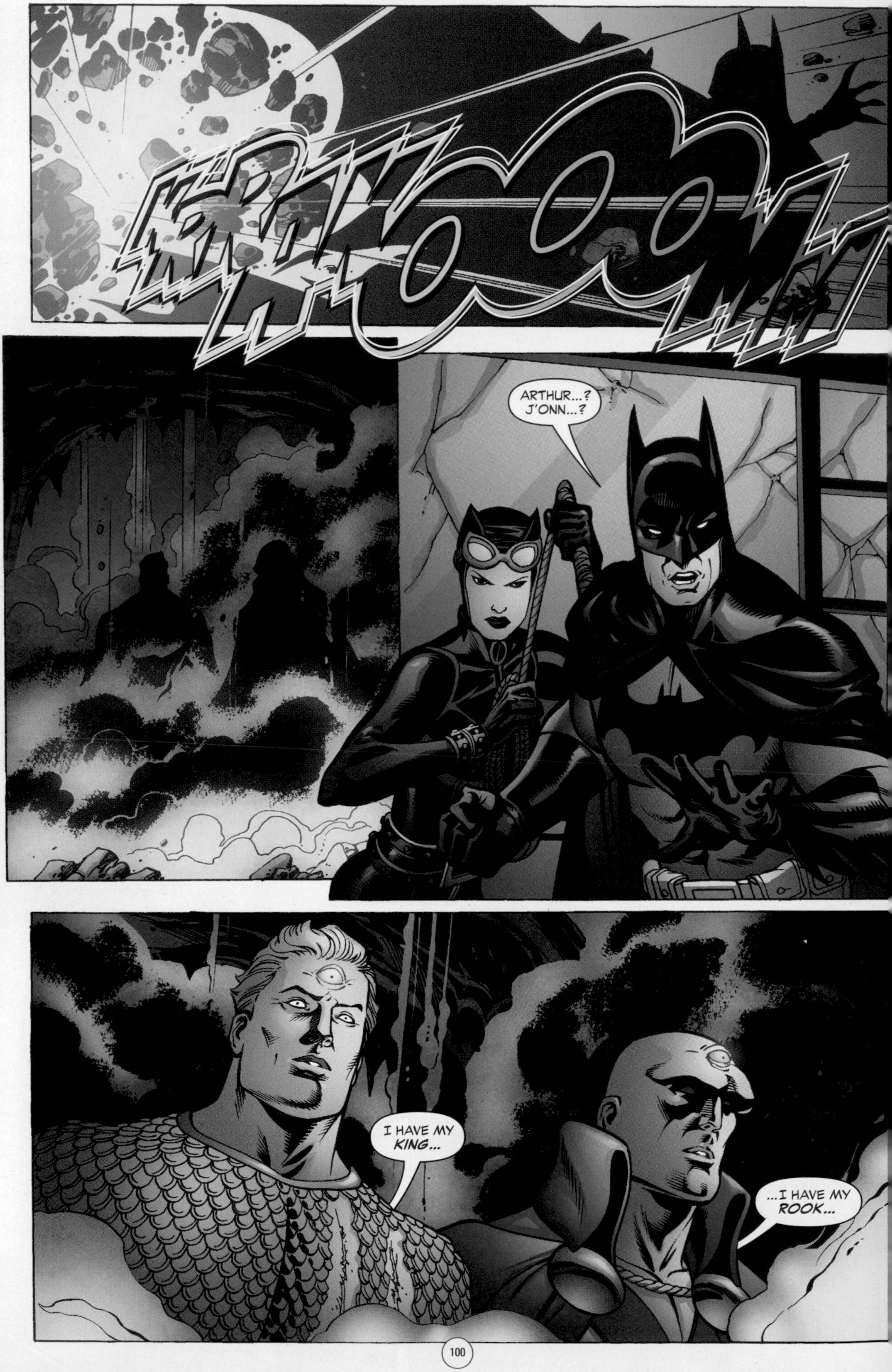
ARTHUR...? J'ONN...?
I HAVE MY *KING*...
...I HAVE MY *ROOK*...

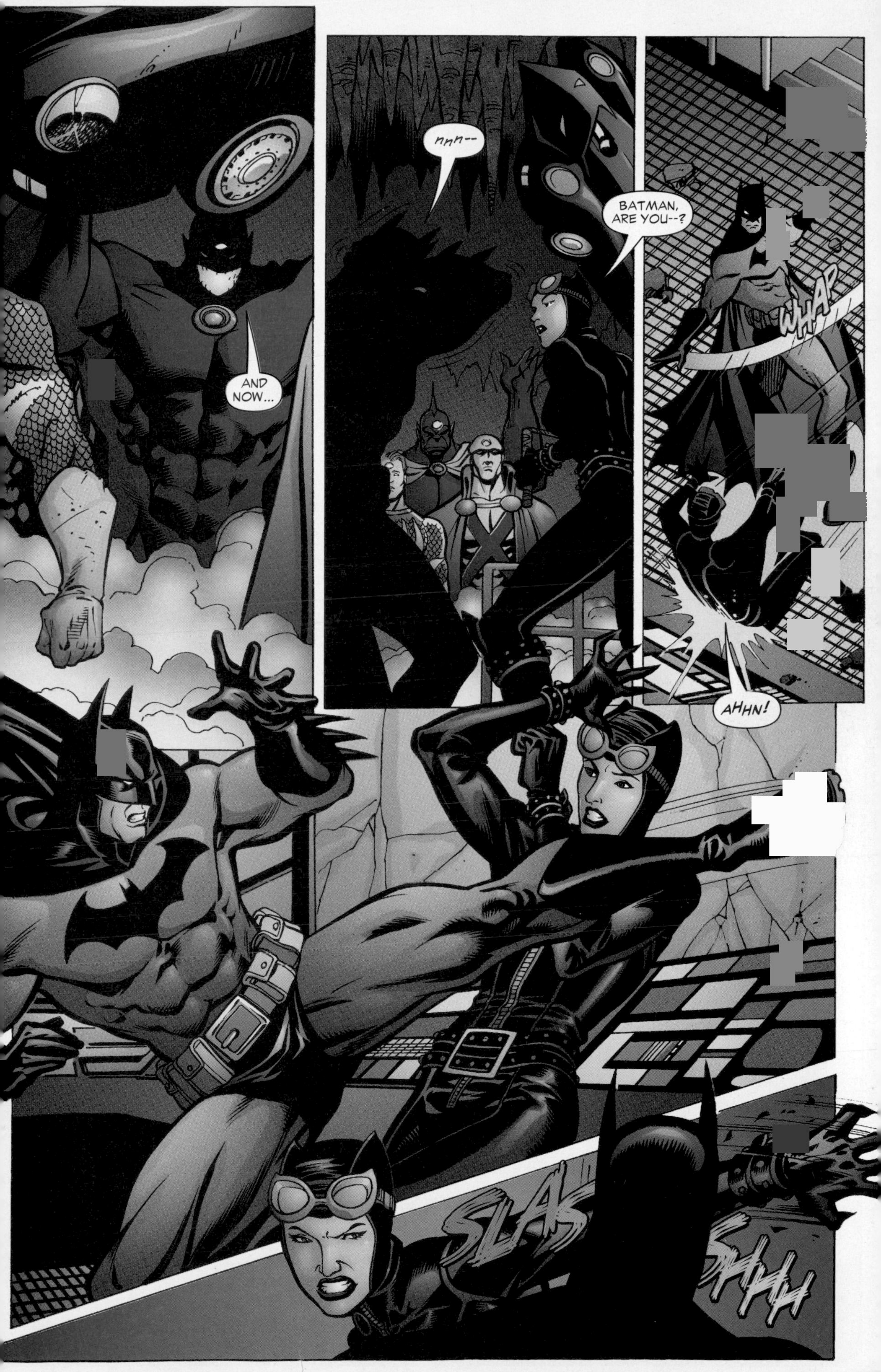
AND NOW...
nnn--
BATMAN, ARE YOU--?
WHAP
AHHN!
SLAS
SHHH

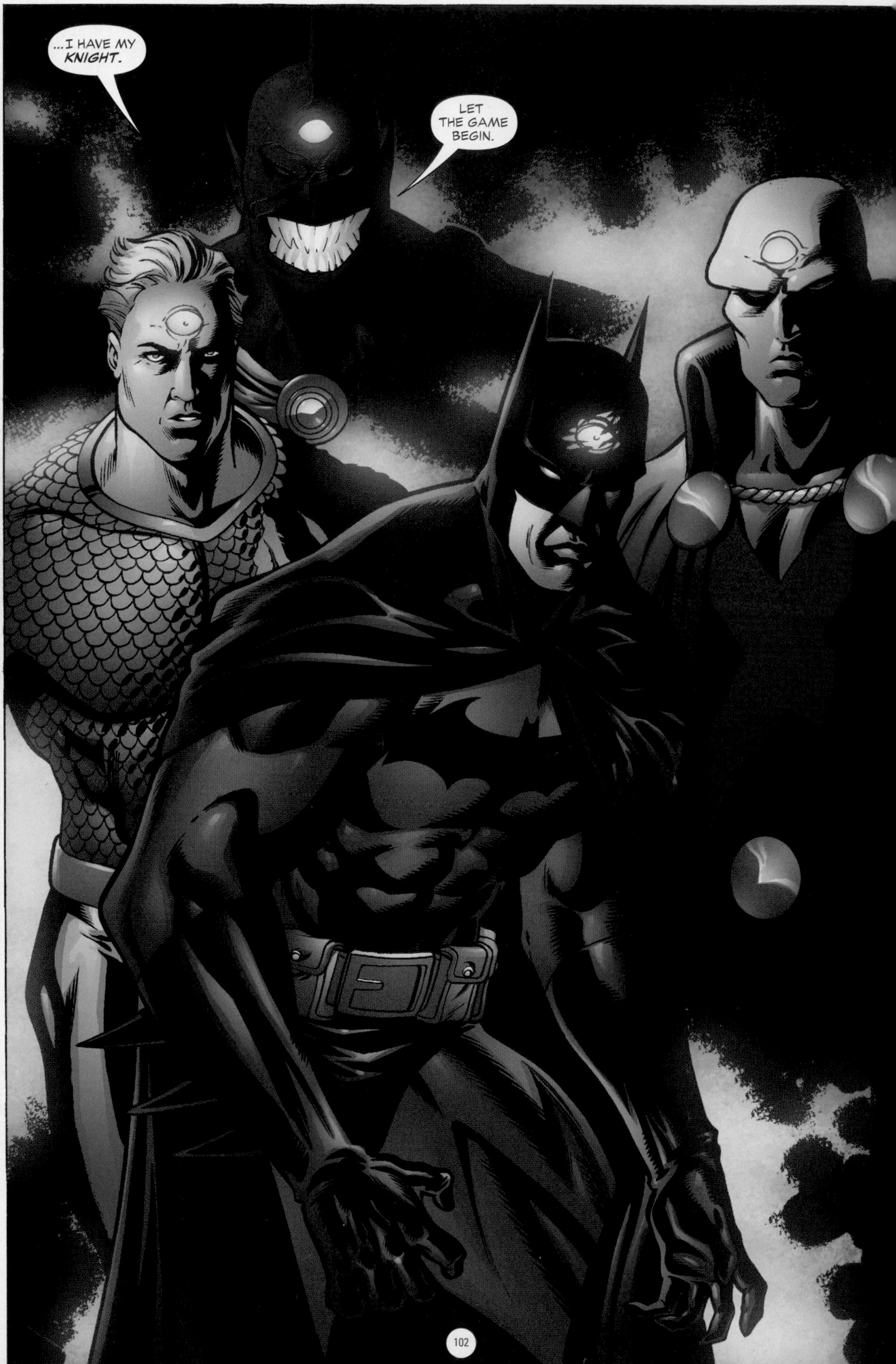
...I HAVE MY KNIGHT.
LET THE GAME BEGIN.

JLA #119
by Rags Morales & Mark Farmer

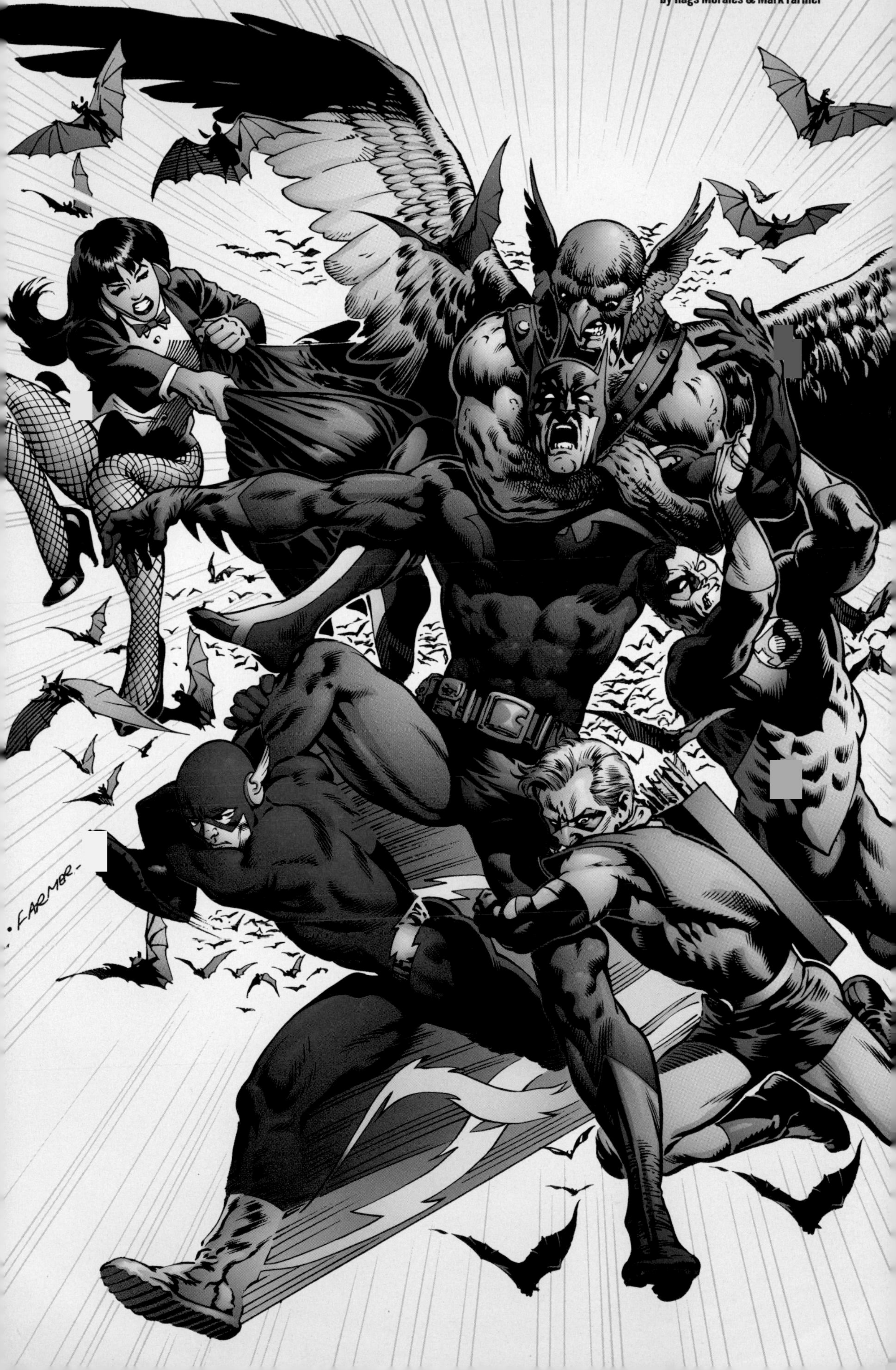
FARMER

JLA

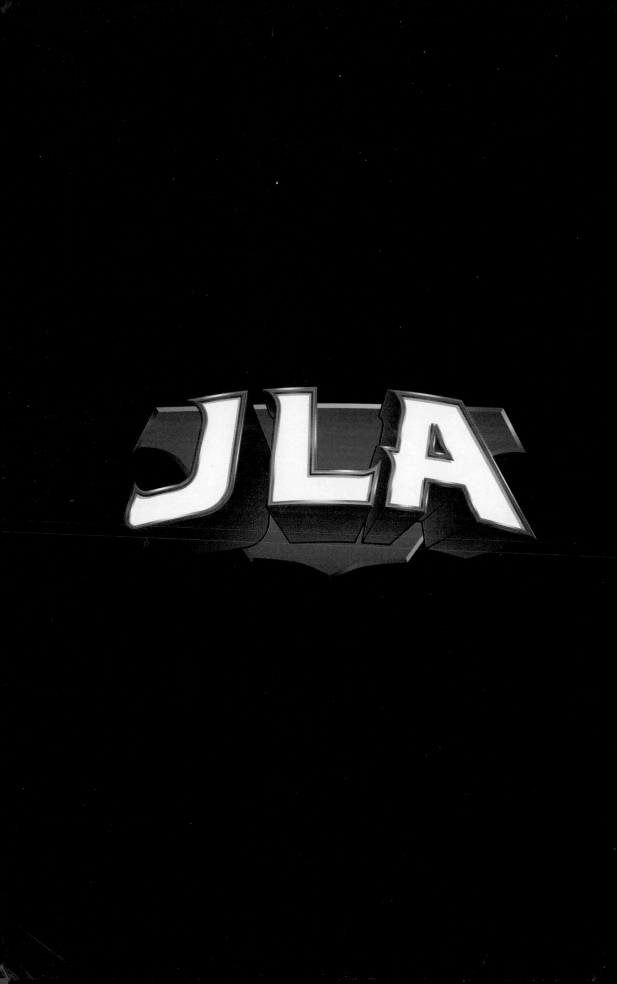

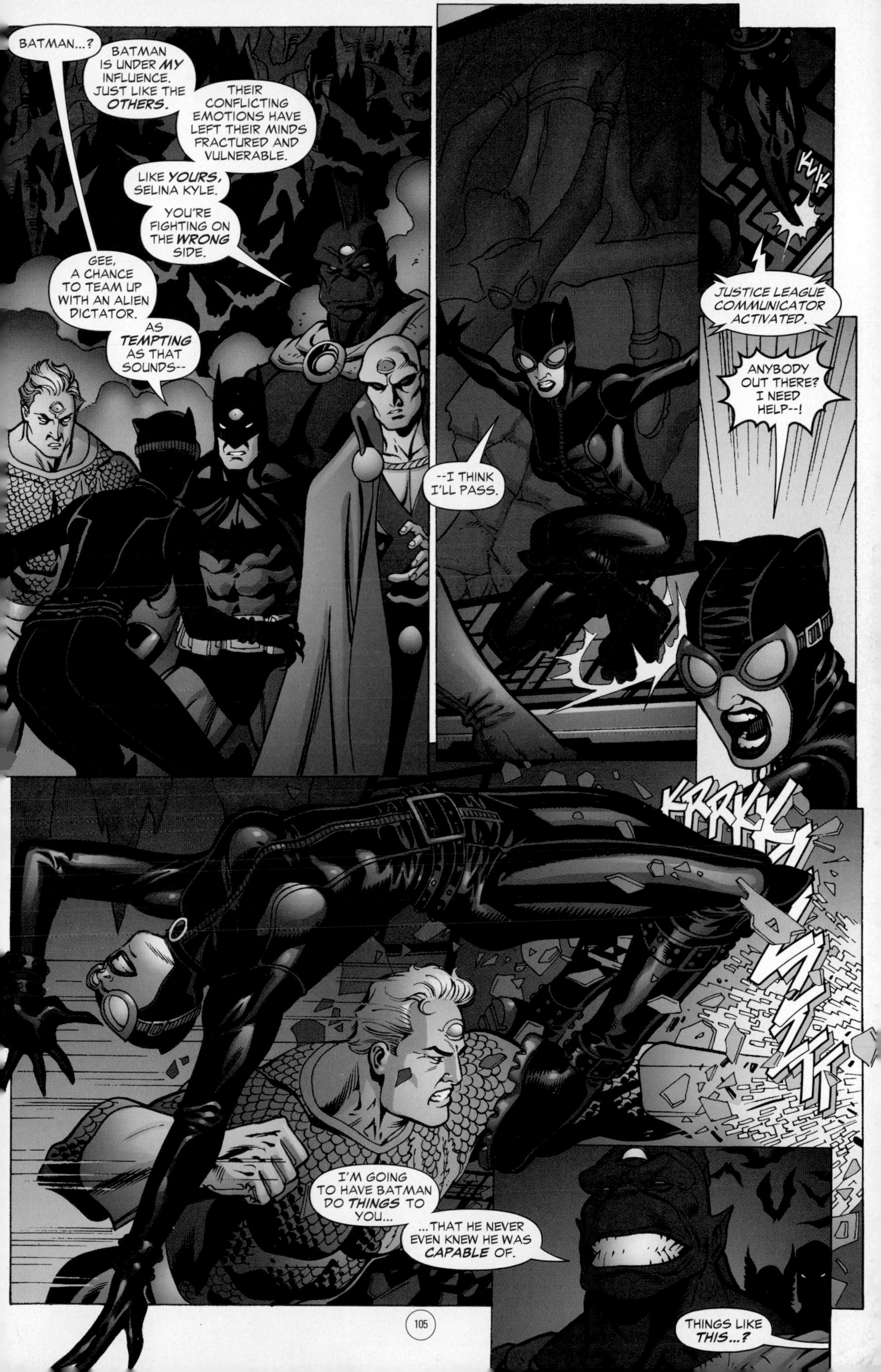

BATMAN...?
BATMAN IS UNDER MY INFLUENCE. JUST LIKE THE OTHERS.
THEIR CONFLICTING EMOTIONS HAVE LEFT THEIR MINDS FRACTURED AND VULNERABLE.
LIKE YOURS, SELINA KYLE.
YOU'RE FIGHTING ON THE WRONG SIDE.
GEE, A CHANCE TO TEAM UP WITH AN ALIEN DICTATOR.
AS TEMPTING AS THAT SOUNDS--
--I THINK I'LL PASS.
KLIK
JUSTICE LEAGUE COMMUNICATOR ACTIVATED.
ANYBODY OUT THERE? I NEED HELP--!
KRRKK
SMAKK
I'M GOING TO HAVE BATMAN DO THINGS TO YOU...
...THAT HE NEVER EVEN KNEW HE WAS CAPABLE OF.
THINGS LIKE THIS...?

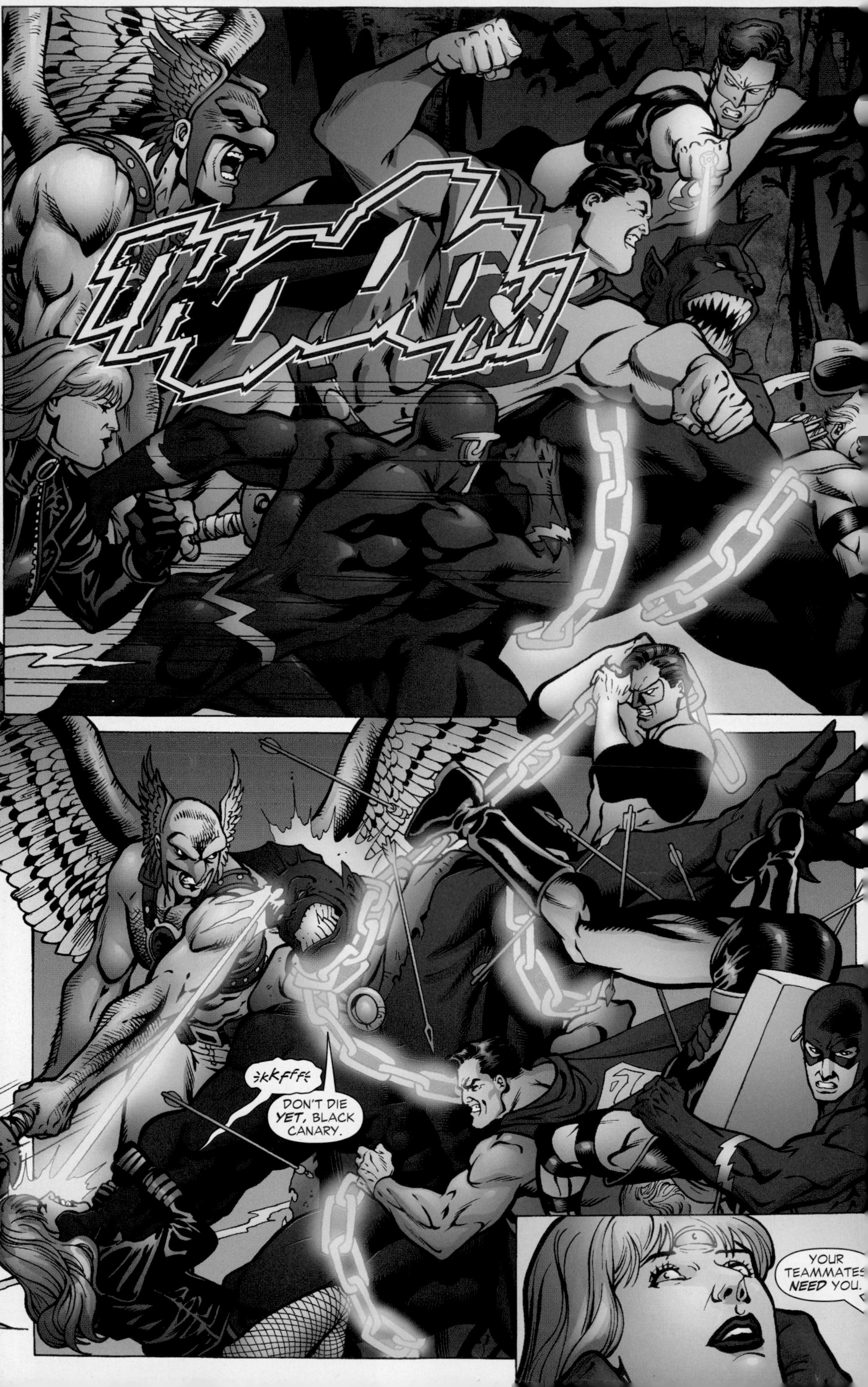

≈KKFFF≈
DON'T DIE YET, BLACK CANARY.
YOUR TEAMMATES NEED YOU.

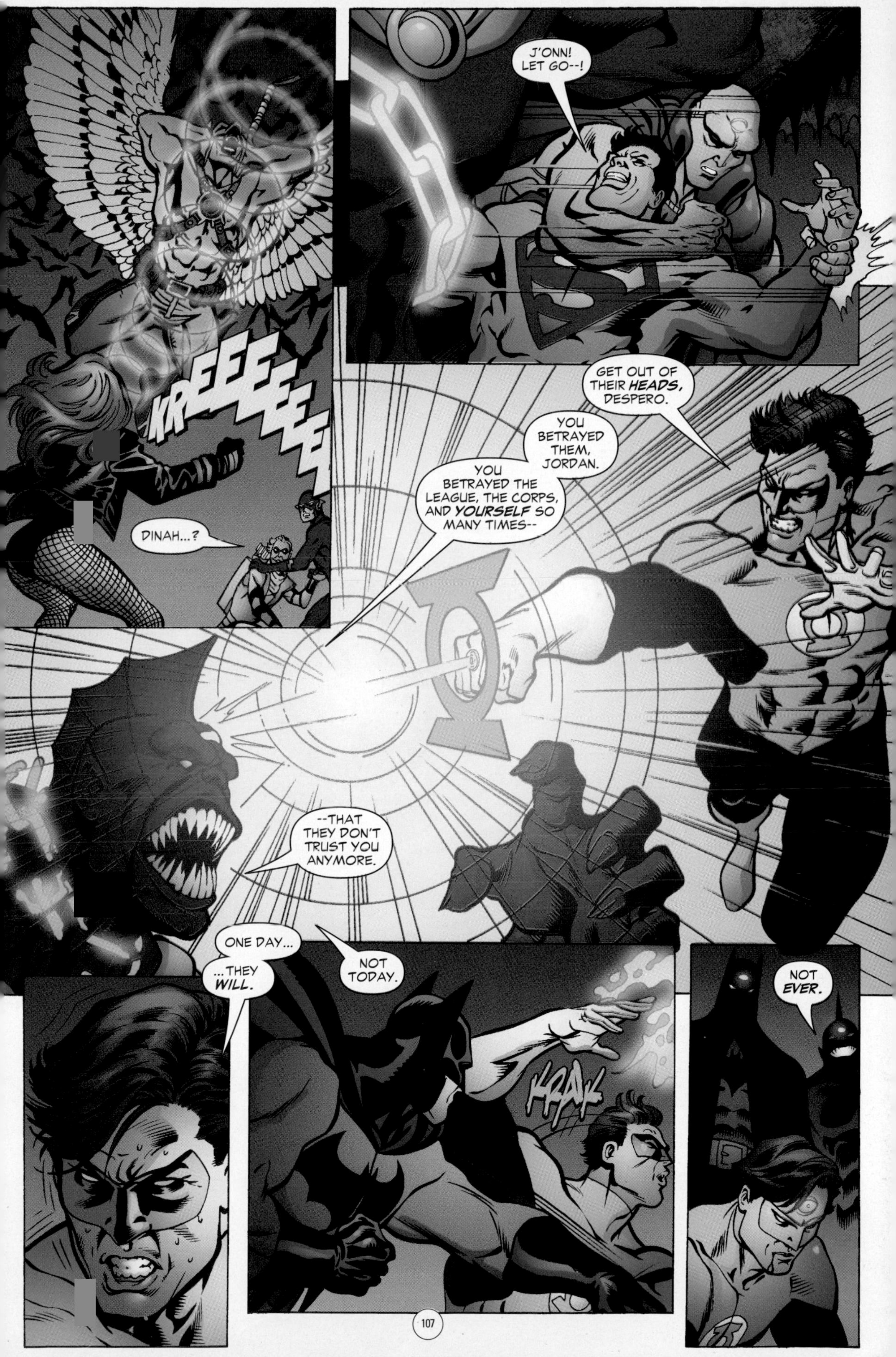
KREEEEEEE
DINAH...?
J'ONN! LET GO--!
GET OUT OF THEIR **HEADS,** DESPERO.
YOU BETRAYED THEM, JORDAN.
YOU BETRAYED THE LEAGUE, THE CORPS, AND ***YOURSELF*** SO MANY TIMES--
--THAT THEY DON'T TRUST YOU ANYMORE.
ONE DAY...
...THEY **WILL.**
NOT TODAY.
KRAK
NOT ***EVER.***

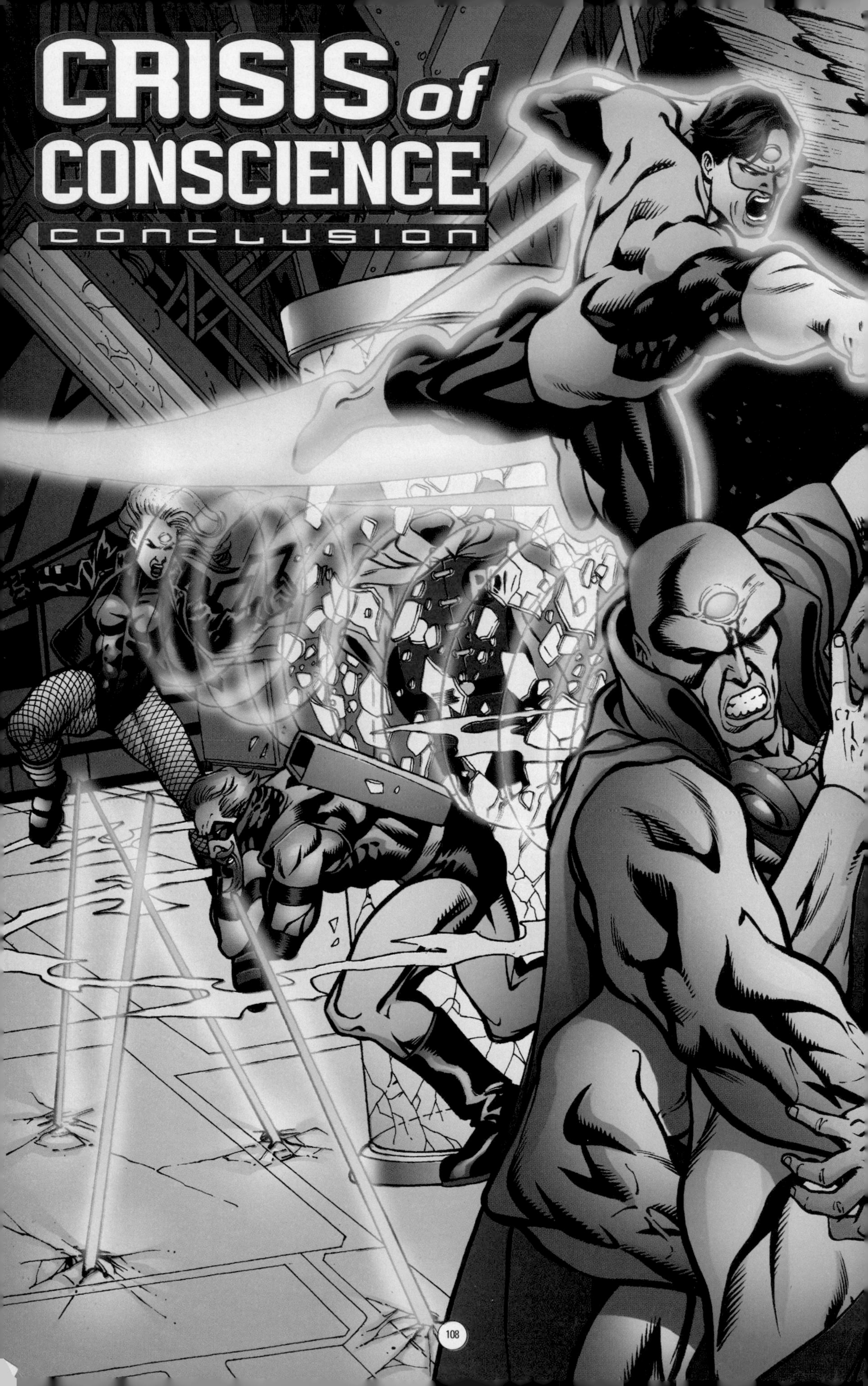
CRISIS of CONSCIENCE
CONCLUSION

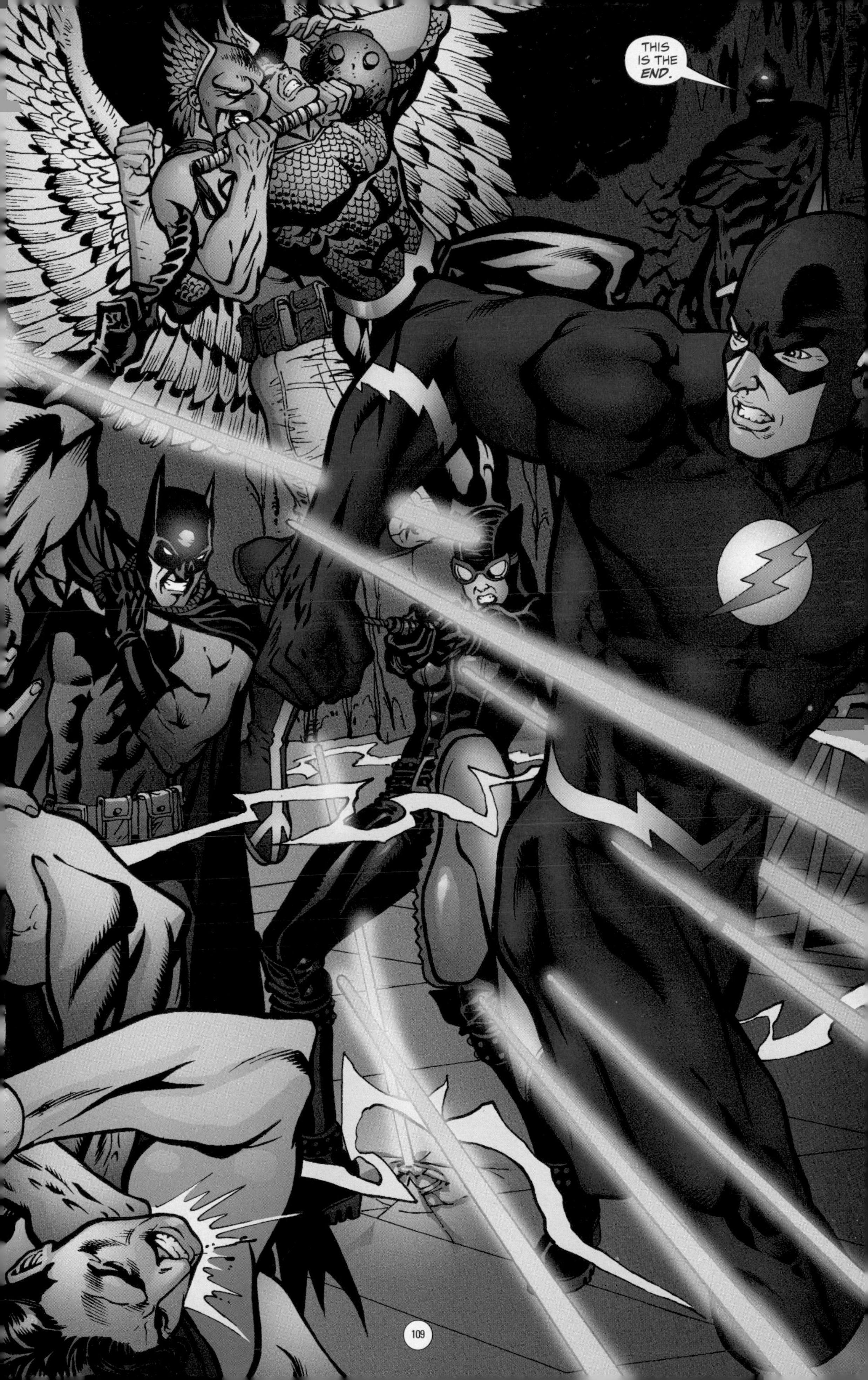
THIS IS THE END.

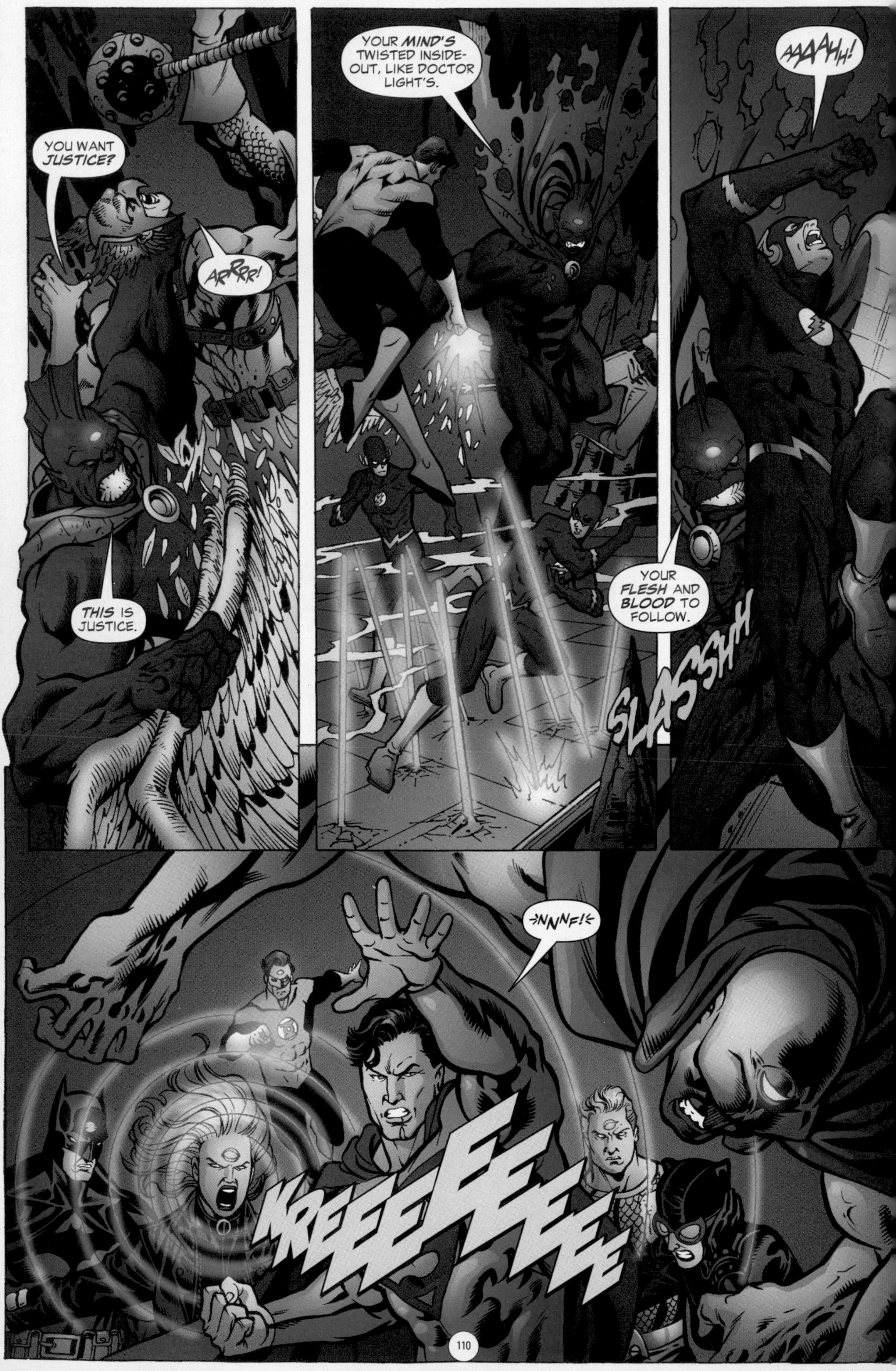
YOU WANT JUSTICE?
ARRRR!
THIS IS JUSTICE.
YOUR MIND'S TWISTED INSIDE-OUT, LIKE DOCTOR LIGHT'S.
AAAAHH!
YOUR FLESH AND BLOOD TO FOLLOW.
SLASSHH
NNNF!
KREEEEEEEEE

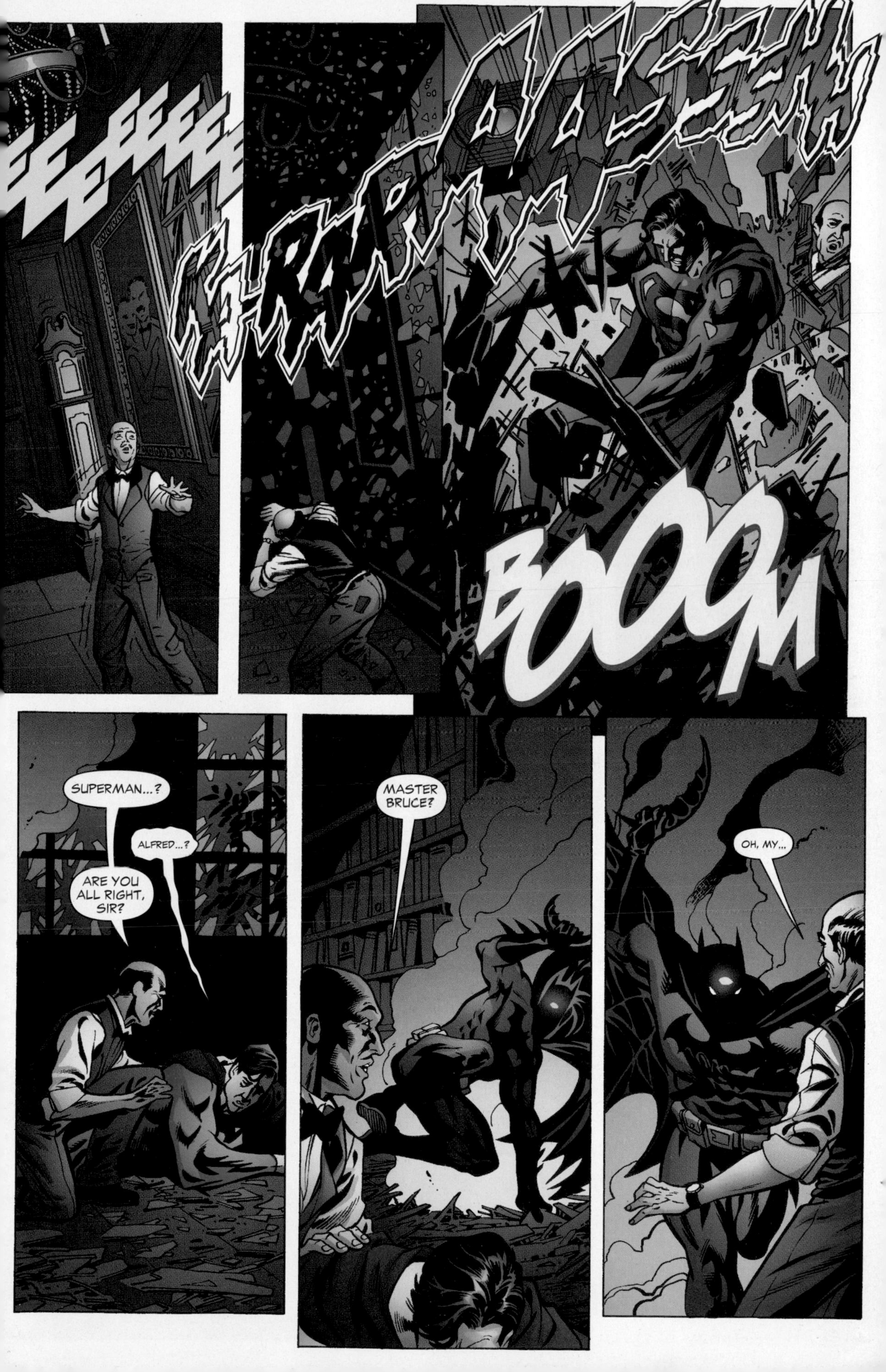
EEEEEEEEE
CRAAAASSSHH
BOOOM
SUPERMAN...?
ALFRED...?
ARE YOU ALL RIGHT, SIR?
MASTER BRUCE?
OH, MY...

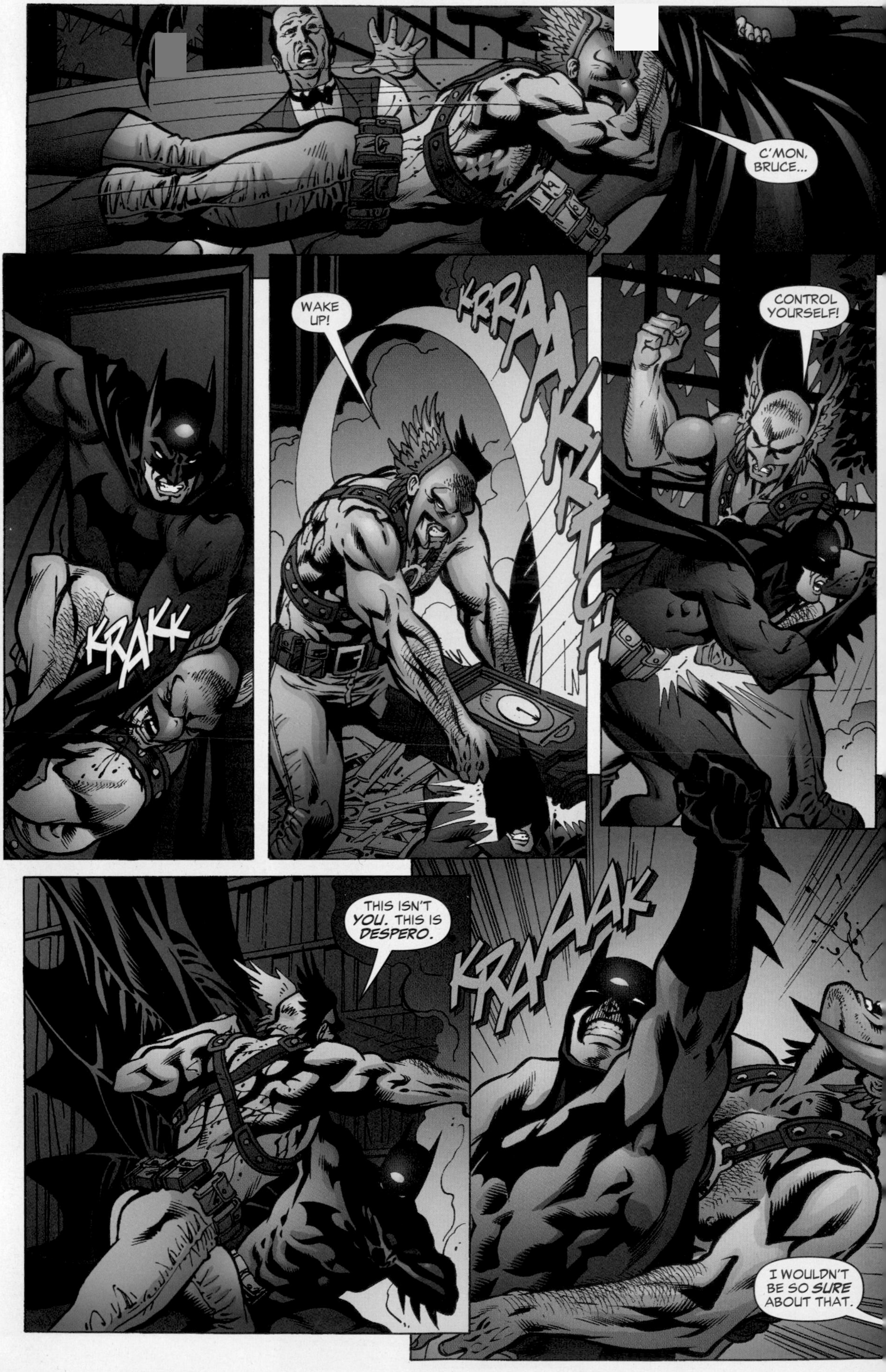
C'MON, BRUCE...
KRAKK
WAKE UP!
KRRAAKKTCH
CONTROL YOURSELF!
THIS ISN'T YOU. THIS IS DESPERO.
KRAAAK
I WOULDN'T BE SO SURE ABOUT THAT.

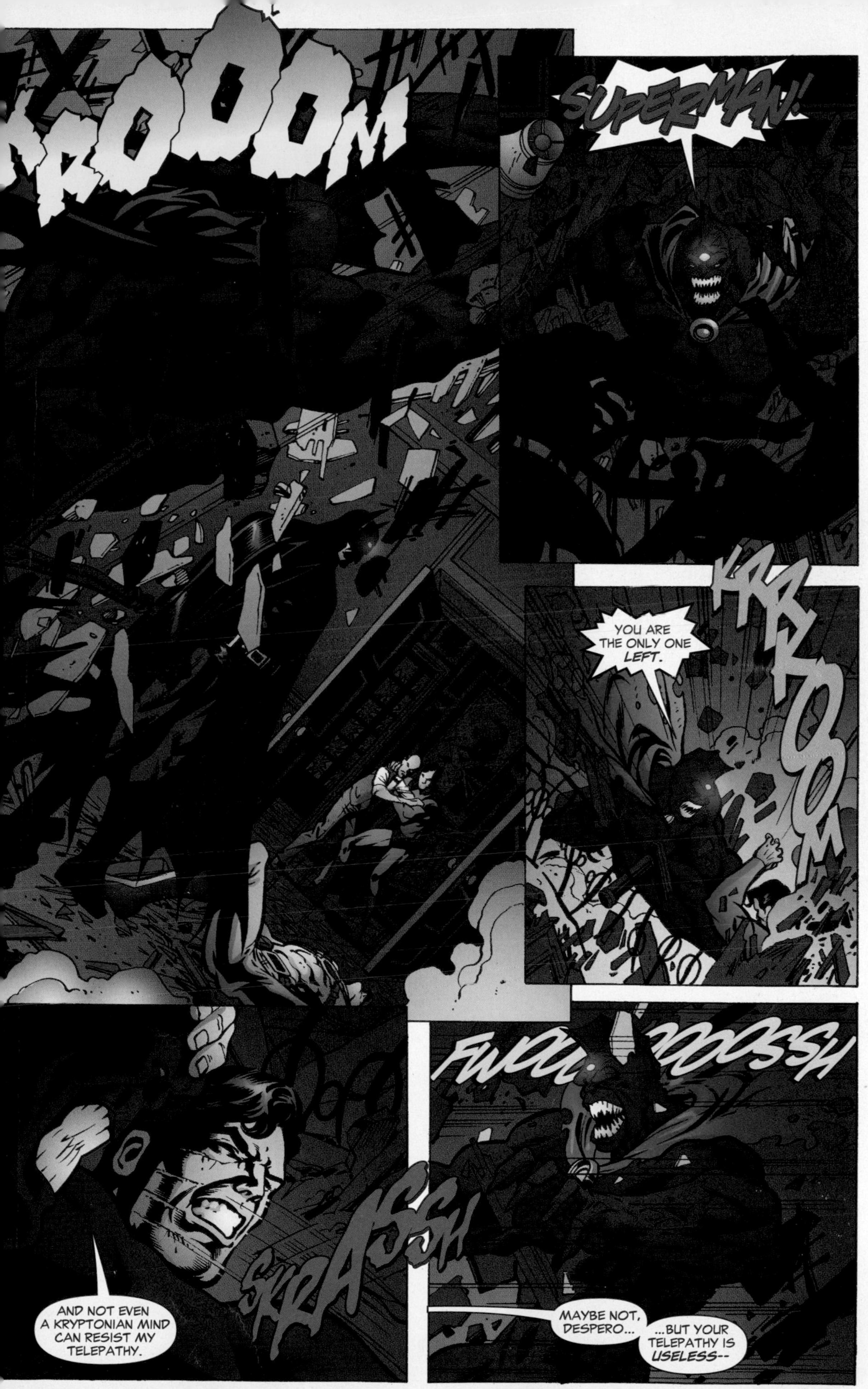
KROOOOM
SUPERMAN!
KRRROOOM
YOU ARE THE ONLY ONE LEFT.
AND NOT EVEN A KRYPTONIAN MIND CAN RESIST MY TELEPATHY.
SKRASSH
FWOOOOOOOSSH
MAYBE NOT, DESPERO...
...BUT YOUR TELEPATHY IS USELESS--

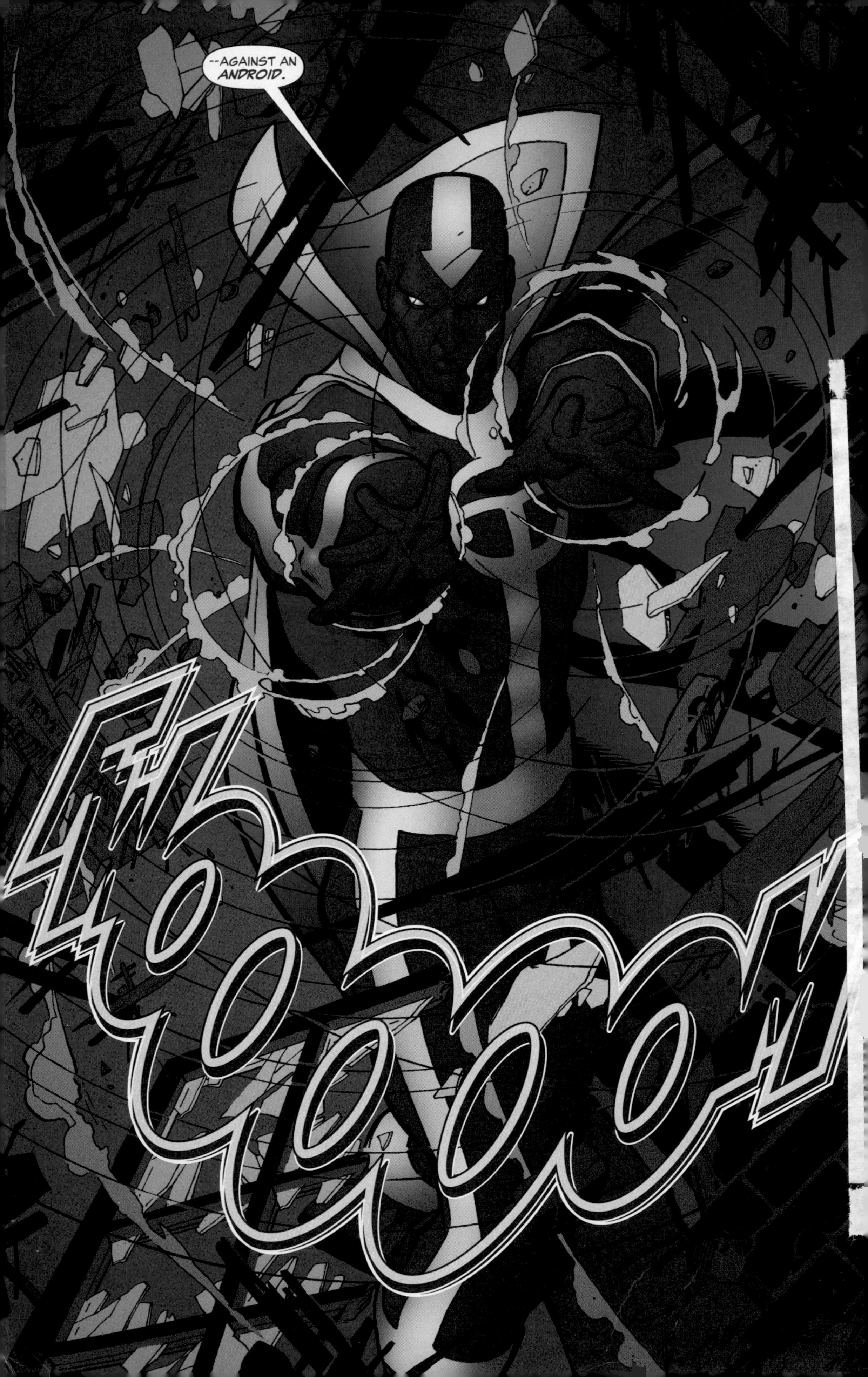
--AGAINST AN ANDROID.

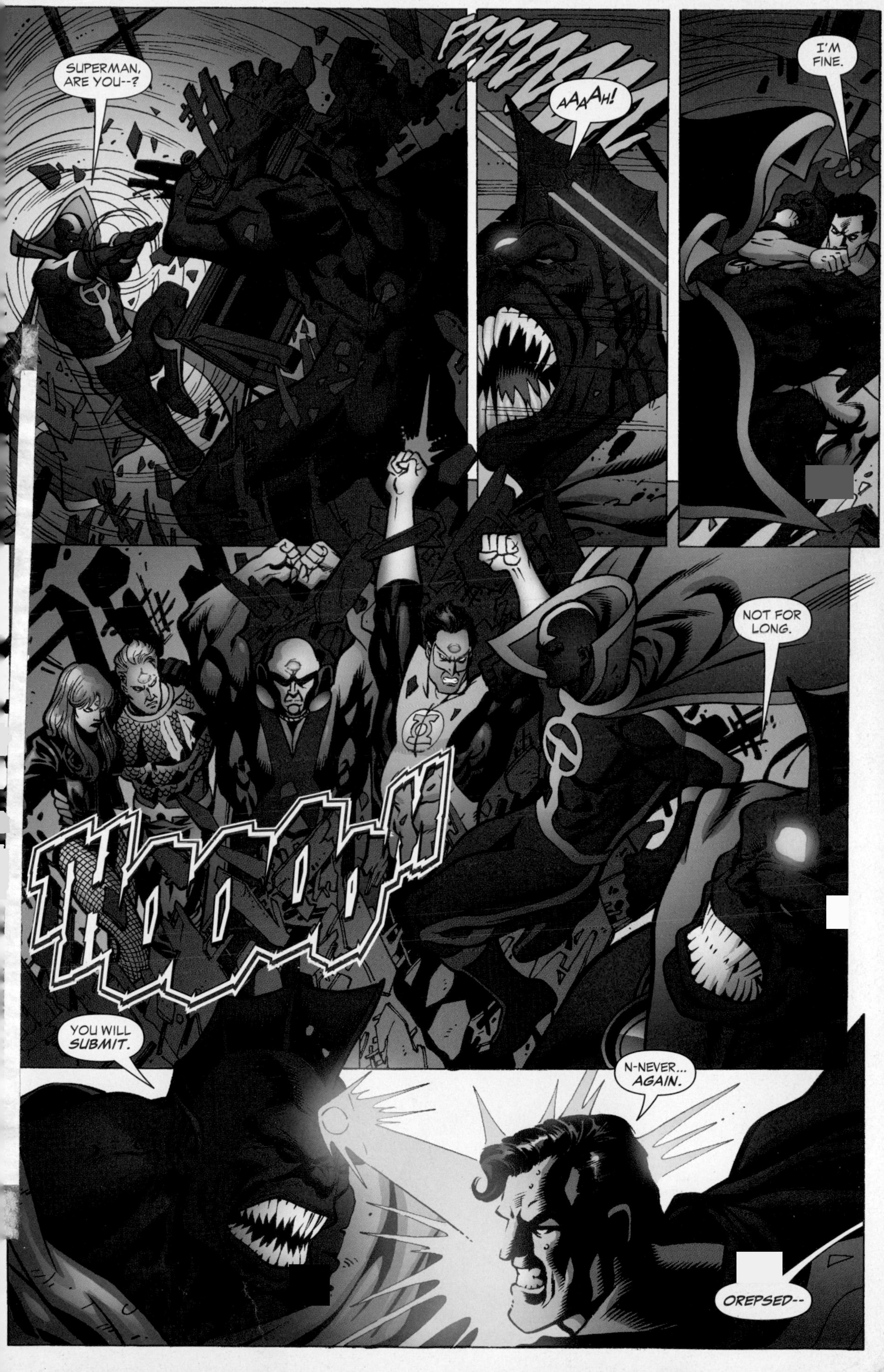
SUPERMAN, ARE YOU--?
AAAAH!
I'M FINE.
NOT FOR LONG.
YOU WILL SUBMIT.
N-NEVER... AGAIN.
OREPSED--

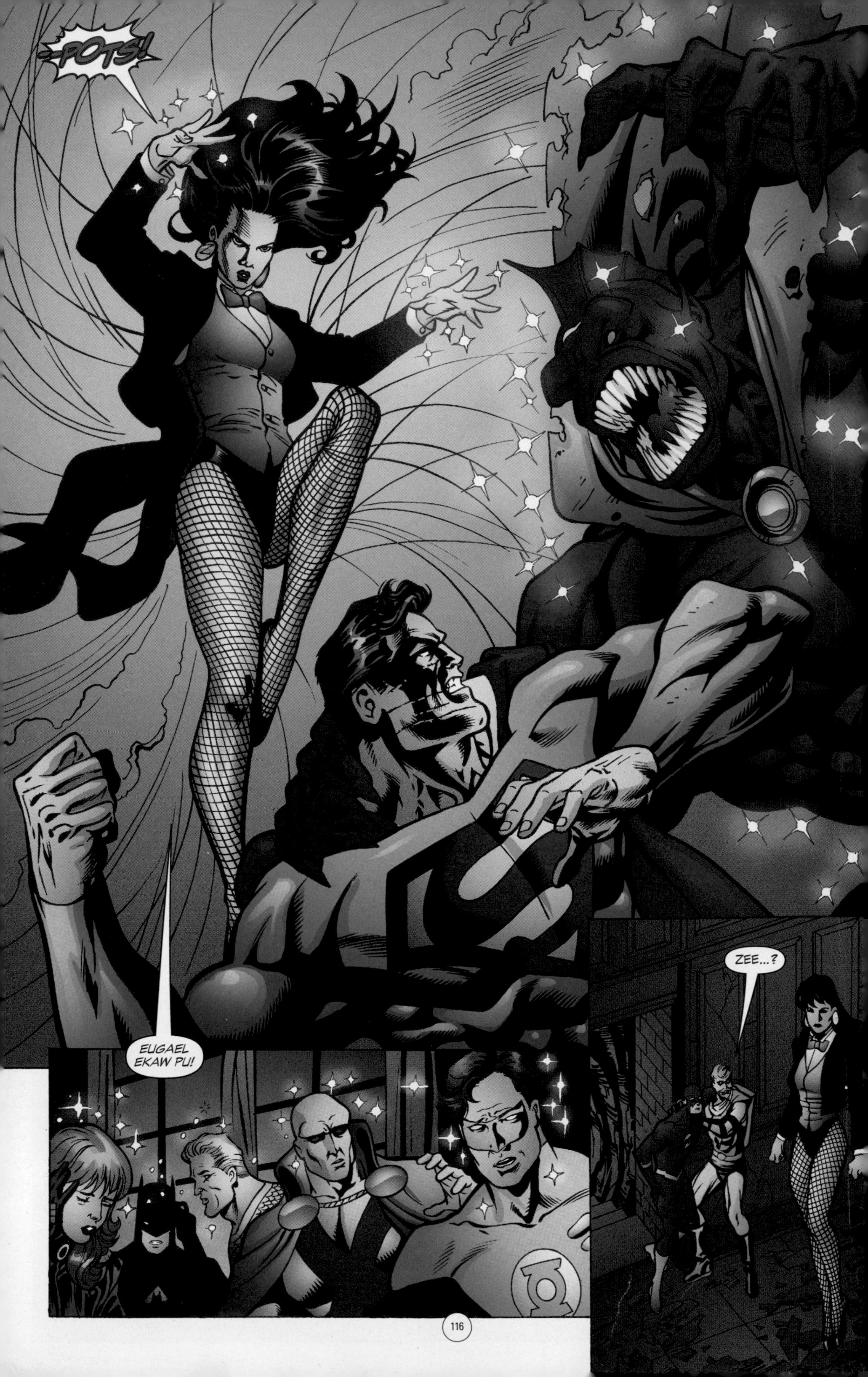

-POTS!
EUGAEL EKAW PU!
ZEE...?

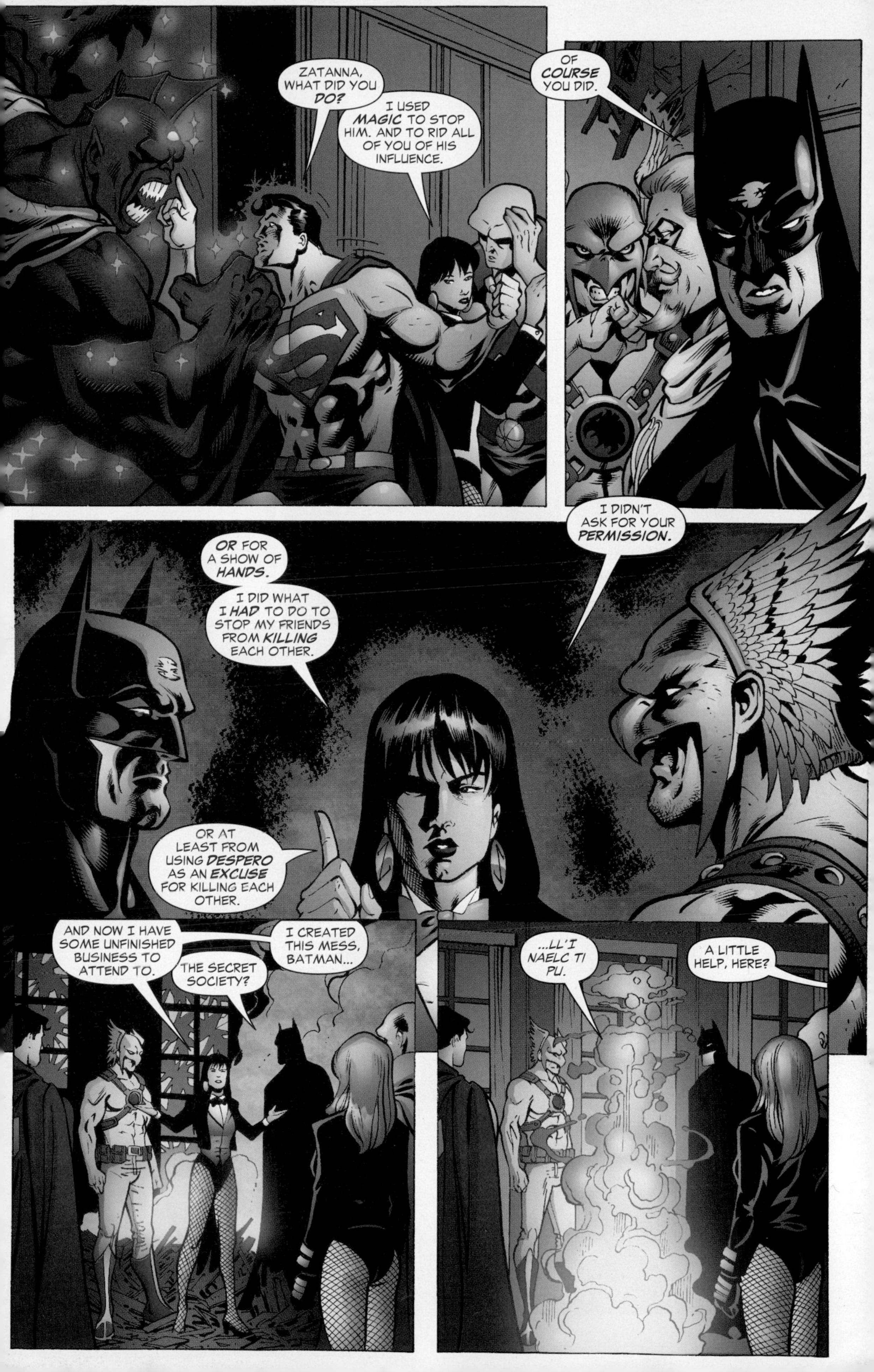
ZATANNA, WHAT DID YOU DO?
I USED MAGIC TO STOP HIM. AND TO RID ALL OF YOU OF HIS INFLUENCE.
OF COURSE YOU DID.
OR FOR A SHOW OF HANDS.
I DIDN'T ASK FOR YOUR PERMISSION.
I DID WHAT I HAD TO DO TO STOP MY FRIENDS FROM KILLING EACH OTHER.
OR AT LEAST FROM USING DESPERO AS AN EXCUSE FOR KILLING EACH OTHER.
I CREATED THIS MESS, BATMAN...
AND NOW I HAVE SOME UNFINISHED BUSINESS TO ATTEND TO.
THE SECRET SOCIETY?
...LL'I NAELC TI PU.
A LITTLE HELP, HERE?

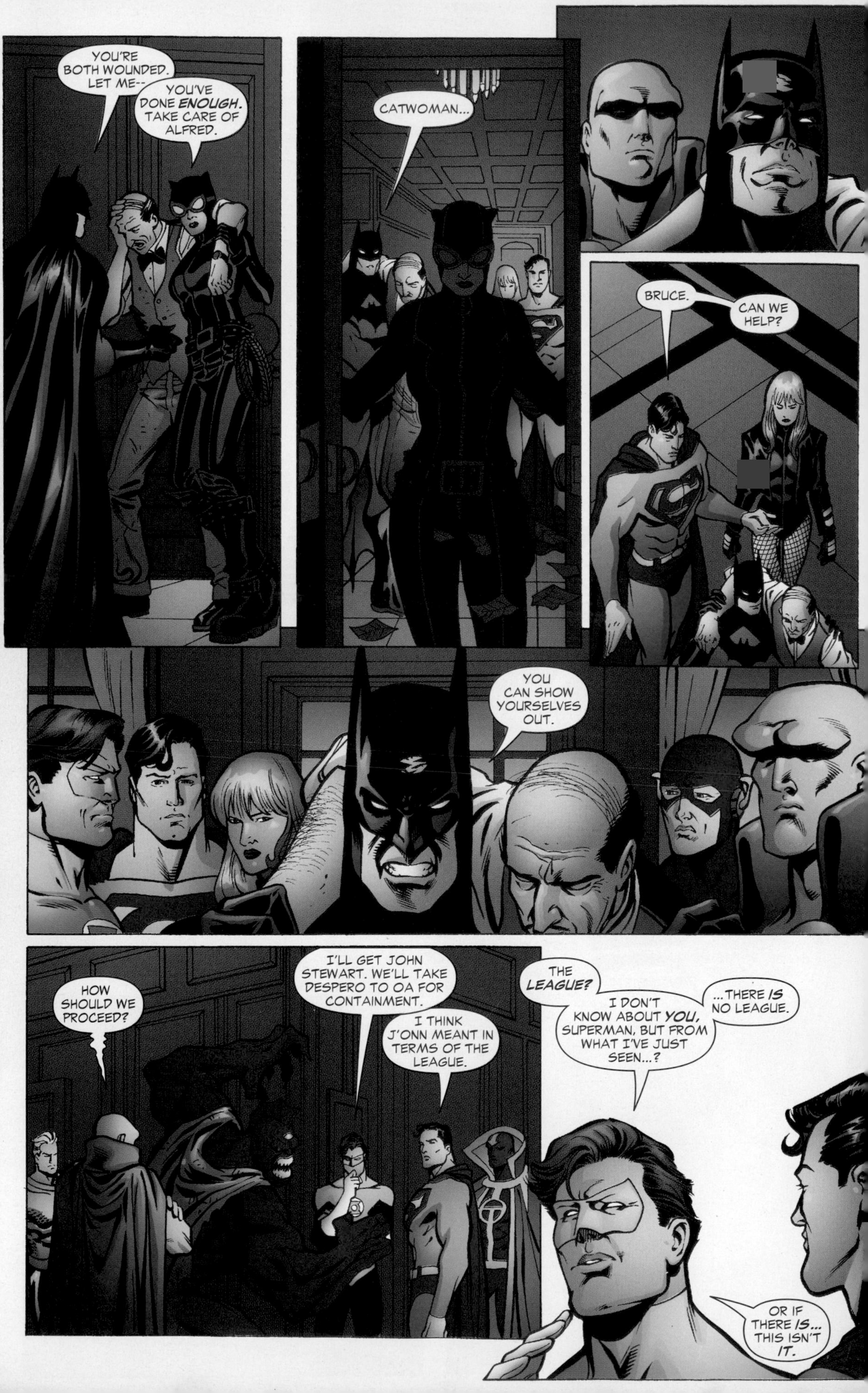
YOU'RE BOTH WOUNDED. LET ME--
YOU'VE DONE ENOUGH. TAKE CARE OF ALFRED.
CATWOMAN...
BRUCE.
CAN WE HELP?
YOU CAN SHOW YOURSELVES OUT.
HOW SHOULD WE PROCEED?
I'LL GET JOHN STEWART. WE'LL TAKE DESPERO TO OA FOR CONTAINMENT.
I THINK J'ONN MEANT IN TERMS OF THE LEAGUE.
THE LEAGUE?
I DON'T KNOW ABOUT YOU, SUPERMAN, BUT FROM WHAT I'VE JUST SEEN...?
...THERE IS NO LEAGUE.
OR IF THERE IS... THIS ISN'T IT.

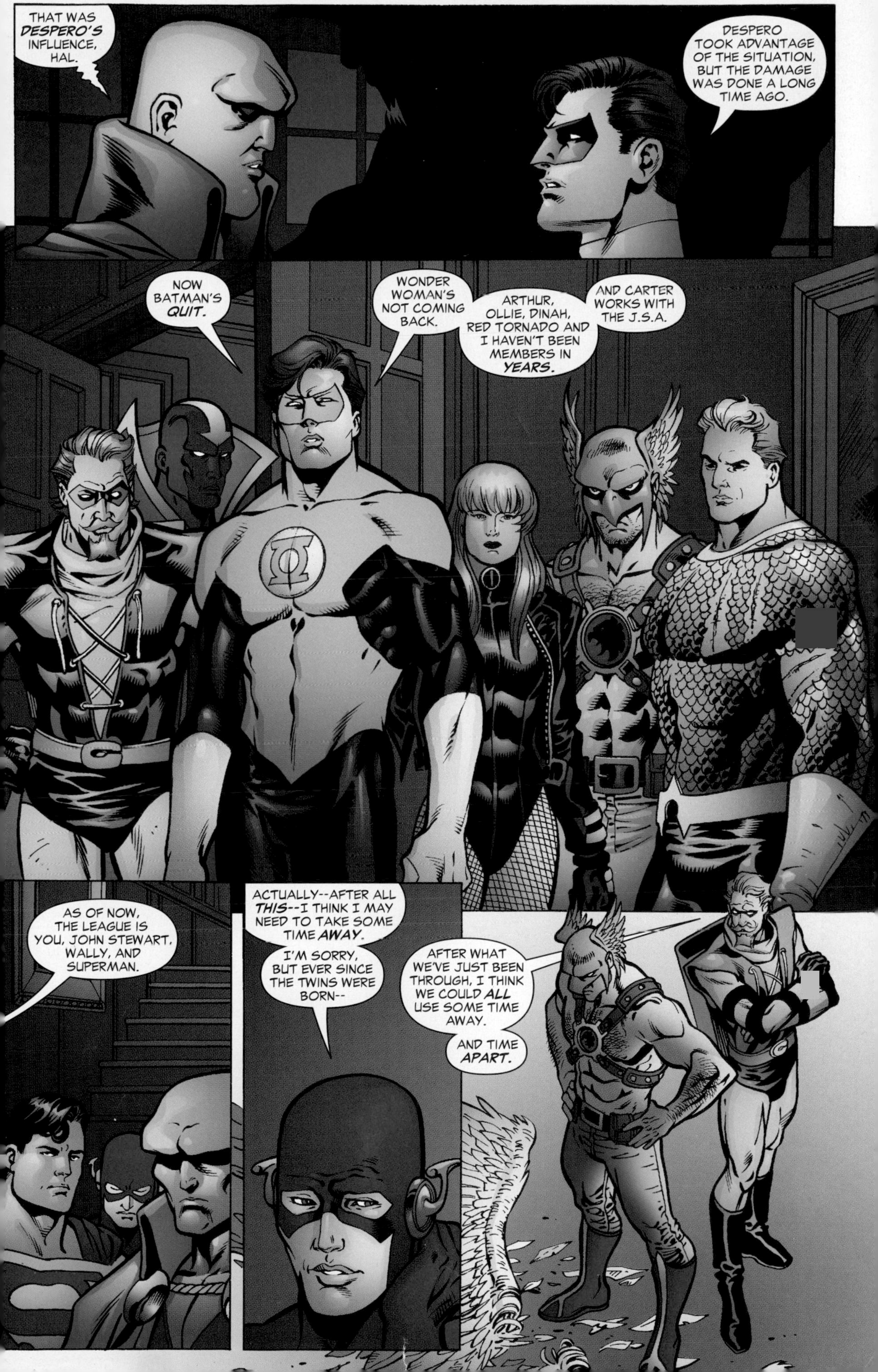
THAT WAS DESPERO'S INFLUENCE, HAL.
DESPERO TOOK ADVANTAGE OF THE SITUATION, BUT THE DAMAGE WAS DONE A LONG TIME AGO.
NOW BATMAN'S QUIT.
WONDER WOMAN'S NOT COMING BACK.
ARTHUR, OLLIE, DINAH, RED TORNADO AND I HAVEN'T BEEN MEMBERS IN YEARS.
AND CARTER WORKS WITH THE J.S.A.
AS OF NOW, THE LEAGUE IS YOU, JOHN STEWART, WALLY, AND SUPERMAN.
ACTUALLY--AFTER ALL THIS--I THINK I MAY NEED TO TAKE SOME TIME AWAY.
I'M SORRY, BUT EVER SINCE THE TWINS WERE BORN--
AFTER WHAT WE'VE JUST BEEN THROUGH, I THINK WE COULD ALL USE SOME TIME AWAY.
AND TIME APART.

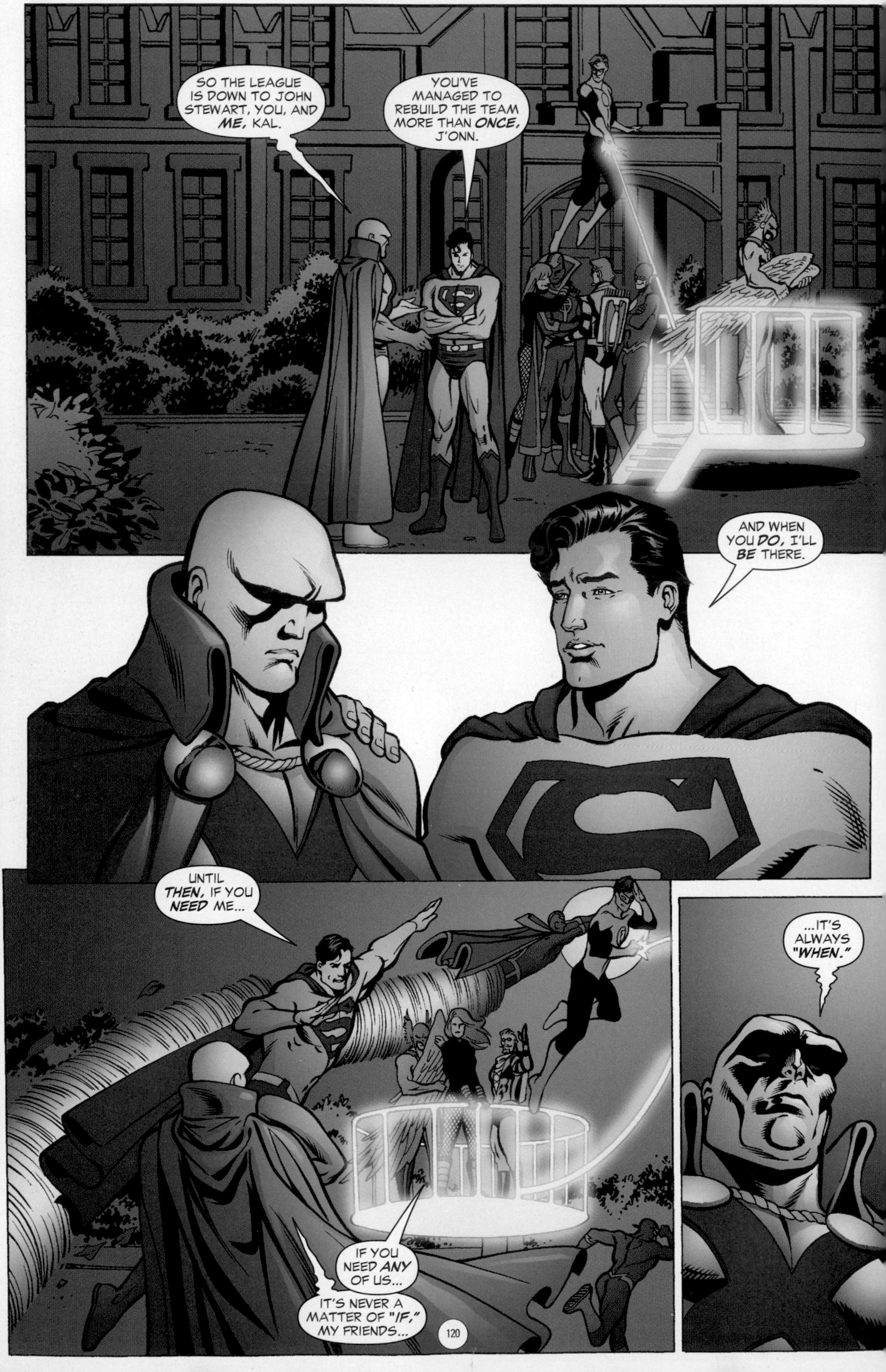
SO THE LEAGUE IS DOWN TO JOHN STEWART, YOU, AND ME, KAL.
YOU'VE MANAGED TO REBUILD THE TEAM MORE THAN ONCE, J'ONN.
AND WHEN YOU DO, I'LL BE THERE.
UNTIL THEN, IF YOU NEED ME...
IF YOU NEED ANY OF US...
IT'S NEVER A MATTER OF "IF," MY FRIENDS...
...IT'S ALWAYS "WHEN."

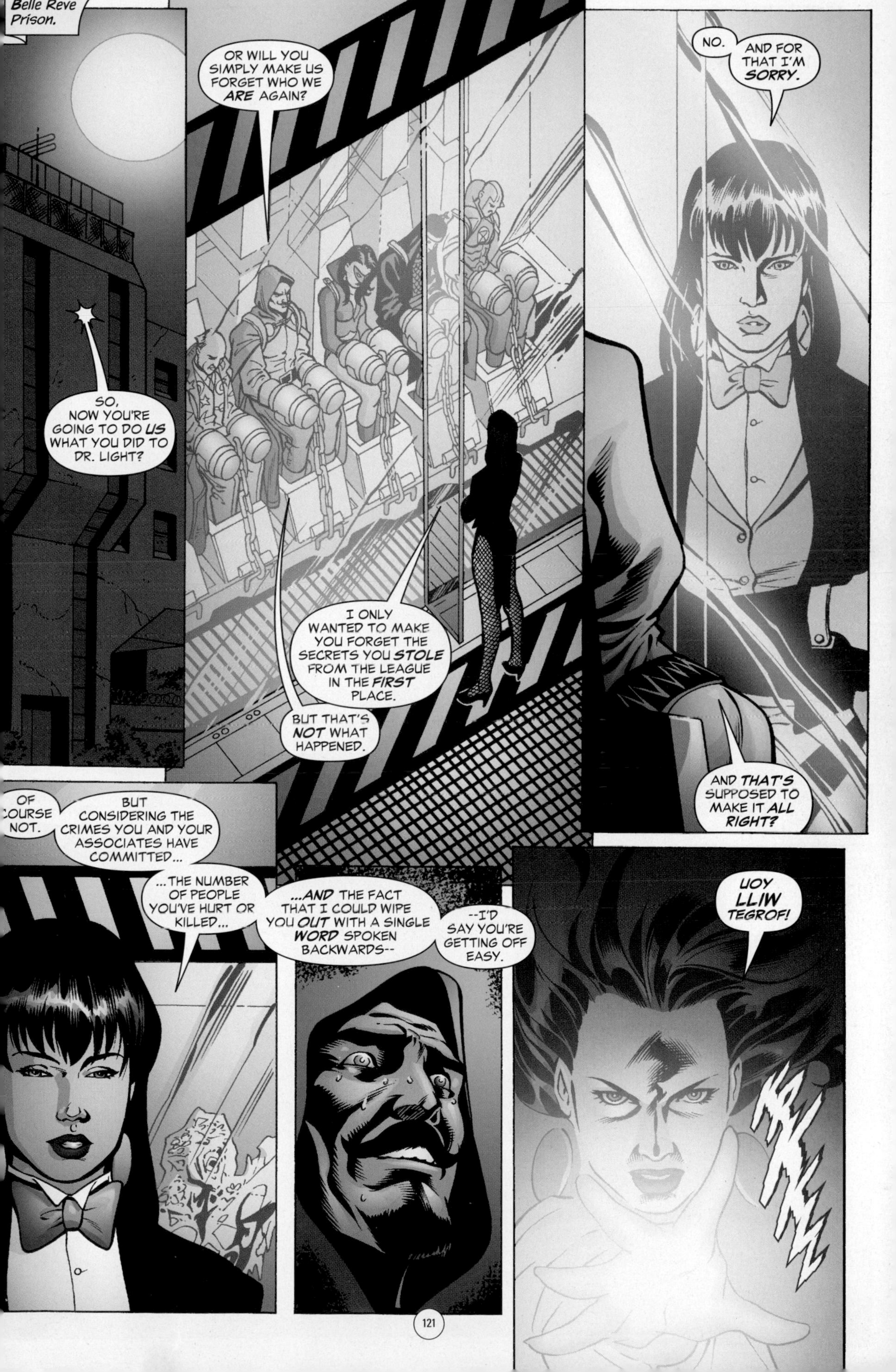
Belle Reve Prison.
SO, NOW YOU'RE GOING TO DO US WHAT YOU DID TO DR. LIGHT?
OR WILL YOU SIMPLY MAKE US FORGET WHO WE ARE AGAIN?
NO.
AND FOR THAT I'M SORRY.
I ONLY WANTED TO MAKE YOU FORGET THE SECRETS YOU STOLE FROM THE LEAGUE IN THE FIRST PLACE.
BUT THAT'S NOT WHAT HAPPENED.
AND THAT'S SUPPOSED TO MAKE IT ALL RIGHT?
OF COURSE NOT.
BUT CONSIDERING THE CRIMES YOU AND YOUR ASSOCIATES HAVE COMMITTED...
...THE NUMBER OF PEOPLE YOU'VE HURT OR KILLED...
...AND THE FACT THAT I COULD WIPE YOU OUT WITH A SINGLE WORD SPOKEN BACKWARDS--
--I'D SAY YOU'RE GETTING OFF EASY.
UOY LLIW TEGROF!

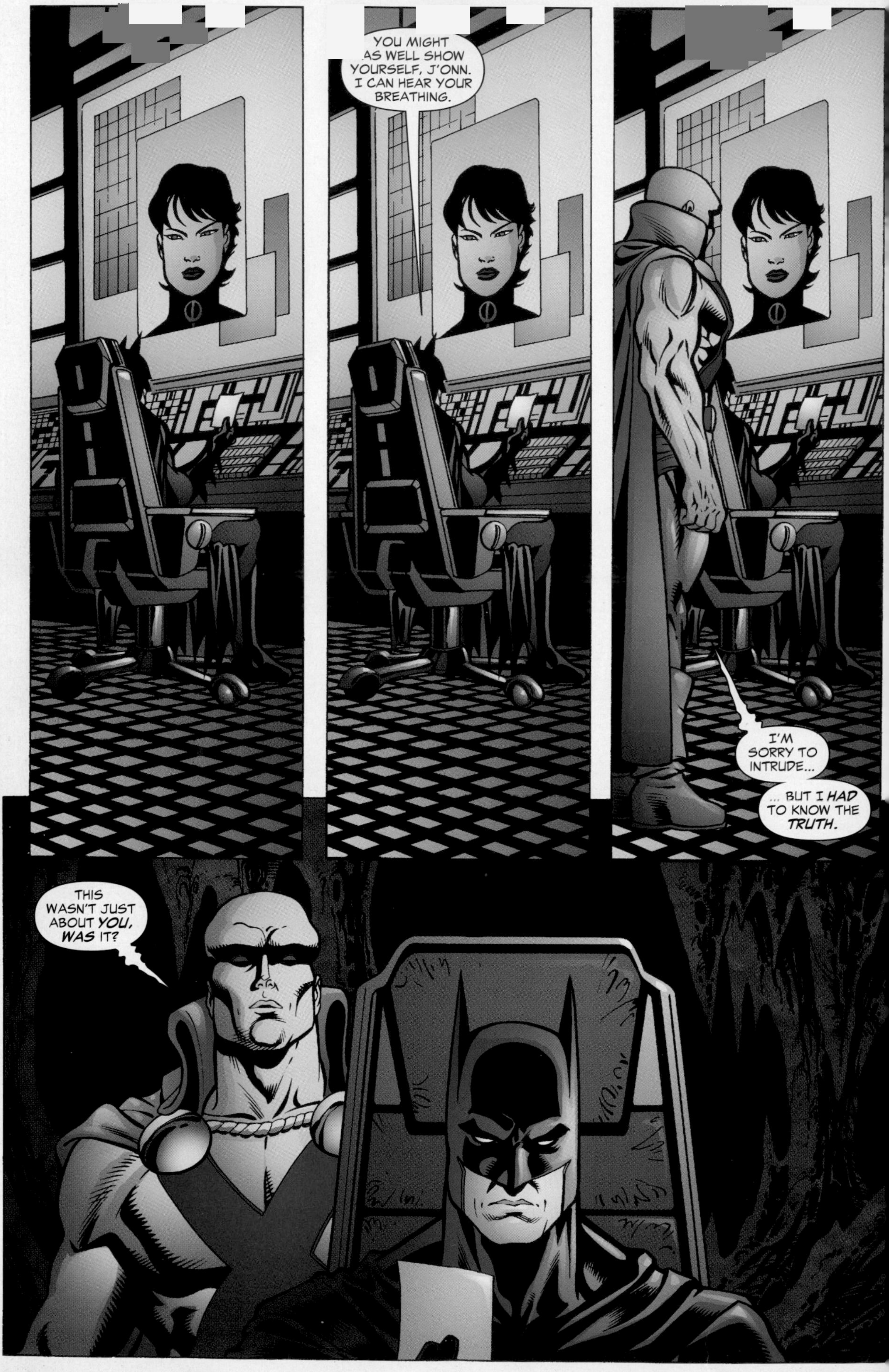
YOU MIGHT AS WELL SHOW YOURSELF, J'ONN. I CAN HEAR YOUR BREATHING.
I'M SORRY TO INTRUDE...
... BUT I *HAD* TO KNOW THE ***TRUTH.***
THIS WASN'T JUST ABOUT ***YOU, WAS*** IT?

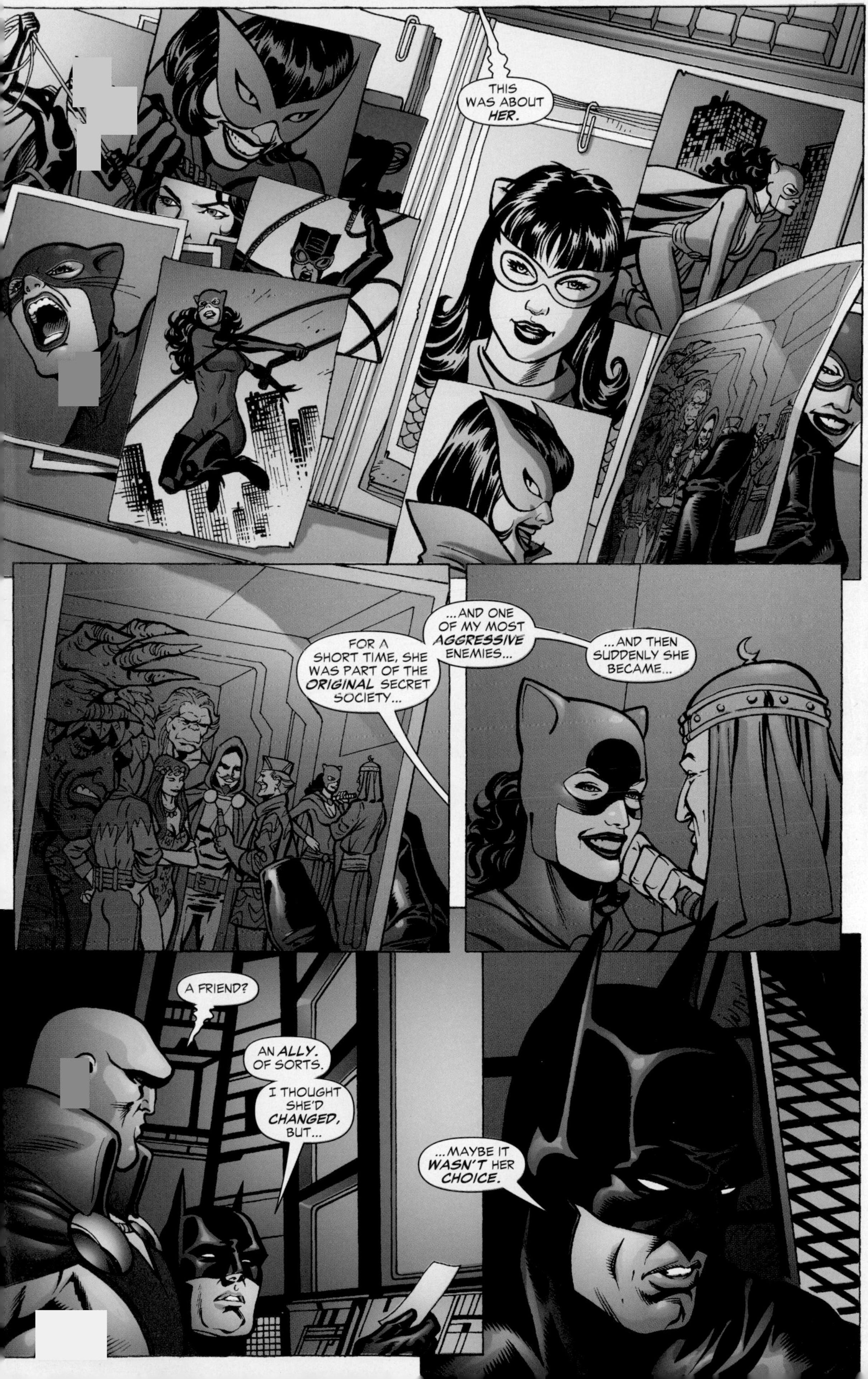
THIS WAS ABOUT HER.
FOR A SHORT TIME, SHE WAS PART OF THE ORIGINAL SECRET SOCIETY...
...AND ONE OF MY MOST AGGRESSIVE ENEMIES...
...AND THEN SUDDENLY SHE BECAME...
A FRIEND?
AN ALLY. OF SORTS.
I THOUGHT SHE'D CHANGED, BUT...
...MAYBE IT WASN'T HER CHOICE.

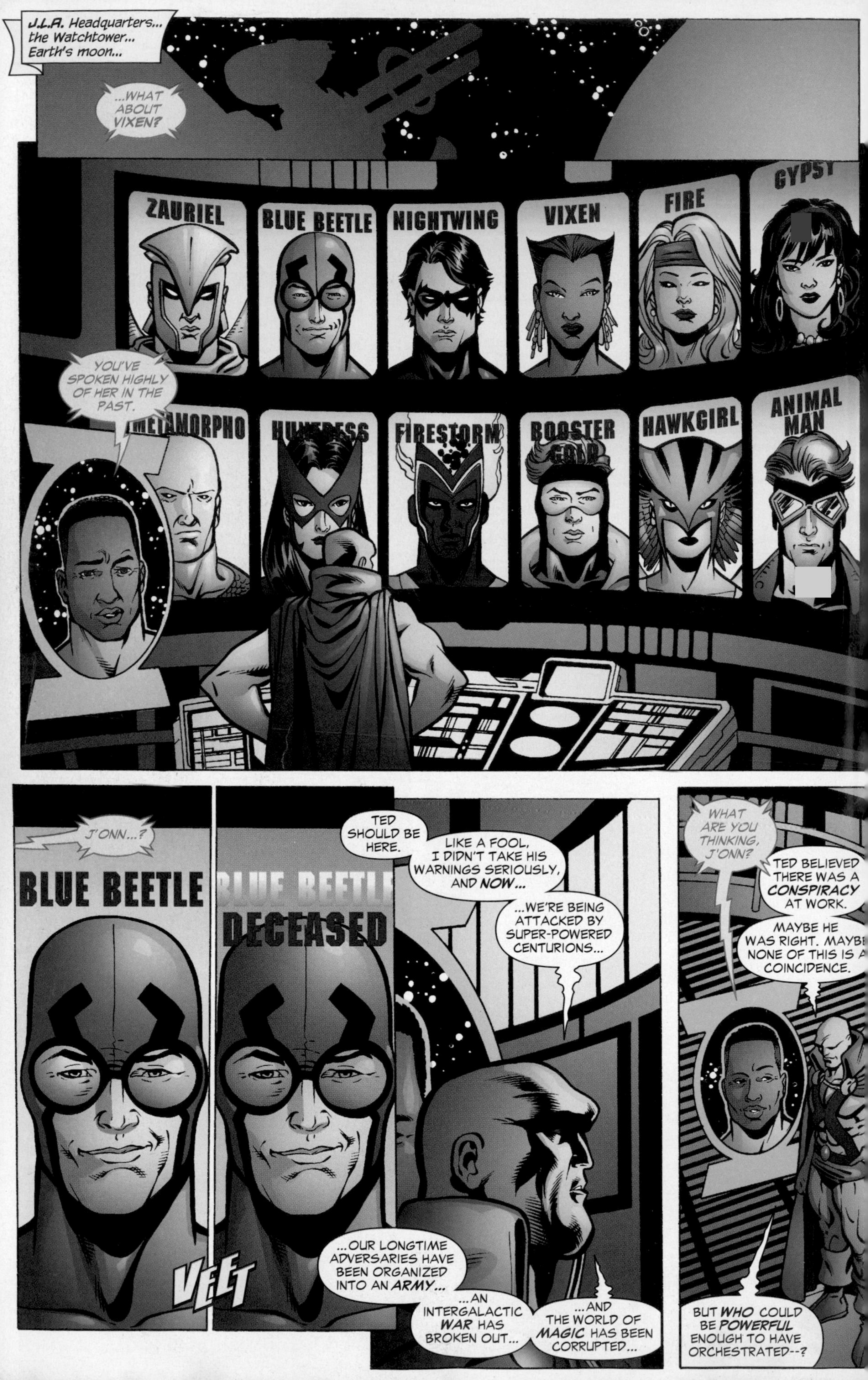
J.L.A. Headquarters... the Watchtower... Earth's moon...
...WHAT ABOUT VIXEN?
ZAURIEL
BLUE BEETLE
NIGHTWING
VIXEN
FIRE
GYPSY
YOU'VE SPOKEN HIGHLY OF HER IN THE PAST.
METAMORPHO
FIRESTORM
HAWKGIRL
ANIMAL MAN
J'ONN...?
BLUE BEETLE
BLUE BEETLE
DECEASED
VEET
TED SHOULD BE HERE.
LIKE A FOOL, I DIDN'T TAKE HIS WARNINGS SERIOUSLY, AND NOW...
...WE'RE BEING ATTACKED BY SUPER-POWERED CENTURIONS...
...OUR LONGTIME ADVERSARIES HAVE BEEN ORGANIZED INTO AN ARMY...
...AN INTERGALACTIC WAR HAS BROKEN OUT...
...AND THE WORLD OF MAGIC HAS BEEN CORRUPTED...
WHAT ARE YOU THINKING, J'ONN?
TED BELIEVED THERE WAS A CONSPIRACY AT WORK.
MAYBE HE WAS RIGHT. MAYBE NONE OF THIS IS A COINCIDENCE.
BUT WHO COULD BE POWERFUL ENOUGH TO HAVE ORCHESTRATED--?

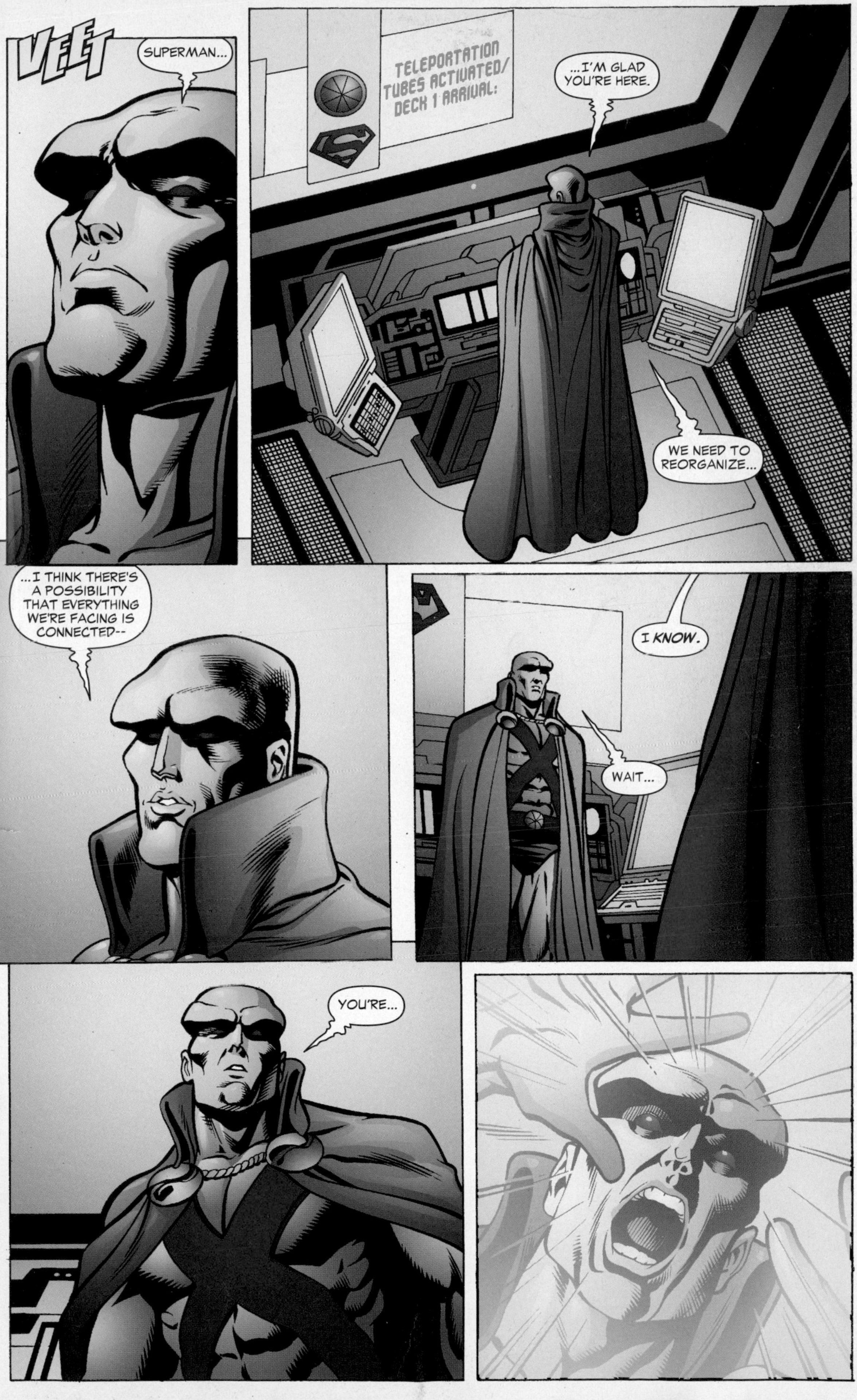
VEET
SUPERMAN...
TELEPORTATION TUBES ACTIVATED/ DECK 1 ARRIVAL:
...I'M GLAD YOU'RE HERE.
WE NEED TO REORGANIZE...
...I THINK THERE'S A POSSIBILITY THAT EVERYTHING WE'RE FACING IS CONNECTED--
I KNOW.
WAIT...
YOU'RE...

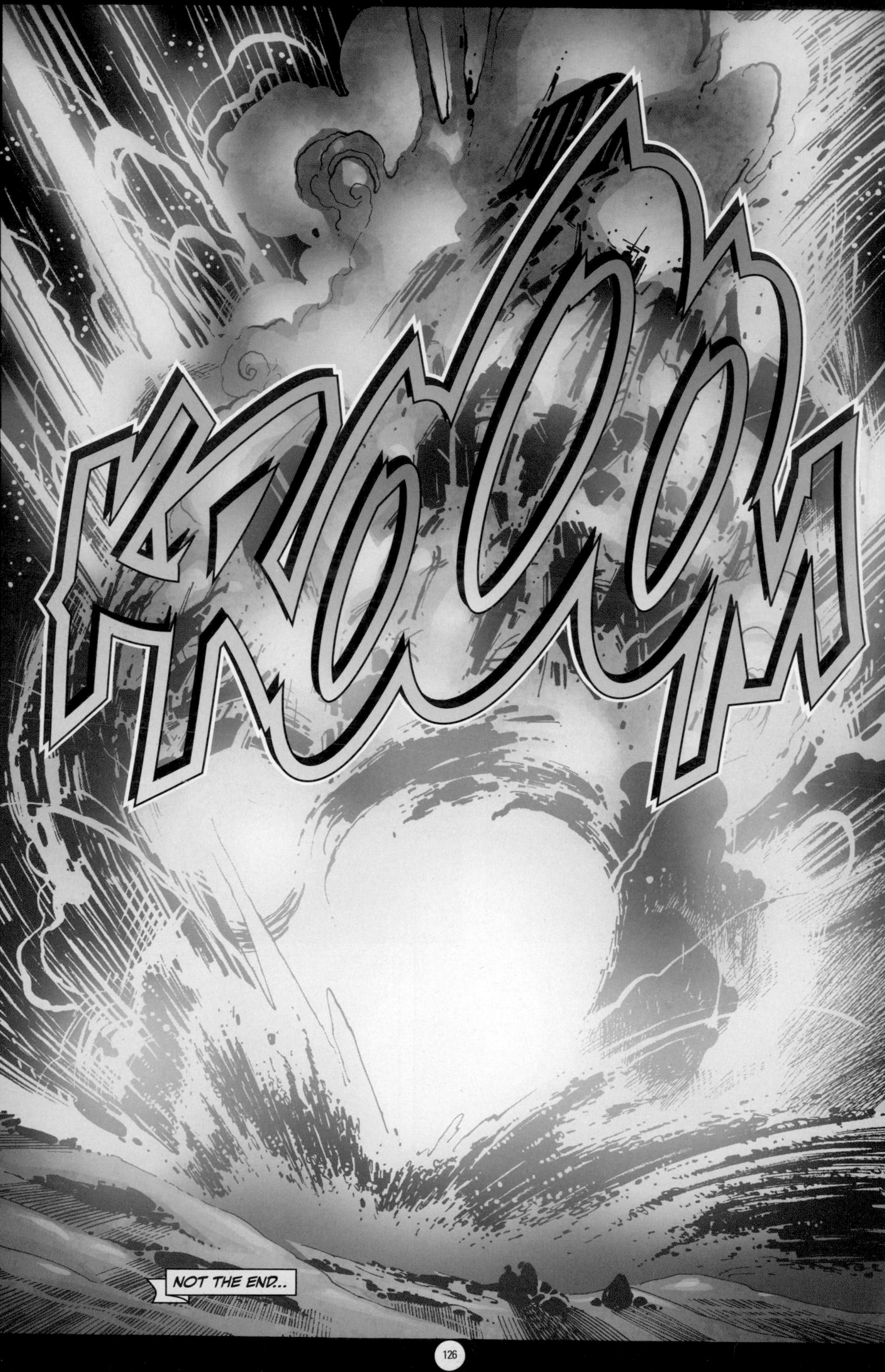
NOT THE END...

READ MORE OF THE JLA'S ADVENTURES IN THESE COLLECTIONS FROM DC COMICS:

JLA
TOWER OF BABEL

The World's Greatest Super Heroes
JLA
TOWER OF BABEL
Mark Waid · Dan Curtis Johnson
Howard Porter · Drew Geraci

Batman's Secret files on the Justice League have fallen into the hands of one of its oldest and deadliest foes — Ra's al Ghul. Now, the JLA faces its greatest challenge — possible treason within their own ranks! Will the JLA survive?

Mark Waid, Howard Porter, Drew Geraci and some of DC's finest talents come together to spin this deadly tale.

JLA:
EARTH 2

JLA
earth 2
grant morrison
frank quitely

GRANT MORRISON
FRANK QUITELY

JLA:
THE TENTH CIRCLE

The World's Greatest Super Heroes
JLA
THE TENTH CIRCLE

CHRIS CLAREMONT
JOHN BYRNE

JUSTICE LEAGUE OF AMERICA:
THE NAIL

JUSTICE LEAGUE OF AMERICA
THE NAIL
ALAN DAVIS • MARK FARMER

ALAN DAVIS
MARK FARMER

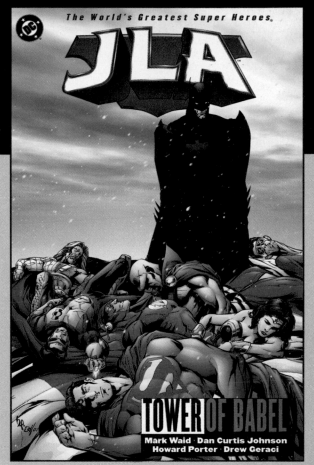

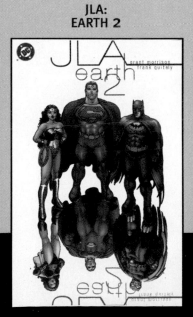

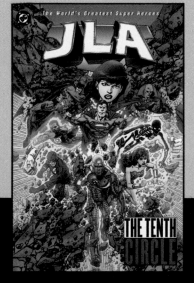

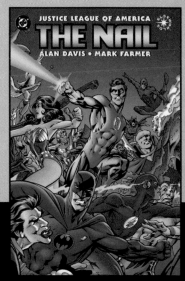